Stories of Peoplehood

How can we build thriving political communities? In this provocative account of how societies are bound together, Rogers Smith examines the importance of 'stories of peoplehood', narratives that promise economic or political power and define political allegiances in religious, cultural, racial, ethnic, and related terms. Smith argues that no nations are purely civic: all are bound in part by stories that seek to define elements intrinsic to their members' identities and worth. These types of stories can support valuable forms of political life but they also pose dangers that must be understood if they are to be confronted. In contrast to much contemporary writing, *Stories of Peoplehood* argues for community-building via robust contestation among sharply differing views. This original argument combines accessible theory with colourful examples of myths and stories from around the world and over 2,500 years of human history.

Rogers M. Smith is the Christopher H. Browne Distinguished Professor of Political Science at the University of Pennsylvania. He has published over seventy articles and is author or co-author of the following books: *The Unsteady March: The Rise and Decline of Racial Equality in America* (with Philip A. Klinkner, 1999); *Civic Ideals: Conflicting Visions of Citizenship in U.S. History* (1997); *Citizenship without Consent: The Illegal Alien in the American Polity* (with Peter H. Schuck, 1985); and *Liberalism and American Constitutional Law* (1985, rev. edn. 1990).

Contemporary Political Theory

Series Editor
Ian Shapiro

As the twenty-first century begins, major new political challenges have arisen at the same time as some of the most enduring dilemmas of political association remain unresolved. The collapse of communism and the end of the Cold War in the east reflect a victory for democratic and liberal values, yet in many of the western countries that nurtured those values there are severe problems of urban decay, class and racial conflict, and failing political legitimacy. Enduring global injustice and inequality seem compounded by environmental problems, disease, the oppression of women, racial, ethnic, and religious minorities and the relentless growth of the world's population. In such circumstances, the need for creative thinking about the fundamentals of human political association is manifest. This new series in contemporary political theory is needed to foster such systematic normative reflection.

The series proceeds in the belief that the time is ripe for a reassertion of the importance of problem-driven political theory. It is concerned, that is, with works that are motivated by the impulse to understand, think critically about, and address the problems in the world, rather than issues that are thrown up primarily in academic debate. Books in the series may be interdisciplinary in character, ranging over issues conventionally dealt with in philosophy, law, history and the human sciences. The range of materials and the methods of proceeding should be dictated by the problem at hand, not the conventional debates or disciplinary divisions of academia.

Other books in the series

Ian Shapiro and Casiano Hacker-Cordón (eds.)
Democracy's Value

Ian Shapiro and Casiano Hacker-Cordón (eds.)
Democracy's Edges

Brooke A. Ackerly
Political Theory and Feminist Social Criticism

Clarissa Rile Hayward
De-Facing Power

John Kane
The Politics of Moral Capital

Ayelet Shachar
Multicultural Jurisdictions: Cultural Differences and Women's Rights

John Keane
Global Civil Society?

Stories of Peoplehood

The Politics and Morals of Political Membership

Rogers M. Smith

CAMBRIDGE
UNIVERSITY PRESS

PUBLISHED BY THE PRESS SYNDICATE OF THE UNIVERSITY OF CAMBRIDGE
The Pitt Building, Trumpington Street, Cambridge CB2 1RP, United Kingdom

CAMBRIDGE UNIVERSITY PRESS
The Edinburgh Building, Cambridge, CB2 2RU, UK
40 West 20th Street, New York, NY 10011–4211, USA
477 Williamstown Road, Port Melbourne, VIC 3207, Australia
Ruiz de Alarcón 13, 28014 Madrid, Spain
Dock House, The Waterfront, Cape Town 8001, South Africa

http://www.cambridge.org

First published 2003

Printed in the United Kingdom at the University Press, Cambridge

Typeface Plantin 10/12 pt.   *System* LaTeX 2$_\varepsilon$ [TB]

A catalogue record for this book is available from the British Library

Library of Congress Cataloguing in Publication data applied for

ISBN 0 521 81303 4 hardback
ISBN 0 521 52003 7 paperback

The publisher has used its best endeavours to ensure that the URLs for
external websites referred to in this book are correct and active at the
time of going to press. However, the publisher has no responsibility for the
websites and can make no guarantee that a site will remain live or that the
content is or will remain appropriate.

To Caroline
Who always wants stories

Contents

Acknowledgments

After the publication of my 1997 book, *Civic Ideals: Conflicting Visions of Citizenship in U.S. History*, I had many occasions to discuss its themes. In doing so I found myself expanding upon that book's explanatory and normative arguments, in ways that led me to write this one. As a result, its writing involves debts to far more individuals than I can list or even recall. My thanks to all who made criticisms and suggestions at panels or talks held at the American Political Science Association; Amherst College; Arizona State University; the Center for Area Studies in Osaka, Japan; the Claremont Colleges; the University of California at Davis; the University of Chicago; the CUNY Graduate Center; the University of Connecticut; Cornell University; Harvard University; the Evangelie Akademie Loccum, Germany; the University of Michigan; New School University; Northwestern University; the University of Notre Dame; Ohio State University; Princeton University; and the University of Wisconsin, among other locations.

Like most of my writing, this book has been heavily shaped by discussions with two of my erstwhile colleagues at Yale University, Ian Shapiro, who prompted me to write it, and Adolph Reed, Jr., who prodded me to do better. "Part I" began as the 1999 Charles E. Lindblom Lecture at Yale. It was my privilege to teach for over two decades in the home department of Ed Lindblom, who, along with Robert Dahl and Robert Lane, provided an inspiring example of what scholars of politics could be, as well as great intellectual stimulation and friendship. The ideas in this book were deeply influenced by many other Yale colleagues, particularly Bruce Ackerman, Nancy Cott, John McCormick, Jennifer Pitts, Peter Schuck, Steven Smith, and Norma Thompson, along with participants in various Yale seminars. Elizabeth Cohen and Sarah Song provided both valuable research assistance and important insights. Without Sarah's work during a Yale-sponsored leave in 2000–2001 the book would not yet be done.

I am also deeply indebted to my new colleagues and students at the University of Pennsylvania, especially Anne Norton, Andrew Norris, Nancy Hirschmann, Brendan O'Leary, Douglas Massey, and the participants in my graduate seminar on citizenship. Penn students David Greene and Jennifer Spiegel provided superb research assistance, funded in part by the Carnegie Corporation of New York. Richard Zinman, David Hollinger, Mary Katzenstein, Joseph Carens, James Hollifield, Denis LaCorne, and Yohann Aucante, offered very useful comments on parts of the manuscript, as did anonymous press reviewers. John Haslam at the Cambridge University Press has been an endlessly patient and helpful editor.

For almost fifteen years, Mary Summers has contributed more to everything I do than anyone else, including me. My children Virginia, Caroline, and Reed do their best to get me to do other things, which makes life better in many ways.

Introduction: on studying stories of peoplehood

Oh, oh, oh, the ancient fairy tale
It is high time to begin it.
The Fairy tale of the olden times
It is just time to remember it.
Opening lines of the Kyrgyz
Manas Epos

Manas and Moses

The Republic of Kyrgyzstan, also termed the Kyrgyz Republic, came into existence after a coup ended the former Soviet Republic of Kyrgyzstan on August 31, 1991. In the year 2002, the Republic maintained an official website linked to a 1992 Decree by Kyrgyz President Askar Akayev. He declared that 1995 would be "a year of national celebration of the millennium of the Kyrgyz heroic epos Manas." Akayev also urged various governmental ministries to submit projects "on the revival of the age-old values and material and spiritual heritage of the Kyrgyz people connected with the epos Manas." Those projects included organizing a single "scientific-propaganda coordinating center in the Republic in order to unite the means of mass media, science, culture and education for restoring the objective historical truth about the Kyrgyz and their historical memory."[1]

This website is revealing on several levels. From academic and cultural viewpoints, reviving and celebrating the epos Manas was a highly commendable act. Twenty times longer than the *Iliad* and *Odyssey* combined, the epos details the history of the Kyrgyz people from ancient times until the eighteenth century. Many regard it as an irreplaceable source of Kyrgyz history, philosophy, ethnography, and spirituality.

Yet in issuing his decree, President Akayev surely aimed at more than a major cultural or intellectual contribution. The Manas narrative had

---

[1] In the year 2002 the website was located at http://freenet.bishkek.su/kyrgyzstan.

1

obvious *political* appeal to the government of a newly independent re-public. It relates the heroic feats of the legendary dragon-slaying Kyrgyz hero Manas, who led his people in ancient times through struggles for national independence against foreign invaders. The epos then pursues Kyrgyz history through the lives and deeds of Manas's son, Semetey, and his grandson, Seitek, forebears of the modern Kyrgyz nation. In propa-gating this epos via various governmental means, President Akayev was not only seeking to promote an artistic masterpiece. He was also seeking to institutionalize a post-Soviet vision of the modern Kyrgyz Republic in his constituents' lives, by presenting the new Republic as the appropriate heir of the grand traditions the Manas epos embodies. And he sought to achieve this strengthening, in turn, by using the epos to reinforce the sense of the Kyrgyz that they *are* a people, and a people that deserves to feel proud of its historical, cultural, and political identity, properly understood.[2]

These political goals are suggested not only by how promptly Akayev chose to decree elaborate celebrations of the Manas, only months after the 1991 coup that ended Soviet rule. It is shown also by his championing of governmental coordination of all major "scientific-propaganda" infor-mation sources. He sought to insure that they assisted in presenting the "age-old values" of the Kyrgyz people in ways that accorded with what the government regards as "objective historical truth." It might seem surprising that the leader of a newly independent nation would turn so quickly and publicly to such a cultural project and take such a central-ized, potentially authoritarian approach to doing so. Yet on reflection, it is understandable why a new regime's leaders would wish its constituents to see themselves as one people and as a rightly proud, independent people. It is also clear why leaders would wish their constituents to identify the new regime with that people's most ancient and glorious values and achievements. And it is clear, as well, why leaders might wish to exercise considerable control over the understanding of their political identity and obligations to which their constituents are exposed.

However understandable, that last aspect of Akayev's efforts may be cause for concern. Governmental deployment of a nation's historical re-sources raises fears of state-sponsored, chauvinistic indoctrination via

---

[2] Breuilly, 1982, 346–348, cites similar Afrikaner, Czech, and Italian examples of ceremo-nial celebrations of earlier events displaying "heroic resistance to aliens" which sought to inspire a people to "return to the heights of the past, though in a transformed fashion." In these cases "Afrikaner," "Czech," and "Italian" identities were all reinforced, if not substantially constituted, by celebrations of the actions of predecessors who would not have defined their peoplehood in those terms. In one form or another, such political ceremonies are, I believe, ubiquitous.

distortion and manipulation of cultural artifacts. Kyrgyzstan is a country with 4.7 million people who belong to some eighty ethnic groups, and it classifies only 58 per cent of its citizens as ethnically Kyrgyz, though all are officially members of the "Kyrgyz people." It is hard to imagine that all the non-Kyrgyz ethnic group members identify themselves fully with the Manas epos, with the new regime that is celebrating it, and indeed with the "Kyrgyz people" – though doubtless President Akayev hoped that through these efforts many would come to do so.

This promotion of a certain vision of Kyrgyz political community has taken place, moreover, in a world where international attention to chauvinistic political projects cannot easily be avoided. Hence the government's globally accessible English-language website walks a tightrope. Perhaps extravagantly, it proclaims the epos "the unique masterpiece of the world cultural treasury." But it explicitly distances the Manas epos from narrow nationalism, even while it affirms popular self-determination within particular nations or peoples. In regard to the international realm, it assures us that "Each nation makes its own contribution to the world cultural treasury according to the peculiarities and richness of its talents and creative abilities." Domestically, it asserts that the main principle the Kyrgyz people employ in governing their ethnic pluralism is that "Kyrgyzstan is our common house," and that their Republic "firmly upholds the equality of all communities" within that house. Those beyond its walls are assured that the Manas "epos sings the values which are common for all people: social justice, honesty, dignity, humanism, care for people." Yet these universal values include particularistic attachments: the Kyrgyz webmasters next list "love for homeland, for national traditions and customs" as sentiments exalted in the Manas. They end by summarizing these promises of harmoniously blended nationalism and humanitarianism, assigning to the epos the espousal of "respect for human rights" along with the promotion of "national unity and tolerance, peaceful coexistence with neighbouring states, people's aspirations and hopes for the better future."

Further suggesting Kyrgyz awareness of world opinion, the site also contains a link to a supportive Resolution of the General Assembly of the United Nations. The Resolution presents the Manas epos as "not only the source of Kyrgyz language and literature but also the basis of cultural, moral, historical, social and religious traditions of the Kyrgyz people." Lest that sound a bit parochial, the UN document adds, "this epos favors the dissemination of humane ideals and value of the humanity." The Resolution goes on to stress "the liberal heritage of this epos for the peoples of the region." Hence it enjoins UNESCO (United Nations Educational, Scientific, and Cultural Organization) to cooperate and assist in celebrating and disseminating knowledge about the epos Manas in 1995 and thereafter.

By most accounts, Akayev's 1992 Manas initiative did spur fresh attention to this cultural work, and favorable responses to such measures contributed to Kyrgyzstan's reputation in the early 1990s as "a showcase of the Central Asian democratic experience." President Akayev has, however, since been criticized for undemocratic measures. His government has raided, threatened, and in some cases shut down independent media; disqualified political opponents from participating in elections; temporarily revoked the registration of the Kyrgyz Committee for Human Rights; and arrested ethnic Uzbek citizens suspected of belonging to "extremist" Islamic groups, a practice that drew sharp criticisms prior to September 11, 2001. Kyrgyzstan's Constitutional Court also permitted Akayev to win a constitutionally questionable third five-year term in October, 2000.[3] When in March 2002 Kyrgyz police shot demonstrators protesting against the jailing of an opposition lawmaker, Akayev did compel his cabinet to resign, saying that "Kyrgyz society is right when it refuses to forgive the authorities . . . for violations of human rights and infringements of democratic freedoms"; but he did not himself resign.[4] Thus, though his celebration of the "humane" and "liberal" Manas epos may indeed have aided Akayev's efforts to win domestic and international support for the new Kyrgyz regime, it has not prevented him from authorizing some quite illiberal measures. Neither, however, does he seem to view his government's frequent invocations of the Manas, and his ongoing protestations of support for democracy and human rights, as superfluous.

This recent episode in the long and politically contested history of an extraordinary epic work, and of modern Asian politics, serves to dramatize the empirical and normative phenomena this book will probe: the generation, maintenance, and transformation of senses of political peoplehood. It may be rare for governments to sponsor a narrative of national identity conducive to their authority over their predecessors and potential rivals quite as explicitly as President Akayev did in 1992 and thereafter. Yet, I will argue, political leaders necessarily engage in such "people-forming" or "people-building" endeavors to a greater or lesser degree all the time, inevitably deploying inherited materials of the sort the Manas epos strikingly exemplifies. In fact, leaders routinely propagate

---

[3] Sergei Glabo, "Politics-Kyrgyzstan: President's Victory a No-Win for Democracy," Inter Press Service, http://www.oneworld.org/ips2/Oct00/07_26_014.html, Oct. 31, 2000; Amnesty International, "Annual Report 2000-Kyrgyzstan," http://www.web.amnesty. org/web/ar2000. See also "Amnesty International Report 2001: Kyrgystan," AI Index: POL 10/001/2001, ISBN: 0862102995, www.amnesty.org.

[4] *The New York Times on the Web*, May 22, 2002, http://www.nytimes.com/apoline/ inter . . . /AP-Kyrgyzstan-Government-Quits.

and institutionalize particular visions of their political communities in broad-ranging ways that do far more both to win and to distribute status, power, and resources among some people and not others than Akayev's more symbolic promotion of the singing of the Manas. His actions thus comprise one of the more colorful, yet far from the weightiest, examples of the fundamental and pervasive role that stories of peoplehood play in political life.

It is a role that, I believe, they have always played, everywhere in our world and throughout recorded human history. Two distinguished archaeologists, Israel Finkelstein and Neil Silberman, have recently argued that in the seventh century BC, King Josiah of Judah undertook actions that seem not unlike those of President Akayev of Kyrgyzstan, under not wholly dissimilar circumstances. Archaeological evidence suggests that Judah, long overshadowed by its northern counterpart, the separate kingdom of Israel, had grown rapidly after Israel's conquest by Assyria in 720 BC. When the Assyrian empire eventually began to decline, opportunities arose for King Josiah, who came to the throne in 639 BC and reigned for thirty years (Finkelstein and Silberman, 2001, 229–282).

Josiah's government sought to win support for throwing off all foreign domination and building a new nation that would encompass both Judah and Israel, if not more. To help achieve these ends, an expanded cohort of professional priests and scribes in Judah's holy city of Jerusalem greatly revised and combined various historical and religious traditions to create five books, Genesis, Exodus, Leviticus, Numbers, and Deuteronomy, known as the Pentateuch, the Torah, or the books of Moses. They culminate in Moses's death just before his people finally enter their promised land. The Pentateuch's magnificent narratives define the history, cosmic significance, laws, and divine mission of what they present as "the people of Israel." Yet that history features Judah over and over again – as the burial place of the ancient Jewish patriarchs, including "the most Judean of patriarchs – Abraham"; as populated by the descendants of the son blessed by Jacob as ruler over all the tribes of Israel; as the place where the idolatrous Canaanites were most fully conquered; as the home of the gloriously successful king David; as far greater than the northern kingdom of Israel and more faithful throughout most of history to the original covenant with Abraham in which both kingdoms shared. In the seventh century, Finkelstein and Silberman argue, the laws and mission conveyed by these books strongly indicated that all participants in that covenant should be politically united and religiously devoted exclusively to the one God of Israel, whose worship centered in Judah's Temple of Jerusalem (Finkelstein and Silberman, 2001, 23, 44, 229–230).

Yet, they maintain, modern archaeology shows it to be far more likely that David was in fact a minor ruler of a Judah that was a mere "marginal, isolated, rural region"; that up until its conquest by Assyria, the northern kingdom of Israel was far wealthier, more populated, and more historically significant than Judah; that neither monotheism nor Jerusalem had ever been so central to religious practices in either Judah or Israel as the government of King Josiah and their Pentateuch insisted; and that few in either Judah or Israel felt any strong religious or political imperative to achieve unification as one political people prior to Josiah's ambitious pursuit of that goal. Finkelstein and Silberman believe that the Pentateuch reinterprets and invents characters, events, and struggles in ways that systematically valorize Josiah (by celebrating Joshua, especially); stigmatize Judah's rivals (the opposing kingdoms of Moab and Ammon are said to be populated by the children of incest); and most of all, urge the political unification of Israel and Judah and the embrace of a common religion centered in Jerusalem, in a manner that served King Josiah's key political goals. The result was a set of literary texts, written when literacy had recently become more widespread in the region, that "dramatically changed what it meant to be an Israelite." This new sense of communal identity not only helped to consolidate Josiah's rule within Judah. It also strengthened popular will to face international threats, and it helped "prove to the native residents of the northern highlands that they were indeed part of the great people of Israel who fought together with the people of Judah to inherit their Promised Land" (Finkelstein and Silberman, 2001, 14, 40, 95, 229–249, 275–283).

The claims of Finkelstein and Silberman are controversial. Though also seeing Josiah as "instituting a sweeping religious reform" that buttressed "Judah's independence and his own religious authority by rigorously restricting sacrificial rites to Jersulem," historian Raymond Scheindlin, for example, contends that it was "Judean elders in Babylonia" under the Persian empire who created the Torah, compiling an "official national history and codification of laws, customs, and religious practices, enabling them to reorganize the national identity around religious behavior and to some extent to turn the national identity itself into a religion." They did so, on his account, precisely to sustain a sense of "peoplehood" or common identity after the Babylonian conquest in 587 BC, and the subsequent heightened dispersal of Jews, had deprived them of "a common political framework, a common language," and "national institutions."[5]

---

[5] Scheindlin contends that it "is from this period that it becomes appropriate to begin speaking of the Jewish people, meaning all those who, throughout history and around the globe, have regarded themselves as linked to one another and to the people of the ancient Israelite kingdom, either by ethnicity, culture, intellectual heritage, or religion" (1998, 27).

This adaptation of Jewish political identity into a form less threatening to the ruling Persians took hold in part because it received active Persian support. It was, indeed, under the authority of the Persian emperor that "the Torah was first officially read in public and promulgated as the law of the province of Judea" itself (Tadmor, 1976, 160; Scheindlin, 1998, 27–32).

It is beyond my scope to try to assess these conflicting accounts of the compilation of the books of Moses.[6] But whatever their origins, it is undeniable that the books portray the formation of a distinct people, and that they have frequently been invoked since by a great variety of leading Jewish figures to foster senses of common political as well as religious identities, purposes, and destinies. It seems likely, then, that the scribes, priests, and other officials of seventh-century Judah, the late sixth- or fifth-century Jewish leaders in Babylonia, and certainly subsequent leaders, have engaged in efforts very similar to modern Kyrgyzstan's promotion of the epos Manas. They, too, have invoked and reinterpreted cultural traditions, often with great artistry, in ways that have helped sustain a sense of shared Jewish peoplehood through many centuries of hardship and often intensely violent struggle that continue today. They also furnished inspirational motifs that would later be woven into many other stories of peoplehood. Just as King Josiah's men may well have transformed a variety of traditions to create their vision of a unified, monotheistic Israel, later political writers would draw upon their work for many different, often surprising purposes.

Finkelstein and Silberman read the book of Judges, for example, as structured during King Josiah's reign to deliver the moral that Israel had been trapped in a cycle of sin and retribution until a redemptive monarchy came to be established (2001, 120). Some 2,300 years later, in 1776, Thomas Paine's classic revolutionary pamphlet "Common Sense" interpreted the ensuing books of Samuel to argue instead that Israel at its greatest had been a republic, and that it had sinned when it turned to monarchy (Jensen, ed., 1967, 410–413). In so doing, Paine drew on deeply entrenched Protestant senses of identity held by colonial British Americans to help inspire their allegiance to the emerging vision of a new, republican nation, the United States of America – for his comparison suggested that the new American nation was, like the ancient Israelites, a "chosen people."[7] Paine was thus engaged in the same sort

---

[6] For a thorough overview of recent debates over ancient Israelite historiography, including the views of "minimalists" who doubt the existence of David and Solomon at all, see Long, ed., 1999. Finkelstein and Silberman, 2001, give the archaeological bases for their disagreements with these still more skeptical views at 128–130.

[7] As a further indication of the wide impact of Israeli people-making, Don Baker notes that many Christian South Koreans today claim this "new Israel," "chosen people" status for themselves (Baker, 1998, 124).

of "people-forming" political endeavor undertaken by Josiah's scribes in the Finkelstein and Silberman account, and by the modern Kyrgyz officials championing the Manas. Doubtless in the course of its long and changing history, the Manas epos, like the Bible, has been interpreted to support political causes just as contrasting as theocratic monarchism and commercial republicanism.

Despite their similarities, however, when read as an innovative seventh-century story of Israeli peoplehood, the Pentateuch and the ensuing books of the prophets in the Bible do stand in contrast to the Manas epos, as presented on the Kyrgyz website, in at least one regard. Though Israel is depicted as in a certain sense a redemptive nation for all humanity, and though a charitable spirit toward outsiders is encouraged, the biblical account of Israeli peoplehood is not crafted to win the approval of foreign observers. Neither does it promise respectful acceptance of diverse religious and ethnic communities within a united Israel. The international and domestic political challenges Josiah faced instead seem to have prompted a strong assertion of Israel's expansionist destiny and a rejection of what were seen as sinful rival cults within the unified nation Josiah sought to build and lead.

Those contrasts suggest that, though the adaptation of cultural and religious traditions for political purposes may be an enduring feature of human life from the time of King Josiah to President Akayev, some things have changed. In many ways, modern economic and technological circumstances and prevalent modern moral traditions work against the open promulgation of senses of peoplehood that can support harsh treatment of both outsiders and insiders who are deemed too "other" by those in power. The questions of whether modern religions, science, technologies, and economics have permanently shifted the politics of people-making in more cosmopolitan, less particularistic directions – or if not, whether they can do so – are topics that the ensuing pages will recurrently explore, though I do not believe a definitive answer can yet be given. Still, whatever the extent of these changes, the ongoing troubles in the Middle East, conflicts with extremist Islamic groups harbored in many Arab and Asian nations, and ethnoculturally charged clashes in too much of Africa, in the former Yugoslavia, in Northern Ireland, in Chiapas, in the Kashmir, in Colombia, and in many other places in the world today, all indicate that a politics generating virulent particularisms and harsh treatment of disdained outsiders and insiders remains hard to avoid.

That leads us to the issues that are central to this book. Human beings have never successfully pursued any of their many aspirations and endeavors – they have never sustained stable families, built prosperous economies, formed organizations for spiritual fulfillment, constructed great buildings and monuments, created enduring works of art, made great scientific and philosophic achievements – without being organized into particular political peoples. These peoples have come in an ever-changing variety of forms, to be sure; but some such political organizations may have always been and may always be essential to human fulfillment and human flourishing. If so, the means by which particular forms of peoplehood are created and maintained are of inestimable human value. Yet, at the same time, the organization of humanity into particular political peoples seems often to be achieved by questionable if not repugnant means and to provide a breeding ground for some of the most bitter human animosities and vicious conduct.

Hence genuinely perplexing issues arise. The dangers of chauvinistic political narratives, xenophobic toward many outsiders and repressive toward many insiders, are so horrific that it is tempting to disdain all governmental crafting of narratives of shared particular political identities as improper exploitations of cultural resources such as the Manas, Israeli religious traditions, and other less formal "stories of peoplehood." Yet this crafting may be unavoidable if we are to sustain vital and deeply cherished political, historical, and cultural traditions and to organize human beings for the productive pursuit of their happiness and welfare. It may, indeed, be one of the tragic dimensions of human life that we can neither do without the political promulgation and institutionalization of "stories of peoplehood" nor can we hope to eradicate entirely their virulent potential.

In any case, we must make choices about how to address this potent dimension of political life. In the electronically interconnected and otherwise "globalized" world of the twenty-first century, should the UN, other international or transnational bodies, other national governments, social groups, and individual citizens play a role in encouraging the sort of political enterprise the Manas millennial celebration represents? If so, must they at the same time somehow seek to insure that such enterprises are genuinely "liberal" and "humanitarian" in their content and consequences? Is this combination even possible? If not, should conscientious groups and individuals simply ignore such worrisome, politically charged activities, in the way we are advised not to look too closely at the making of sausages? Or, as in the case of the production of genuinely toxic foods, should we actively oppose those activities as much as we can?

These are questions that, in one way or another, are being vigorously pressed within many countries and across countries today, for excellent reasons. The forging of enduring, productive forms of political community does seem essential to human flourishing, and for the foreseeable future, at least, these forms must be varied and distinctive. Yet in locales around the globe, that forging continues to occur in white-hot fires of political conflict involving atrocities that ought to be unimaginable. I believe, however, that precisely because these questions are so painfully immediate in so many contexts, we may need to step back from immersion in specific controversies and seek ways to reflect more generally about the kinds of phenomena we are now confronting. We need to reframe the questions by pursuing something that, somewhat surprisingly, political scientists have not much sought: an explicit general theory of the ways senses of political peoplehood are generated, maintained, and transformed.[8]

The need for a theory of people-building

Internationally, no political development during the second half of the twentieth century was more important than the fall of the Soviet Union and of Communist domination in Eastern Europe, the events that gave birth to the Kyrgyz Republic and many others. Domestically, no political development in the United States during the second half of the twentieth century was more important than the banning of the Jim Crow system of public and private racial hierarchy, followed by other domestic "liberation movements." Both these developments wrought fundamental transformations in existing forms of political membership, status, and identity, and they also set in train further sweeping changes. So, too, did other developments almost as momentous as the end of the Soviet era.

[8] David D. Laitin's *Identity in Formation: The Russian-Speaking Populations in the Near Abroad* (1998), which begins with a chapter entitled "A Theory of Political Identities," is the outstanding example of a recent work in political science that approaches such a general theory (even as it also skillfully employs survey data, ethnographic studies, and discourse analysis). Laitin's theory stresses interactions of politically entrepreneurial elites and rational constituents, constrained by contextual conditions, in ways that are generally compatible with the framework I develop here. But to keep his empirical work manageable, he focuses rather strictly on the phenomenon of language assimilation; and theoretically, he is chiefly concerned to elaborate a rational choice "tipping" model. He seeks to delineate circumstances in which it does or does not become rational for individuals to choose to switch languages in sufficient numbers to create a "cascade" that results in effective political identity transformation. Because of his substantive focus on the (undeniably vital) category of language, and even more because of his overriding aim to show the usefulness of models of instrumental rationality, Laitin does not identify or explore different substantive types of "stories of peoplehood" (of which linguistic identity is only one example), as I do here. His acceptance that calculations of identity involve concerns of "status" and "honor" as well as "wealth" interests does provide space for recognizing the role of such stories; and though Laitin focuses on those categories as more behavioral expressions of in-group and out-group acceptance, his discussion of different strains of Russian nationalism shows that the underlying conceptions of group identity do invoke these kinds of stories (Laitin, 1998, 1–35, 300–321, 366). For a critique of Laitin as focusing too narrowly on language and the relatively unfruitful "tipping" model, and for not obtaining empirical results consistent with his theory, see Motyl, 2002, 237–241.

These include what was in some ways the international counterpart to the end of Jim Crow, the dismantling of most of the Western European empires and the rise of "new nations" in Africa and Asia after World War II. They include also the construction of new forms of transnational political membership, most notably the United Nations and then the far more intensive regional consolidation of the European Union.

Stirred by this series of historic events, popular writers, political activists, and scholars in many disciplines have in the last two decades devoted increasing attention, both normative and empirical, to what are widely termed issues of "identity politics." This attention stands in contrast to the focus on issues of popular government and personal rights versus aristocratic and autocratic rule that characterized much European and American thought in the seventeenth and the eighteenth centuries, reflective of political struggles to replace kingships with government by the people and for the people. It differs too from the concentration on issues of state power and economic production and distribution that pervaded many nineteenth- and earlier twentieth-century works on politics, when questions of capitalism versus socialism came to dominate all others. Certainly, one can find pertinent analyses and, especially, prescriptions for the construction and maintenance of political communities in the writings of seminal figures in modern western thought like John Locke and Jean-Jacques Rousseau, Adam Smith, John Stuart Mill and Alexis de Tocqueville, Karl Marx and Max Weber. Still, their central concerns lay elsewhere, and so have those of the great bulk of modern western theorists and social scientists who have pursued the paths they began.

The political, economic, and social issues that preoccupied all these analysts were and remain tremendously important. The recent turn instead to questions of political "identity" has therefore been legitimately controversial in many ways (e.g. Lind, 1995; Rorty, 1998; Reed, 2000; Barry, 2001). Many writers fear that, analytically, an undue focus on "identity" misses deeper, often economic causes of political action. Many think also that this focus operates to deflect attention from material inequalities and to heighten divisive, essentialist understandings of political actors. Most such critics contend that the increased concern with "identity politics" has been at best undesirable, at worst deeply immoral.

These considerations have force, and they have shaped the arguments here. Yet the events of the latter part of the twentieth century have made greater focus on both empirical and normative questions about the politics of memberships and identities inescapable. Indeed, it is a premise of this book that modern scholars of politics, including identity politics, still have not taken such questions seriously enough. Political scientists in particular have paid far more attention to questions of state structures and issues of the distribution of resources and power than they have to issues of how, in general, political memberships and identities come to exist and become institutionalized, and how they are then sustained or transformed. They have addressed the latter topic largely by focusing on particular phenomena, such as racial, ethnic, gendered, class, or national identities, rather than addressing the generation of political identities per se. Against what one would think to be their disciplinary self-interest, political scientists have also tended to draw on economic, sociological, cultural, and psychological theories rather than formulating explicitly political ones.[9]

One sign of that relative neglect is the strange sound of the title of this section, "The need for a theory of people-building." We are accustomed to hearing of state-building and of nation-building, but not "people-making" or "people-building. Yet most scholars agree that the creation and maintenance of political communities is not simply a matter of creating and maintaining states. Most scholars also concur that not every political community should be termed a "nation." "Nations" are defined in many ways, but whatever definition one prefers, it virtually always includes some human political communities but leaves out some others.

But some other – what? What is the more encompassing genus of which "nations" are a species? "Polity," "political unit," and "political

---

[9] For a similar critique, see Schnapper, 1998, 12, 145–149. To be sure, there are outstanding exceptions to these generalizations. Unlike Schnapper, I see Armstrong (1982) as stressing the political origins of ethnic and national identities, though how far is unclear as he explicitly eschews much general theory-building (3). The resistance of political scientists to portraying identities as deeply politically constructed may have reflected the wariness of many post-World War II western liberal scholars toward perspectives that appeared to dismiss individual autonomy, in ways associated with both fascist and Communist abuses. In the years of Marxism's greatest prestige, moreover, many writers on the left generally took economically determined class identities to be most important and treated other identities as epiphenomenal, as have many social scientists influenced by liberal forms of political economy. Thus no theory of political identity formation beyond Marxism or economic theory more broadly seemed necessary. If so, it is not surprising that theoretical explorations of the politics of identity have proliferated after the fall of Communism.

In one such effort, Alexander Wendt (1999) offers an insightful "general, evolutionary" model of collective identity formation on which I draw extensively here. Wendt does so, however, out of recognition that we scholars with "constructivist" views of social identities do not clearly possess a general theory of their creation (317), and his effort, too, is a partial one. He is specifically concerned with the formation of "state" identities rather than the senses of political "peoplehood" examined here. I regard my endeavor as complementary to his, both partial contributions to a more truly general theory of political identity formation and transformation. Still, as elaborated below, my approach does treat the construction of "state" identities as but a particularly important element in "people-building" politics, rather than either as an independent phenomenon or as the central phenomenon in "people-building." Wendt might disagree.

community" are all rather stuffy academic terms, and the first seem to focus too exclusively on state institutions; while the term "community" alone has many quite different connotations. In English, the broader term most often used instead of "nation" is probably "people," as in the Declaration of Independence: "When in the course of human events, it becomes necessary for one people to dissolve the political bands which have connected them with another." So, too, the US Constitution opens: "We the People of the United States." The French Declaration of the Rights of Man and Citizen similarly begins: "The representatives of the French people" ("Les Représentants du Peuple Français..."). And the 1949 Basic Law of the Federal Republic of Germany also presents itself as adopted by the German people ("Deutsche Volk").[10] We have already seen that official documents of the Kyrgyz Republic are translated into English as referring to the "Kyrgyz people," at least as often as to the "Kyrgyz nation"; just as the Torah is translated as the history of "the people of Israel." Such phrasing can be found in the authoritative political documents of many other "peoples" also. Indeed, as terms like "tribes" and "nations" have come to have controversial connotations, designations of political communities as "peoples" have become if anything more widespread in recent political documents, reference works, and explicitly normative theoretical works.[11]

Yet though the terms "people" and "peoples" are very commonly employed, the quest for a "theory of people-building" has been so little perceived to be a central challenge for political analysis that the very phrase sounds odd (as do synonymous alternatives that I will use, like "people-forming" and "people-making").[12] That state of affairs, to be sure, may

---

[10] Both English and French versions of the French Declaration can be accessed at http//:www.justice.gouv.fr/navig.htm. Both English and German versions of the German Basic Law can be accessed at http//:www.jura.uni-sb.de/law/GG.ggo.html.

[11] See e.g. Rawls, 1999; Annan, 2000; Diagram Group, 2000; Ivison, Patton, and Sanders, eds., 2000); Young, 2000, 9–12. Gilbert, 2000, is a useful overview of current debates that often uses "peoples" as the more inclusive category for "races," "ethnic groups," and "nations," as I do here. Gilbert does not, however, ever explain this usage or analyze how "peoples" come to exist. Liah Greenfeld (1992, 6) accurately notes that prior to the modern era the term "people" often referred to the lower classes, but that the term has also always had more general referents that included elites and masses alike. Schnapper (1998, 23) describes "people" as a "political" rather than a "scientific" term, but it is precisely those groups that tend to assert some claim to political authority that I wish to designate.

[12] Bernard Yack defines "peoples" in a distinctive way, as the imagined pre-political sovereign that authorizes legitimate governments in some ideological traditions, and he suggests this ideological role may explain the absence of theories of "people-building." He acknowledges his usage is designed to distinguish analytically between distinct conceptions of community and does not map on to all the ordinary usages I am invoking here (Yack, 2001, 520–521).

be entirely proper. Even if peoples are "made," at any given point in history a large number of established forms of peoplehood already exist. It may therefore be sensible to focus on politics within the parameters they establish, attending at most to specific new types of peoplehood that may be emerging, which is what most writers have done. Furthermore, the many historical varieties of peoplehood may be so different from one another that trying to generalize across them could represent a hopeless "apples and oranges" exercise. A more general theory of "people-making," or put more grandly, some sort of "Unified Field Theory of Political Identity Formation," may just be too general to be of real use.[13] That may be why scholars have focused on more particular topics, such as ethnicity, racial formations, class consciousness, construction of gender identities, formation of religious groups, linguistic politics, and the like. Political scientists and sociologists have especially devoted attention to "nations," "nationalism," and "nation-building."[14] That emphasis has been understandable, since until recently, the "nation-state" has seemed to most analysts to be the dominant form of political membership in the modern world, now and for the foreseeable future. It seemed sensible to focus on the nation-state's emergence from older varieties of peoplehood, its distinctive characteristics, and its destiny, rather than seeking theories that could encompass forms of political community now obsolete.

Still, in most other areas of inquiry, scholars do not shrink from seeking as general a theory as possible of the phenomena that they study. And today, many are inclined to argue that the era of the "nation-state" is over (if it was ever so dominant as some have asserted); so that attention to "nations" and "nationalism" seems plainly insufficient to address the topic of the formation and transformation of the kinds of political memberships, communities, and identities that will matter in the twenty-first century. As the examples of ancient Israel and modern Kyrgyzstan suggest, moreover, it is perfectly conceivable that there are important common elements to the processes through which different types of

---

[13] For a historian's sharp and reasonable critique of exactly the sort of general theorizing I am engaging in here, see Breuilly, 1982, 2. Yet in an attempt to avoid too general an approach, Breuilly and others have to define their topics, in his case "nationalism," in plausibly but eminently contestable ways that generate lengthy and often unfruitful debates over what "nationalism" (or "ethnicity," or "class," or some other category) "really" is.

[14] See e.g. Smith, 1983, 191; Turner, 1986, 18–19; Brubaker, 1992, 35. As Will Kymlicka points out, many liberal theorists, at least, have long neglected issues of "nation-building." Most now analyze them, at most, in terms of state nation-building and minority groups rights, as Kymlicka himself does very usefully (Kymlicka, 2001, 4).

political "peoples" have been generated in different times and places. If so, these elements are surely fundamental for both empirical and normative political analyses. There can hardly be any topic more richly significant for explanatory political inquiries than the questions of how people come to have the senses of political affiliation and allegiance that they possess and how those senses of belonging change. There can hardly be any topic more profoundly important to normative political debates than the question of the forms of political membership and identity we ought to embrace as our own.

The initial argument of this book is that political analysts should see whether we can achieve a theory or theories of processes of "people-making," understood as the generation of shared beliefs, among outsiders and insiders alike, that certain human populations comprise a political "people." But it goes beyond my ambitions and my competency to provide such a full-fledged "Unified Field Theory" here, much less to test rigorously the speculative notions I will advance. Instead, my aims are first, to sketch what I believe to be some if not all of the fundamental elements of any credible theory of people-making. Second, I argue for the particular importance of certain sorts of stories, especially types I call "ethically constitutive stories," as components of the politics of peoplehood. Finally, I use this tentative explanatory framework to critique some prevailing normative arguments concerning political memberships and identities as politically unrealistic, and to suggest instead a different approach to moral evaluations of political affiliations and community allegiances. Whereas the thrust of many contemporary writers is to seek to push particularistic "ethically constitutive stories" to the margins of politics, I seek to check their dangers while also energizing politics by calling for a politics of contestation among multiple constitutive stories of peoplehood, both more particularistic and more universalistic.[15]

I cannot pretend that the pages that follow contain systematic evidence for my ideas. The aim of this small book is simply to lay out what I hope to be stimulating empirical and normative conceptual claims. In support of my aspirations to generality, I exemplify these arguments with discussions of the politics of people-making in many times and places. Still, these references to actual human communities are meant only to illustrate and

---

[15] Perhaps surprisingly for a scholar whose chief normative commitments have been to certain forms of liberalism and anti-racism, this puts me on many issues closer to postmodernist democrats like William Connolly than to "mainstream" liberals like John Rawls. Even so, as discussed in the last two chapters, I stress the need for positive, stable forms of people-making more than most postmodernists do.

clarify, not to test, the claims made here. But if these pages do not undertake everything that should be done to meet the need for empirical and normative theories about the generation of political peoples, they nonetheless pursue a potentially far-reaching and, I think, worthwhile agenda. There are, of course, many virtues that a book that merely aims to sketch out ideas cannot claim; but one to which its author ought to aspire is brevity. So, on we go.

Part I

Explaining the political role of stories
of peoplehood

1 Elements of a theory of people-making

Varieties of political peoples

Theories must be theories of something. One of the goals of this book is to persuade contemporary American political scientists that they should take as central to their theorizing some topics that have long been treated as marginal or beyond their disciplinary concerns. When American political science underwent what scholars call its "behavioralist revolution" in the 1950s, many outstanding scholars came to believe that the study of politics should be understood as the empirical analysis of the behavior of human "interest groups." Others preferred to study the conflicts of "classes" in Marxist fashion. Some analyzed the functions of "systems" in imitation of the sociologist Talcott Parsons. Others focused on the often-irrational workings of individual psyches; and some continued to stress the internal traits and tendencies of human institutions and of bodies of ideas. Today many study politics as the preference-driven actions of instrumentally rational individuals.[1]

Without disdaining any of those enterprises, I suggest that an intellectually adequate political science must also focus on what I regard as a quite basic dimension of all political activity, one that has not been so directly addressed by prevailing approaches: the making, maintaining, and transforming of senses of political peoplehood. Sometimes this activity dominates political life. Often it is an important but muted component of political action, and at times it is more marginal. In the final analysis, however, it structures politics – and human beings – too fundamentally to be ignored. It is a type of activity that is carried on not by members of all human associations, groups, and communities, but by participants in what is still a rather larger and unruly subset of those groups. I term that subset "political peoples."

A human group can be of great importance to its members, as many cultural, recreational, and social associations are, without its being the

---

[1] Pertinent discussions of the history of political science include e.g. Seidelman and Harpham (1985), Farr (1988), and Gunnell (1993).

sort of "people" I am concerned with here. I define a group as a *political* people or community when it is a potential adversary of other forms of human association, *because* its proponents are generally understood to assert that its obligations legitimately trump many of the demands made on its members in the name of other associations. This definition excludes many forms of human community: though doubtless many persons feel great loyalty to their football clubs, singing groups, or Girl Scout troops, neither the leaders nor members of such associations are ever likely to assert seriously that the obligations of those memberships justify them in violating governmental laws.

To be sure, it is also true that usually not all, and often not even most, members of a "political people" will fully accept such claims to its primacy. Most will feel that they have a number of other affiliations and identities with claims on them that are also very important. Many may in fact feel they have been to some degree been directly or indirectly coerced into their putatively "primary" political membership. Yet so long as most acknowledge that their membership presents them with these sorts of claims on their allegiances, the group is a "political people" as I am using the term here.[2] "Political peoples" are forms of "imagined community," in the famous phrase that Benedict Anderson (1983) has applied to nations. I am stressing, however, that they are "political" because they are communities "imagined" to impose binding obligations and duties; and many human associations beyond those that Anderson calls "nations" fall under this definition.

To see why, we need to recognize that the potency of senses of "political peoplehood" can vary in two ways. First, a particular group's supporters may believe that its obligations can override the demands of a lot of or only a few other associations. Second, a group may assert its primacy over a wide range of issues, or only certain ones. Clearly, actual groups will often fall somewhere in the middle in the strength of the demands made in their name, the number of issues over which they assert priority, or both. We can thus imagine a wide variety of "political peoples," from those that advance "strong" claims to allegiance over a "wide" range of issues down to those more politically trivial groups that advance only "weak" claims to allegiance over a "narrow" range of issues. Displayed in that favorite

---

[2] The existence of such senses of political peoplehood can therefore be substantiated empirically by evidence such as speeches of leaders and legislative and judicial proclamations of members' statuses and obligations, and by opinion surveys of members' beliefs about their community and its claims upon them. I do not seek to provide such evidence in systematic fashion in this theoretical work, but the concepts laid out here are useful in part because they can easily be operationalized in this fashion.

Table 1

Strong & Wide (China, US)	Strong & Midrange (Quebec)	Strong & Narrow (Jehovah's Witnesses)
Moderate & Wide (Belgium, Navajos)	Moderate & Midrange (Wales, Antioquia)	Moderate & Narrow (AFL-CIO, Greenpeace)
Weak & Wide (Puerto Rico, Ecovillages)	Weak & Midrange (Brooklyn, Hong Kong)	Weak & Narrow (Oxfam, PEN).

tool of social scientists, a multi-celled table, and with some contestable examples provided, this variety looks as shown in Table 1.

This table could be expanded indefinitely by including gradations indicating further degrees of strength and breadth for senses of peoplehood, along with the additional permutations that would result. But for our purposes, these two dimensions of "the potency of peoplehood" are not the same. The most politically important feature of a group is the degree to which its proponents assert its priority over other associations, whether over many issues or few. It is such assertions that most often entail political conflict. These senses of political peoplehood might therefore instead be arrayed along a spectrum ranging from "strong and wide" through "moderate" versions and finally to "weak and narrow," to wit: *Strong/Wide* → *Strong/Midrange* → *Strong/Narrow* → *Moderate/ Wide* → *Moderate/Midrange* → *Moderate/Narrow* → *Weak/Wide* → *Weak/Midrange* → *Weak/Narrow*.

I will discuss the various types of political peoples listed in Table 1 in this order.

Strong political peoples

The various types of "strong" political peoplehood are, unsurprisingly, the ones that pose the greatest challenges to achieving a peaceful, constructive "politics of people-making," and so they will feature most prominently in the ensuing discussion. To clarify their problematic character, let me emphasize that even "strong and wide" senses of membership are still conceptions of particular forms of human community, in which certain sorts of persons and activities rightly have places and others do not. Even if such a view of political community is presented as properly extendable to all of humanity, as when Alexander the Great sought to conquer the world, it still represents a type of political association that requires its members to accept certain identities and affiliations and to abandon others (Armstrong, 1982, 133). "Strong and wide" senses of political membership are thus ones that present a particular form of community as "inherently limited" in some respects that make it distinctive, but as nonetheless "sovereign" (Anderson, 1983, 16–17).

Indeed, at the extreme, the champions of a "strong and wide" political people depict it as a distinct society entitled ultimately to override the claims of not just many but *all* other groups, and entitled to do so not just in regard to a few issues but *all* issues. When officials of modern regimes like the People's Republic of China or the United States hold that their members are obligated to obey all of their national laws, to forswear all allegiances to any foreign powers, and to accept obligations for military service against whomever the government designates as an enemy, they are asserting senses of peoplehood that are both strong and wide.

It is tempting, in fact, to identify such "strong and wide" conceptions strictly with the "peoples" and officials of widely recognized "sovereign" states. But that would be a mistake; many leaders who articulate such strong senses of peoplehood are not even aspirants to formal state offices, at least not openly. They may be religious leaders, such as the sword-wielding popes of the late Middle Ages and clerics like the Ayatollah Khomeini. They may be spokesmen for radical racial and ethnic groups, like the contemporary Aryan Nation and Marcus Garvey's United Negro Improvement Association at its most extreme. Often such figures combine religious and ethnic appeals, as Osama bin Laden has done with horrifying effectiveness. They can be working-class activists, such as the various Marxist strategists who have seen their ultimate community of allegiance as the transnational proletariat. They can also be linguistic or cultural adherents, as in the case of some strongly separatist Quebecois; or regional loyalists, like the antebellum American southerners who believed their obligations to their states and region overrode the claims of the Union. At times, leaders of radical environmentalist and feminist groups and other social movement organizations similarly contend that duties to their association and its cause deserve to outweigh all rival obligations. Many more such examples could be added.[3] Whenever any such leaders contend that the church, group, community, gender, association, class, or "people" for whom they profess to speak deserves the allegiance of

---

[3] These conceptions of peoplehood might be seen as various forms of what many analysts, following Cornelius Castoriadis (1987) as well as Anderson, refer to as "social imaginaries." They also certainly include what are often termed "myths" of identity. But it is not possible to explore here the relationship between my term "peoplehood" and the many and varied scholarly uses of "social imaginary" and "myth" without a lengthy excursion into semantic swamps where, I fear, many readers would be lost permanently.

all who belong to it in cases of conflict with virtually all rivals, they are promulgating a "strong" version of political peoplehood as defined here. It might be thought that any "people" whose leaders advance "strong" claims to sovereignty in regard to some issues will ultimately seek to do so in regard to all. It is indeed likely that they will act this way under many circumstances. But not all; today there are many political communities that firmly brook no challenges to their rights to self-determination in many important matters but that nonetheless agree to form semi-autonomous entities within broader societies whose decision-makers speak for them in other regards, often especially in foreign affairs. As suggested on the preceding chart, with secession and independence apparently rejected for the time being, Quebec (or at least its Francophone majority) forms one such "political people" today. Though Quebec continues to act as a member of Canada's federal system, it officially denies that it is a province. On December 7, 2000, moreover, the self-styled National (not provincial) Assembly of the "Quebec State" passed Bill 99, asserting "that the Quebec people, through their political institutions, have the right to rule on the nature and extent of their right to self-determination" and on its exercise. The bill also specified that "no parliament or government may reduce the powers, authority, sovereignty or legitimacy of the National Assembly."[4] These are direct assertions of "strong" political peoplehood, even though Quebec voters have thus far refused to ratify referenda explicitly endorsing full sovereignty. At the same time, Quebec chiefly insists on autonomy in regard to language education and use, issues with broad ramifications to be sure, but still sufficiently confined to term this a "strong but midrange" sense of peoplehood.[5]

Finally, many forms of political community claim primacy over a few issues, but not very many. Devoted Jehovah's Witnesses pursue ways of life that are, to be sure, comprehensively shaped by their religious beliefs, and many Witnesses believe that the obligations defined by their faith unquestionably outweigh their duties to any governments that claim power over them. But apart from a relatively small range of issues such

---

[4] These official English translations of the provisions of Bill 99 can be found at http://www.premier.gouv.qc.ca./premier ministre/english.

[5] As Joseph H. Carens notes in a forceful defense of Quebec's policies from a liberal democratic point of view, "the only distinctive cultural commitment...that Quebec requires...is knowledge of French." Neither immigrants nor native-born citizens are required to "prove their loyalty to Quebec by proclaiming an attachment to its symbols or an identification with its history." People "can be full members of Quebec's distinct society even if they look and act differently from the substantial segment of the population whose ancestors inhabited Quebec and even if they do not in any way alter their own customs and cultural patterns with respect to work and play, diet and dress, sleep and sex, celebration and mourning, so long as they act within the confines of the law" (Carens, 2000, 131).

as proselytizing, flag salutes, and in some cases military service, most Jehovah's Witnesses have no trouble accepting governmental authority, and indeed some hold civic offices.[6] Their religious membership amounts to a "strong but narrow" kind of political peoplehood that can at times involve them in intense political conflicts, but not nearly so routinely as in the case of the more wide-ranging forms of "strong" peoplehood.

Moderate political peoples

The categories of "strong and midrange" and "strong but narrow" political peoples are analytically distinct from, but in practice merge into, various forms of "moderate" political peoplehood. The key distinction is whether a people's officials claim to be the final authorities over some range of matters, or whether they are content to share even final decision-making. The boundaries between having a meaningful "share" in decisions and being "final" over some of them are, however, often hard to draw.

Even so, one of the most striking phenomena in the world today is the growth of apparently stable forms of "moderate" political peoplehood, in which leaders of various communities are willing to recognize themselves as significantly authoritative on certain matters without claiming full and final "sovereignty" over most or any. Such circumstances are, to be sure, far from unprecedented. In the European "Middle Ages," from the fall of the Roman Empire to the rise of monarchs claiming absolute power over the members of their "nations," most people lived within multiple structures of authority – including diverse orders of clerics, local lords, more distant kings, sometimes village or town officials, sometimes Holy Roman Emperors – all of which asserted certain prerogatives but not absolute sovereignty. Despite the tensions and disorderliness inherent in such a structure of overlapping authorities and memberships, many legacies of this past survived the consolidation of monarchical and then republican European nation-states from the fourteenth century through the twentieth. Today, Europeans are simultaneously constructing a heightened supra-national system of power and membership in the form of the European Union and devolving certain powers back to older forms of political community such as Wales, Scotland, and Corsica. Some analysts see in these developments the potential for a modernized, democratized variant of the Middle Ages' world of "moderate" political memberships (Held, 1995, 31–38, 136–140, 235–237).

---

[6] For an overview of political and legal controversies involving the Witnesses, see Peters (2000).

To assert, as I do in Table 1 above, that Belgium today advances only a "moderate" sense of peoplehood is perhaps overstated. Belgium can still plausibly be perceived as a traditional sovereign state. It is so treated in the United Nations, the Olympics, and many other "international" arenas. Yet it is at least equally plausible to hold, like the Belgian scholar Liesbet Hooghe, that with the constitutional reforms of 1988, further formalized in the 1992 *Accord de la St Michel*, "official Belgium decisively abandoned the nation-state idea. According to the new definition of stateness and state–society relations no level of government can claim absolute priority. Sovereignty has lost its absolute character; it is now shared by the regions, the national state and Europe" (Hooghe, 1991, iii; Fitzmaurice, 1996, 3, 145). Many leaders of Belgium's more federalized modern government have indeed firmly supported increasing the European Union's supervening authority over a growing list of issues. Belgium has also always had substantial linguistic, ethnic, and religious diversity, creating tensions that were curtailed initially chiefly by opposition to Dutch rule in the early nineteenth century, and that have often festered since. As a result, today Belgians have sought to control their linguistic and economic conflicts via assigning extensive authority for governance to the levels of the quite varied regions and communities, provinces, communes, and cities that have made up Belgium throughout its modern history (Hooghe, 1991, 3–5, 22–23; Fitzmaurice, 1996, 268; Strikwerda, 1997, 27–63). Hence many Belgians today, leaders and citizens alike, are content to define the obligations of Belgians to Belgium in ways that are more tolerant of multiple allegiances, some more expansive, some less expansive, than champions of state sovereignty elsewhere can comfortably abide.

Similarly, leaders of the Navajo Nation in the US formally claim sovereignty and subject an even wider range of their members' affairs to distinctive regulation than Quebec does (though Quebec may be closing the gap). The Navajo people rely heavily, however, on funding from the US government, and they seek it in the name of their rights as equal American citizens, as well as in the name of treaty agreements.[7] Unlike Quebec, they are not now asserting any general right to annul federal legislation. Thus the Navajo, the Belgians, and some other communities today seem to accept stable, "moderate but wide" senses of political peoplehood.

[7] See, e.g., Navajo President Kelsey A. Begaye (1999, 6): "The Indian allocation is usually one half or less of the non-Indian allocation . . . We can no longer accept being treated like second class citizens in our own country. This allocation of limited resources to Native American Nations goes back to the heart of the Jim Crow laws; 'Separate but Equal' . . . the principle of equal justice under the laws must apply to the Native American Nations in America." Available at http://www.navajo.org.

Moving to the next "moderate" gradation: even after devolution, the Welsh government claims less yet in the way of sovereign powers than does either Belgium or the Navajo Nation. The sense of Welsh political peoplehood is real; it, too, now has a National Assembly; but neither most Welsh leaders nor most residents view Wales as highly demanding or authoritative over a very broad range of issues. The Welsh government's mandate is to address more local concerns distinctive to the people of Wales, while the Welsh continue to be represented in the UK and European Parliaments and to act as loyal citizens of the UK and the European Union in the broad areas of those governments' acknowledged jurisdictions. In the same way, citizens of the relatively prosperous Antioquia region of Colombia, who often presented themselves in the past as Antioquians far more than they did as Colombians and who maintained significant measures of self-governance, now acknowledge Colombian identity. Antioquia acts only as a particularly powerful department or province within the Colombian state. Most state or provincial citizens in most stable federal systems probably have similar "moderate, midrange" conceptions of their state or provincial "peoplehood."[8]

Finally, in contrast to the "strong but narrow" senses of politically potent identity held by groups like the more fervent religious denominations, most labor unions and environmental groups are willing to accept that they must ultimately yield to governmental authority even on the specific issues that most concern them. They do not have especially "strong" senses of their group obligations. Yet their politically pertinent senses of group identity are not terribly weak, either. Many leaders and members are willing to engage in some measure of civil disobedience to certain laws to attain their rather specific ends and to regard contrary rulings as illegitimate. They will picket without permits, hold sit-in demonstrations in areas where they have no legal right to be, and sometimes sabotage industrial operations, to dramatize their causes.[9] This belief that they

---

[8] On Wales see e.g. Jones and Balsom, eds., 2000, esp. 282–283. Ann Twinam details how, due chiefly to their prosperity, inhabitants of Antioquia, called Antioqueño or *paisa*, have long been "reviled" as "Jews" by others in Colombia, many of whom have actually asserted that Antiqueños are predominantly of Jewish descent. The Antiqueños responded in the late nineteenth and twentieth centuries by advancing various countermyths claiming that they "form a special race, a distinct culture, and a probably superior people within Colombia" (Twinam, 1980, 81, 84, 90–94; quote is from 94).

[9] For example, at this writing, Greenpeace, which says its mission involves "nonviolent, creative confrontation to expose global environmental problems," has activists facing criminal charges for violating a safety zone in one of their many protests against American military and nuclear tests (details at http://www.greenpeace.org and http://www.greenpeaceusa.org). Unions involved in the AFL-CIO have long histories of sometimes militant strike actions, a history celebrated at its website; and the organization currently professes its broad commitment to finding "creative ways" to give "workers a say in all the decisions that affect our working lives," not just their contracts (http://www.aflcio.org/about/mission.htm).

are justified in disobeying some state laws is what leads me to classify groups such as the AFL-CIO and Greenpeace as having a "moderate but narrow" sense of political peoplehood. Both examples suggest, moreover, that at times some leaders and members of such organizations may advance and act on much stronger claims for their right to override other authorities.

Even so, all these diverse "moderate" forms of peoplehood are of particular interest because, much of the time, they can inspire allegiance from and participation by their members while accepting that those members simultaneously belong to a wide variety of other deeply valued communities. These senses of peoplehood are often conducive to a more pacific and productive "politics of people-making" than "strong" conceptions. Throughout the ensuing analysis, I seek to explore the strategies and conditions that can generate and sustain such "moderate conceptions" against what I depict as powerful political pressures to assert more extreme, demanding, and conflictual notions. Though moderation is admittedly not a virtue in all regards, when it comes to assertions of rightful authority by would-be leaders of political peoples, it generally is.

Weak political peoples

The various "weak" forms of political peoplehood receive less attention in this book. After all, they are weak. Still, they cannot be dismissed as politically irrelevant, if only because they represent forms of membership that can sometimes be mobilized into stronger versions. To dramatize that fact, and also to clarify the distinction between a strong sense of cultural peoplehood and the sort of political peoplehood I am considering here, I have listed Puerto Rico as an example of a rare "weak but wide" political people. Many Puerto Ricans on the island and in the mainland United States feel their Puerto Rican cultural identity very keenly; and island officials regulate quite a wide variety of issues affecting the lives of their residents. Yet all know that these officials do so only at the sufferance of the US government, a government in which island Puerto Ricans are not represented. Unlike the Navajo and other Indian Nations, Puerto Rico has never had treaties with the US designating it as an at least putatively sovereign nation. To the contrary, nothing in American law permits Puerto Rican officials credibly to claim any ultimate sovereignty over any topic (Ramos, 2001, 11–14). Unsurprisingly, many Puerto Ricans object to this "weak" status, and it has the potential to be a basis for a form of peoplehood that will assert much more standing in relationship to the United States. Still, such assertions are as yet not powerful enough to produce any major political conflicts, in part because many Puerto Ricans seem satisfied to have a strong sense of distinctive cultural identity but only a weak form of political peoplehood. The situation of Puerto Rico thus resembles that of the various small "ecovillage" communes that exist in a number of American states and other countries. These are "countercultural" communities with institutions of collective property, organic farming, and distinctive environmentally oriented religions that establish quite comprehensive ways of life for their members; but they do not claim any exemptions from any supervening governmental authorities, making them "weak though wide" political peoples.[10]

Similarly, being a member of the "people of Brooklyn" cannot be dismissed as a politically inconsequential identity. But though the public policies of Brooklyn have fairly substantial consequences for the lives of the borough's citizens, no one claims that Brooklyn is sovereign over and above the government of New York City, much less the State of New York or the United States of America. Indeed, it is less broadly significant in the lives of its inhabitants than Puerto Rico's government or the communal institutions of ecovillages. Brooklyn's "weak, midrange peoplehood" correspondingly forms part of the politics of people-making in the United States, but not a major part.

It is more controversial to characterize Hong Kong as a "weak, midrange" political people, since it has long had a distinctive identity and a significant measure of functional autonomy, despite having been a British colony. The Basic Law that now defines it as a Special Administrative Region of the People's Republic of China, moreover, includes guarantees of a "high degree of autonomy," continuation of most existing laws, and maintenance of a capitalist economic system for fifty years. Still, appointment of the chief executive and interpretation and amendment of the Basic Law rest with the Central People's Government, so that like Puerto Rico, Hong Kong has no authority that cannot be altered by direct national legislation. In fact Hong Kong citizens have even less discretion over vital matters like the selection of their top administrative officials than Puerto Ricans do; so they can reasonably be classified as a "weak and midrange" political people.[11]

Even organizations that do not claim any authority to override claims made on behalf of other human groups, and who concern themselves with a relatively narrow range of human affairs, cannot be entirely dismissed as irrelevant to the politics of peoplehood. A transnational organization like the charitable group Oxfam International may work to relieve suffering in ways that lead its members to question existing governmental policies

---

[10] On Puerto Rico's legal status, see e.g. Ramos, 2001. On ecovillages, see e.g. Jackson, 2000.

[11] The text of the Basic Law can be found at http://www.info.gov.hk/basic_law/fulltext.

and allegiances, even if such questioning rarely escalates to civil disobe-dience, much less active rejection of the legitimacy of various regimes. The political tensions bound up with such memberships are exem-plified in Oxfam International's "Strategic Plan, 2001–2004," entitled "Towards Global Equity." It proclaims that "Oxfam people are global citizens" and that its members "participate in, support and promote the emerging movement for global citizenship."[12] In so doing, Oxfam Inter-national inevitably fosters challenges to claims of the primacy of other forms of citizenship, even if its members devote themselves to advocacy and non-violent protests, not revolutionary activity. Similarly, Interna-tional PEN, the worldwide association of writers, professes itself to be strictly "non-political" and claims no authority to violate any law. Still, it urges its members to "champion the ideal of one humanity living in peace in one world" and to "oppose any form of suppression of freedom of expression . . . throughout the world wherever this is possible."[13] The or-ganization frequently invokes these principles to challenge the legitimacy of many policies of existing political communities.

All such memberships therefore warrant notice here, both because just as they are, all such groups can play significant roles in the politics of people-building, and because these classifications of various communi-ties as "strong," "moderate," or "weak" political peoples are subject to dramatic change over time.[14] The ancient Babylonian Jews may have re-defined Jewish identity as fundamentally religious and compatible with subjectship in a Persian province, as many Jews would later do under the Ptolomies and Rome; Jews may have functioned as stigmatized eth-nic "corporations" within the corporatist structure of feudal Christian Europe; Jews in the United States may have often accepted identifica-tion as simply another religious group among the many American cit-izens have embraced; but modern Zionists have successfully advanced stronger and more sharply political views of Israeli peoplehood (Ettinger, 1976, 727–1092; Scheindlin, 1998, 27–56). As noted, in some centuries Catholic popes riding at the head of armies clearly engaged in quite

---

[12] "Towards Global Equity: Strategic Plan 2001–2004," Oxfam International, available at www.oxfaminternational.org.
[13] "International P.E.N. Charter," available at http://www.oneworld.org/internatpen/home.htm.
[14] Florencia Mallon has argued similarly (1995, 6): "In families, communities, political or-ganizations, regions, and state structures, power is always being contested, legitimated, and refined. Some projects, stories, or interpretations are winning out over others; some factions are defeating others. The interaction among different levels, locations, or orga-nizations in a given society – say, between families and communities, communities and political parties, or regions and a central state – redefines not only each one of these political arenas internally but also the balance of forces among them."

coercive forms of "people-building" in Europe, conquering populations who were then subjected to direct church governance. Even during the antebellum era in US history, important leaders of the Catholic Church in Europe (and a few in the US) repeatedly denounced American republican institutions in favor of rather repressive forms of monarchy. They thereby implied, at least, that church allegiances opposed and trumped the loyalties of Catholic Americans to the US government, making the Church a "strong" political people (Smith, 1997, 209). But in the twentieth century, Catholic leaders and members have overwhelmingly accepted that church membership provides no legitimate basis for generally disavowing the authority and laws of the US government or those of most other governments in whose jurisdiction Catholics reside. Catholicism thus rarely if ever represents a "strong" form of political peoplehood today.

That does not mean, however, that the modern Catholic Church is never a significant actor in the politics of people-making in the US, as it clearly is elsewhere. In certain regards, American Catholics have quite plausibly continued to see themselves as threatened by political forces advancing Protestant or secular visions of the American nation. Examples include Protestant attacks on the presidential candidacy of John F. Kennedy, policies denying public funds to Catholic schools, and rulings permitting abortions. In response, Catholics have sometimes taken group actions to resist these rival positions, and a radical few have claimed that their religious identities and allegiances justify violating at least some US laws. These stances are, to be sure, quite rare within the American Catholic Church and generally quite narrow in the breadth of their challenges to US laws, authority, and membership. Hence it makes sense to continue to classify that Church as at most a "moderate" and "midrange" form of political peoplehood, often a rather "weak and narrow" form. The same is true of most of the other civil associations that comprise what many writers call "civil society." But because the politics of peoplemaking is an ongoing dimension of human life, and even "weak" political peoples are not likely to escape the pressures it generates indefinitely, the statuses of all such groups are always subject to transformation.[15]

As I have noted, today many scholars see a pattern of transformation that they regard as quite encouraging. They are predicting empirically and hoping normatively that forms of membership advancing strong claims

---

[15] In a valuable analysis of the political construction of Mexican – American social movement organizations that has parallels with the arguments here, Benjamin Marquez observes that some are constructed in ways that support moderate, integrative civil rights agendas; others, in ways that express support for racial autonomy; and some in ways that inspire radical revolutionary activity. But groups can over time be transformed from more moderate to more radical (Marquez, 2001).

of absolute sovereignty are in fact disappearing in favor of more moderate varieties of peoplehood, as a result of processes of globalization and the decline of nation-states (Held, 1995; Linklatter, 1999; Bosniak, 2000; Young, 2000). In many cases, such as federated societies like Switzerland and Canada; countries with semi-autonomous indigenous peoples like the United States and Australia; and societies with religious groups that claim partly autonomous status like the Amish and some Orthodox communities in Israel, it does indeed seem that populations can simultaneously maintain enduring allegiances to more than one political "people" without necessarily generating any severe clashes.

Still, those same examples, like the bloody history of medieval Europe, also indicate that the potential for severe conflicts usually persists in such arrangements. As discussed in Part II, I agree broadly with those who wish to see a complexly federated world of "moderate" to "weak" political peoples in which individuals can freely choose to belong to many such roughly equal and only "semi-sovereign" communities at once – so long as these forms of peoplehood are still capable of serving as locales of human economic, cultural, and political flourishing. In this Part, I argue nonetheless that the political dynamics of people-building make the achievement of such arrangements on an enduring basis difficult and precarious, though not impossible. The point is to show how those of us with normative reservations about absolutist senses of allegiance face major, identifiable challenges in considering how we can forge stable forms of political membership that eschew them.

The wellspring of those challenges is the fact that, precisely because there are many forms of human association whose leaders are tempted to claim their members' allegiances in cases of conflict, political tensions between advocates of different actual and potential political communities will inevitably arise and sometimes escalate. When an existing government's authority is challenged by a movement leader or by officials of a rival regime, those clashes are likely to prompt the rival forces to advance "strong" senses of peoplehood, to assert sovereignty strenuously on behalf of the "political people" they claim to champion. The Kyrgyz conception of "peoplehood" is presented to the web-surfing world, perhaps sincerely but doubtless also self-consciously, as one that does not threaten either law-abiding domestic minorities or neighboring peoples. But the tenacity with which President Akayev has held on to his power suggests that, should the new Kyrgyz Republic's leaders come to believe their regime faces serious struggles to maintain its independence from any such sources, such as the ethnic Uzbek Islamics it is already policing stringently, matters may well change. It is likely that they will stress more in symbols and in policies the aspects of the Manas story and their other traditions that justify repression of such opposition. These measures may in turn produce intensified struggles and even more radical assertions of distinctive political identity by groups like Uzbek Islamics in Kyrgyzstan. Throughout the world, the outcomes of such struggles do much to define the forms of human association, membership, and identity that prevail, though always, only for a time. That is why I characterize "people-making" processes as fundamentally political.

Premises of a "positive" theory of people-building

My account of the elements of these political processes of people-making rest on four assumptions about *all* senses of political peoplehood, from very strong to very weak. These assumptions can certainly be disputed; but even without elaborate defense, I believe they are sufficiently plausible to make attention to the arguments built upon them worthwhile. Simply stated, the premises are:

(1) No political peoples are *natural* or *primordial*. All are the products of long, conflict-ridden histories, and all must be understood as human creations, formed by participants in preexisting forms of peoplehood.

The core evidence for this claim is historical: no extant sense of political peoplehood can be shown to have endured over long periods of time without quite fundamental transformations. None has been free from historical periods of intense internal and external contestation in which partisans of rival visions of political community have sought to dispute and to transform the political identities and allegiances of some or all putative members of that "people."

(2) Political peoples are created via *constrained, asymmetrical* interactions between actual and would-be leaders of political communities and the potential constituents for whom they compete.

This assumption rejects views suggesting that senses of peoplehood emerge organically or evolve out of people's particular economic, territorial, demographic, ancestral, religious, linguistic, or cultural identities in some fairly automatic, unconscious process. All those factors do shape individual senses of personal identity, but precisely because many factors do so, none can automatically serve as the basis of a conception of political community. Instead, they must be explicitly espoused as such a basis in ways that effectively mobilize constituencies to embrace them and institutionalize them. That is why the processes of people-making must be analyzed as resting on interactions between leaders and constituents; and the interactions are *asymmetrical* because it is actual and would-be leaders who most directly articulate and seek to institutionalize conceptions of political peoplehood.

That asymmetry means, moreover, that there is always a dualistic character to such conceptions. Indeed, at one extreme, leaders may articulate and impose such sharply differentiated, vertically structured conceptions of peoplehood that leaders and constituents are portrayed as having virtually nothing in common. Those in power form a ruling class that defines itself as a distinct group or "people" entitled to rule over one or more lesser groups or "peoples." Even in such accounts, let me stress, both rulers and subjects are still understood to be members of a larger political order that represents a kind of common political "peoplehood." It is, however, a kind in which the different classes occupy very different places and are presented as possessing sharply different characteristics.[16] The great French historian Marc Bloch captured well what he termed this fundamental "dualism" of hierarchical forms of political membership. He wrote, "serfdom made a man at once the subject of his chief and a member of an inferior and despised social class, near the bottom of the scale" (Bloch, 1970, 88–89). As the peasant revolts that Bloch went on to discuss indicate, the occupants of such lower ranks often object passionately to the stigmatized statuses and identities imposed on them, but they cannot deny their existence; and over time many may at least partly internalize those identities. Not only feudal aristocrats governing bodies of peasants who often did not even speak the same language, but also European colonial governments imposing subjectship on diverse African and Asian populaces, and southern white supremacists governing American blacks in the days of slavery and Jim Crow, all display versions of such "vertical, differentiated" forms of peoplehood.[17]

But the asymmetrical relationship of leaders and followers need not be so one-sided. At the other extreme, leaders may instead articulate a fully horizontal, unified conception of membership in which they claim to be no more than representative members and humble agents of their "people." Bloch also called attention to how in the towns, villages, and rural communities of the late Middle Ages, many sought to form "communes," legally recognized political entities bonded not by "the old oaths of fidelity and homage ... perpetuating ties of dependence" but by "an obligation among equals" to provide each other with mutual aid (1970, 172). From such communes would eventually emerge political, economic, demographic, and intellectual support for achieving more

---

[16] That is one reason why my category "peoples" is broader than Benedict Anderson's definition of "nations." He envisions the latter as "always conceived as a deep, horizontal comradeship," whatever "the actual inequality and exploitation that may prevail" (1983, 16). In contrast, a "people" may include an elite group that presents itself more like shepherds looking after lower orders of sheep, adults supervising children, or owners managing their property.

[17] See e.g. Gellner, 1965, 1983; Frederickson, 1971.

egalitarian forms of political community more generally, as supporters of political hierarchies feared from the start. In the last two centuries, many modern nationalist leaders have advanced such "horizontal, unified" visions of peoplehood as justifications for their authority, especially but not exclusively democratic ones. In the nineteenth century, many white Americans advanced horizontal, unified accounts of US peoplehood that were logically in deep tension with the vertical racial structures of membership they simultaneously endorsed.[18]

As that example indicates, the distinction between "vertical, differentiated" and "horizontal, unified" forms of peoplehood is always a matter of degree, and most actual communities display elements of both.[19] Claims of horizontal equality and homogeneity are usually actually applied to a more or less large ruling group, while hierarchical accounts define the different statuses of all those denied full membership within a political community who are still treated as belonging to it. Only if a "ruling group" consisted either of one person alone, or of all members of a political people, would we find a political community that did not combine vertical and horizontal forms; and such extremes are rarely if ever to be found.

Even at such extremes and in all cases in between, the asymmetrical interactions between leaders and led should be seen as *constrained* in several ways. Most importantly, leaders' choices are always to some degree restricted by what their potential constituents will accept. Even in instances when leaders are relying extensively on coercive power to impose a political membership on recalcitrant subject populations, obstacles to arbitrary rule are likely to exist that cannot safely be ignored forever.

The source of these obstacles is the fact that, though no political "people" is natural or eternal, the forging of senses of peoplehood never takes place *de novo*, in a state of nature. Aspiring leaders always confront populations already endowed, individually as well as collectively, with a great variety of senses of membership, identity, and affiliation, with entrenched economic interests, political and religious beliefs, historical and cultural attachments, and animosities. What we might then loosely term "the three I's" – preexisting senses of identity, interests, and ideals, all of which inform each other – are themselves partly the products of past politics of people-making. But they are also the products of biological needs and historical developments, such as evolving economic systems, geographical units, communications, transportation, military and medical

---

[18] See Smith, 1997, for what is meant to be overwhelming evidence of this claim.

[19] This distinction corresponds to the contrast between "ranked" and "unranked" multiethnic groups made in Horowitz, 1985, 21–36, though here the identities of rulers and ruled need not be defined in ethnic terms.

technologies, and climactic and demographic trends that are shaped but not simply created or directed by politics. These conditions set more or less stiff boundaries to the senses of peoplehood leaders can advance successfully: they provide the resources and will both for the maintenance of routinized arrangements, practices, and affiliations that cannot easily be altered without generating chaos, and for conscious resistance to existing and proposed forms of political community.

Furthermore, leaders are themselves endowed with certain conceptions of their possible identities, interests, and ideals and not others. As a result, they are far more likely to be inclined to pursue visions of peoplehood reflective of those established commitments than any alternatives. To the degree that this is so, perhaps we can say that they are "constrained" in their aspirations internally as well, as analysts of power influenced by Michel Foucault tend to suggest.[20] To many others, of course, it seems peculiar to argue that leaders are "constrained" to do what they want to do, or to be what they feel themselves to be. The assumption here is that aspirants to leadership are constrained but not fully determined by the discourses and traditions that contribute to their senses of identity and purpose.

Potential constituents are similarly restricted by all these factors in seeking active grass-roots alliances with their present or potential fellow members. Furthermore, they must always operate within existing structures of political, military, and economic power, headed by current leaders; and in more repressive, hierarchical societies, those structures can greatly limit their abilities to join new coalitions or new political memberships, or even to express openly their dissatisfactions with the prevailing order. To be sure, these structures of power also affect established leaders, but they are likely to limit ordinary people to a greater degree.

And perhaps even more importantly, most people simply do not have the same personal aspirations as would-be leaders in many respects, including their desires to organize efforts for political change. The division between leaders and constituents is one that reflects personal goals, values, and inclinations as much as it does the objective possession of resources or statuses, because these can be sought and sometimes acquired, if sufficient will to do so exists. But some persons are admittedly better situated to lead than others, and some wish to do so far more than others. Here too, whether the lack of a desire to lead counts as a "constraint" can be debated; but for all these reasons, mass publics rarely if ever act

---

[20] See, for example, Foucault's contention that modern criminal court judges are more "subordinate" to systems of "normalizing," "carceral" punitive mechanisms and discourses than those systems are "subordinated" to them (Foucault, 1979, 307–308).

consciously to create a new form of political community unless they are organized to do so through mobilizing leaders.

(3) Ordinarily, however, these various "constraints" are not so powerful, individually or collectively, as to determine entirely the sorts of accounts of peoplehood that leaders can effectively advocate and that people can successfully support. *Both leaders and constituents possess meaningful political agency.*

Because they always have available to them a range of alternative senses of identity and interest that they and various potential constituents might plausibly embrace, leaders have meaningful discretion in regard to the conceptions of peoplehood they advance and institutionalize. In democratic systems, moreover, constituents exercise political agency by deciding for whom they will vote. More fundamentally, in all systems constituents can resist voluntarily providing other forms of crucial aid, especially their labor and their military service, to elites whom they oppose.[21] More generally, as Dominique Schnapper has noted, the more members "cease to participate in the values, practices, and institutions" established as elements of a particular form of peoplehood, the more weakened it becomes (Schnapper, 1998, 41). Thus, even when membership in a political society is imposed by conquest, unwilling subjects can usually resist it while sustaining some quite distinct, alternative conceptions of the "people" to whom they inwardly profess their allegiance, and for whom they seek to act. Even when medieval rural peasants were not officially recognized as forming "communities," they still sometimes forged senses of common identity and common cause (often led by country priests) and rose up to attack their lords, seeking to set up leaders of their own (Bloch, 1970, 169–170). The types of alternative orders they sought to create, moreover, varied widely. Even entrenched economic interests of the sort that drove peasant revolts, interests which are often rightly thought to be especially politically potent, still can be advanced by a range of forms of political community (Jung, 2000, 30–31). Whatever stance one takes on philosophic questions of free will, in these regards leaders and constituents generally experience themselves as having meaningful agency in the forms of peoplehood they imagine, articulate, endorse, and institutionalize.

(4) But agency to do what? What do those who advocate or endorse certain forms of political membership hope to accomplish? As just suggested, I presume that political communities are constructed for many

---

[21] David Laitin (1998, 27) provides the example of parents who support nationalist language laws in former Soviet republics but who also undermine them by continuing to send their children to Russian-language schools until a critical mass of their fellow Russian speakers can be persuaded to accept change.

purposes, which must ultimately be understood to grasp any particular politics of people-building. Economic concerns are always present and often integral, but other goals are sometimes still more potent. The common denominator shared by virtually all of them is that *architects of all forms of peoplehood are engaged in political projects that seek to create stable structures of power* enabling them to accomplish their varied ends. Hence, although the actors in this politics have a range of aims that we must in the end comprehend, we can analyze them as all concerned in the first instance to achieve and maintain power adequate to pursue those aims.

Though an exhaustive literature survey would be distracting here, it is worth pausing to indicate how these premises situate the ensuing analysis in relation to other scholarly perspectives. First, I am clearly siding with the many and varied writers who see political group memberships such as national, ethnic, and racial identities as fundamentally humanly "constructed," against "primordialists" who understand these identities as in some sense natural products of human sociobiological development. In so doing I am taking a position that, while not uncontested, is predominant in modern scholarship. As David Laitin has remarked, "Construction and choice, rather than blood and inheritance, is now the standard story line about identities" (Laitin, 1998, 12). At the same time, I do not presume that support for a particular form of peoplehood is always merely "instrumental" to some other end. Often it may be; but many political actors may instead see the construction of a certain sort of common life as their highest ideal.[22]

---

[22] One influential work championing "primordial" views of ethnicity is Van den Berghe, 1981. A prominent if controversial contemporary work championing biological theories of racial groups is Rushton (1995). The Indian sociologist T. K. Oommen (1997, 66) accepts the biological reality of races but not what he sees as ideologies of racial superiority. The "constructivist" or "instrumentalist" opponents of ethnic and national "primordialism" and biological racialism include classic modern writers like, e.g., Hans Kohn (1957) and Elie Kedourie (1961) on through Donald Horowitz (1985), Eric Hobsbawm (1990), Etienne Balibar and Immanuel Wallerstein (1991), and Michael Omi and Howard Winant (2nd edn., 1994).

Anthony D. Smith has criticized some of these writers for overemphasizing how national identities, in particular, have been crafted by elites, instead of recognizing the large degree to which modern nationalism has been a "popular" phenomenon (e.g., Smith, 1995, 40). He and Hobsbawm and Gellner, among others, also purport to differ over a question related to both the "primordialist/constructivist" and "popular/elitist" controversies. This is the issue of whether modern nationalities are fundamentally constructed and *novel* or whether they are built on long-enduring traditions, ethnic ties, and myths in ways that involve considerable continuity with older forms of political community (for a fair-minded overview, see A. D. Smith, 1999, 3–19).

As the discussion of Omi and Winant in the text indicates, I defend a middle ground in these debates that I regard not as a waffle but as more intellectually defensible than either extreme. I believe useful answers to these questions come from determining what,

Among those who agree in seeing political identities as "constructed," I am also siding against those who stress processes of "social construction" more than processes of explicit "political construction." Again, I do not dismiss the importance of culture, language, discourses, social groups, religious affiliations, economic interests, territoriality, folkways, unconscious norms, and other such elements as factors that often contribute to senses of political membership. I regard much scholarship exploring these topics as complementary to the analysis here. But my approach is undeniably opposed to that of scholars who would treat such factors as fundamentally determinative of political identities while dismissing the "high politics" of law-making, organized political movements, conquests, and confederations as ultimately of secondary importance.

And among those who do stress processes of "political construction," by casting my analysis in terms of aspiring leaders and potential constituents, I am pursuing an approach reminiscent of, among other writers, the Italian Marxist Antonio Gramsci.[23] Much like his greatest Italian predecessor, Niccolò Machiavelli, Gramsci argued that the "first element" of politics was "that there really do exist rulers and ruled, leaders and led" (Gramsci, 1971, 144).[24] He contended that "intellectuals,"

in each particular context, is constructed and novel in specific stories of peoplehood, and what is instead inherited and maintained, either due to the enduring popular appeal of the elements in question or for other reasons. At the general theoretical level, the answer is surely that elite construction of distinctive conceptions of common identity; their popular opposition or embrace; *and* the maintenance by elites and masses of longstanding traditions of identity are always and everywhere present, but in greatly different degrees in different cases. I therefore agree with A. D. Smith that the construction of senses of peoplehood draws on and is constrained by preexisting, widely espoused senses of identity that, though not "primordial," are deeply entrenched. But most of those he criticizes, except perhaps Hobsbawm in his least balanced formulations, would also concur; and Smith himself gives great weight to the innovating and mobilizing roles of elites in his concrete historical analyses. Hence I am not sure how deep these theoretical differences actually run.

[23] I am grateful to Roger Rouse for stressing this similarity to me. Dominique Schnapper builds on Weber's conception of the nation as a political creation to reach a similar conception of "political projects," though she distinguishes herself, as I would do, from any notion that such projects stem wholly from "will to power" and is necessarily devoted to *Machtpolitik* (Schnapper, 1998, 11, 21, 37–40).

[24] Gramsci was in fact self-consciously continuing a long line of political theorizing that includes figures like Gaetano Mosca, Vilfredo Pareto, Thomas Hobbes, and most seminally, as Gramsci recognized, Machiavelli (Gramsci, 1971, 6, 125–136). I am grateful to Norma Thompson for stressing the Machiavellian structure of my argument to me; but I also acknowledge that these predecessors are generally understood to advocate far less democratic forms of politics than I ultimately want to defend. The normative positions I defend in the last portion of this book are, however, "Machiavellian" in the sense expounded by John McCormick (2001): though they accept a fundamental elites/mass populace distinction, they express convictions that people can and should be politically active in guarding against elite abuses.

for him a broad category that included aspirants to governmental office and all who worked with ideas, played key roles in creating senses of self-awareness and homogeneity among various groups. He looked, for example, to black intellectuals to "give a 'national' character" to the prevailing African-American "sentiment of being a despised race" (5, 21). In so doing, Gramsci was defining the sort of asymmetrical relationship in the propagation of senses of peoplehood that I am positing here. In fact I go further than Gramsci by arguing throughout the ensuing analysis that differences in the interests and aspirations of "leaders and led" profoundly shape the politics of people-building in a number of ways he did not address.[25]

It is notable that one of the most influential contemporary formulations of a "constructionist" perspective on group identities, Michael Omi and Howard Winant's account of racial identities in *Racial Formation in the United States*, is explicitly Gramscian in this way.[26] For Omi and Winant, races are created when "intellectuals" engage in racial "political projects," seeking either to transform or to rearticulate existing group statuses by explaining their problems or their virtues "in racial terms." As groups have sharply different, often opposed interests, more than one such "racial project" is likely to be underway in a society like the US at any one time. "Racial formation, therefore, is a kind of synthesis, an outcome, of the interaction of racial projects on a society-wide level." When projects challenging "the pre-existing racial order" reach "a certain level of intensity," an "unstable equilibrium" or crisis that can precipitate racial transformations occurs (1994, 60–61, 68, 86).

Despite some real similarities, there are three important differences between the approach my premises suggest and the views of both Gramsci and these contemporary Gramscians. The first is that Gramsci himself (more than Omi and Winant) understood all groups in fundamentally Marxian terms. For him groups are rooted in economic relations, "coming into existence on the original terrain of an essential function in the world of economic production," even if the politics of those groups can then proceed with some relative autonomy from "the terrain of economic life." He insists firmly that though a "leading group" must take account of "the interests and tendencies of the groups over which hegemony is to be

---

[25] McCormick (2001, 298n2) notes that there are both naturalistic and class explanations of the differences in elite and mass behavior that Machiavelli perceived and upon which he premised his political analyses. Here I am, like McCormick, chiefly interested in exploring the consequences of such differences in aspirations rather than in discovering their origins.

[26] Other explicitly Gramscian accounts of political identity formation from which I have benefited include Hanchard, 1994, Mallon, 1995, and Ramos, 2001.

exercised," so that a "certain compromise equilibrium" must be formed in which the powerful make "sacrifices of an economic-corporate kind," still these concessions "cannot touch the essential." Though "hegemony is ethical-political, it must also be economic, must necessarily be based on the decisive function exercised by the leading group in the decisive nucleus of economic activity" (1971, 5, 140, 161).[27]

In many contexts, my differences from this perspective are minor. I agree that a political people can never be created or sustained without some viable economic arrangements that can largely meet the felt material needs and wants of, at least, that people's core constituents, its "hegemonic group" or "ruling class." As a result, perhaps more than any other sort of human interest, economic interests are always integral and often primary in senses of peoplehood. A Gramscian analysis will therefore often capture most vital features of people-making.

Nonetheless, economic interests can usually be advanced through many forms of peoplehood, so that economic motives alone cannot be completely determinative of political outcomes. Indeed, the very notions that both "elite" and "mass" actors use to define their economic interests are to some degree shaped by concepts that vary in different social contexts: many Elizabethan landed gentry thought a static economy best served their interests, while many contemporary landholders feel they can profit most from participation in fast-growing market economies. Historically many individuals pursued wealth chiefly by seeking to amass precious metals, others thought it lay more reliably in the ownership of land or productive enterprises.

Both leaders and constituents, moreover, generally have driving interests and values that go well beyond material concerns. Though some would-be leaders may seek to govern in order to acquire wealth for themselves and key supporters, others can plausibly be seen as more devoted to gaining personal glory, or to achieving goals they see as morally compelling, or simply as impelled by raw desires to dominate. And though many constituents value material prosperity, many place at least as much emphasis on physical security, spiritual fulfillment, opportunities for familial and social activities, and other less tangible goods. In consequences, at times the politics of people-building simply cannot be adequately addressed by presuming all are most driven by economic interests. And though they are far from routine, the occasions when forms of political membership are restructured in ways that are not

[27] For a "historical-materialist" argument that Omi and Winant's racial formation theory and postmodernist and poststructuralist perspectives on race lack grounding and that analysts need to return more fully to Gramscian Marxism, see San Juan, Jr., 1999, 39–45.

dictated by economic concerns can be among the most seminal political developments.[28]

My second difference is with Omi and Winant's notion of racial projects, though here my argument may well represent an elaboration of themes implicit in their position rather than an opposition. Their account does not really explain why "intellectuals" embark on specifically racial political projects, though it is clear that these projects arise from efforts to sustain or oppose preexisting systems of inequality, subordination, and repression, which are often already structured in racial terms. But why were "racial" projects first adopted as means of "structuring and signifying" the historical systems of inequality that, on Omi and Winant's account, originated in European expansionists' encounters with African and American "Others" (1994, 61–63)? Why do they continue to be deployed? Like a number of other scholars, I argue that such projects can best be understood as elements in broader *political* projects of "people-formation," projects that aim to construct communities that are also enduring structures of political power; and I try here to elaborate a more explicit structure of analysis for those projects than others have done.[29] On this view, specifically racial notions of identity are seen as examples of one standard type of story of peoplehood – "ethically constitutive stories" – that serves certain political purposes other types of stories do not serve so well.

Finally, at least at times, both Gramsci and Omi and Winant seem to focus more exclusively on the agency of elites or "intellectuals" alone than seems plausible.[30] What leaders can do is, again, substantially constrained

---

[28] I therefore resist the strong economic determinism toward which some neo-Marxist analyses, including Wallerstein's, tend; and also the related suggestion that some see in the work of Ernest Gellner (1965, 1983). He is often understood to argue that the spread of modern economic systems makes large-scale, relatively uniform educational systems necessary, and hence these systems demand something like the nation-state. There are indeed powerful pressures in that direction, but they could be and to some degree were long met via "multinational" empires, and other arrangements now appear possible. To reject neo-Marxian economic determinism, however, is not necessarily to oppose political strategies based on stressing class interests.
      Alexander Wendt has distinguished between "Darwinist" accounts of the evolution of personal and group identities, which overwhelmingly stress adaptations to material conditions, and "Lamarckian" accounts, which instead emphasize ideas and "the variability of cultural forms under similar material conditions" (1999, 320). My view is clearly "Lamarckian" in his terms.

[29] In the course of writing this book, I have come to see that my approach particularly resembles that of Schnapper, 1998 (orig. 1994), though she, too, is concerned with "nations," not "political peoples" more generally; and there are other differences that I note in passing. I am grateful to Yohann Aucante for calling this comparison to my attention.

[30] This characterization is less true of the 1994 second edition of Omi and Winant's justly influential *Racial Formation in the United States*.

by a variety of contextual conditions, including what their potential constituents are willing to support. At times, these authors write as if there were little practical difference between the role of rulers in what I have termed vertical, differentiated forms of peoplehood and more horizontal, unified ones. Politics is always a matter of elite struggles and little more. I believe instead that mass publics play a meaningfully larger role in some political communities than others, and that even in the most hierarchical and authoritarian regimes, mass populations retain some meaningful agency. In this vein James C. Scott has argued compellingly that rural peasants and other subordinated groups show much greater capacities to grasp and resist elite efforts to impose hegemonic political orthodoxies on them than Gramsci appeared to allow (e.g., Scott, 1985, 314–350, 1990, 90–93).

Along with mass pressures, elites are also limited by the broader structures of power, resources, and technological capacity in which they operate, as well as by their own constitutive commitments. Philip Klinkner and I have contended, for example, that only when certain rare combinations of extraordinary international and domestic pressures have been present has it been possible for egalitarian racial reforms to gain significantly successful champions in the US (Klinkner with Smith, 1999). Those pressures include substantial social protest movements, but also international political, intellectual, and economic conditions that particular elites can create and control only to a limited extent. To be sure, the asymmetrical view of the politics through which senses of peoplehood are generated and sustained that I am defending here still stresses the role of elites and their capacities to shape the political imaginations of constituents more than analysts like Scott would do.[31] That makes it all the more imperative for me to underscore the premise here that mass populations have varying but real power to decide which of the memberships available to them will receive their true embrace. Hence they are indeed crucial players in the politics of people-building in every society, if not always to the same extent.

Six elaborations and some digressions

If these assumptions about the processes through which political peoples are created are plausible, then we can flesh out the resulting portrait of the politics of people-formation in a number of significant ways. But to make

---

[31] For an argument by a prominent Southeast Asia scholar that Scott underestimates how much prevailing moral codes "must be invented and reinvented by the ruling elites," see Ong, 1999, 70.

those elaborations convincingly, we need also to address some concerns thoughtful readers will have.

(1) First and most fundamentally: political projects of people-making are likely to be pursued by two general means: *coercive force* and *persuasive stories*. Both serve to constitute institutions of membership and exclusion that structure and distribute power and resources in unequal ways. Both therefore contribute to the ongoing constitution, maintenance, and trans-formations of political identities. Though she focuses like most scholars on "nationhood," the political theorist Margaret Canovan has offered a rare direct statement on how a "people" comes to be. Her pithy summa-tion of the lessons of historical experience with the forging of political communities captures this initial, foundational point perfectly. "Much the most common solution," she writes, "has been rule by one man at the head of an army, buttressed by as much support from religion as can be mustered" (1996, 22).[32]

It is incontrovertibly true that force has been fundamental to the cre-ation and maintenance of most political memberships, and nothing in the ensuing analysis is intended to minimize that vital reality. If Europeans had not conquered native populations largely through force in North and South America, the English, Spanish, and Portuguese-speaking and largely Christian political communities in those territories would almost certainly not exist. If they had not conquered large portions of Africa and Asia, many of the now-indigenously governed societies on those conti-nents would probably not have either the boundaries or the forms of government that they possess. Furthermore, I believe that the stronger and more demanding the sense of political peoplehood being advanced, the more it claims primacy over other memberships and allegiances, the more likely it is that it will have often have to be advanced and defended by forceful coercion. China needs an army more than Brooklyn does.

But political scientists, at least, have attended extensively to the role of force in human affairs. In this schematic analysis I therefore largely leave force aside and concentrate instead on the second element Canovan signals: the support mustered via elite deployment of certain sorts of ac-counts or stories. I devote attention to Thomas Paine's "Common Sense," not to George Washington's battle strategies; to Korean accounts of their ancient forebear Tan' gun, and not to the international military struggles that eventually expelled Japanese rule. This focus is likely to raise some very reasonable worries that may distract readers if I do not address them here, before proceeding to some further elaborations of the politics of people-building.

---

[32] For a similar formulation see Miller, 1995, 34.

One might ask, why this broad category of "stories," rather than something that sounds more particular to the politics of people-formation? Though Canovan is right that such stories have most often been religious or quasi-religious, nonetheless a wide variety of doctrines or ideologies has been used to buttress the exhortations of leaders for constituents to accept particular political memberships. Hence it is appropriate to use a broadly inclusive term. Political science does not clearly offer one, I believe, because political scientists have dealt less well with this dimension of politics than they have with the exercise or threats of force. Perhaps because it seems a more "humanistic" than "scientific" enterprise, many have been reluctant to focus on the prominent role that is *necessarily* played by competing narratives, accounts, or stories of peoplehood in generating and sustaining both more vertical and more horizontal political communities. This role is inescapable, for even if warlords largely strive to define the boundaries of their political community and the statuses of those within it by brute force, they always need at least some members who are persuaded to fight for them by words, not by arms alone. It is very likely that times of armed conflict in fact generate the greatest pressures to advance stories of shared membership and identity that can inspire the enormous risks and sacrifices that wars often demand. Those pressures have evoked responses, from Pericles's Funeral Oration to the Blitz radio speeches of Churchill, that echo down through the histories they help to create (Turner, 1986, 70; Klinkner with Smith, 1999, 3–4). And in times of peace, persuasive accounts play a more pervasive if generally less dramatic role in shaping the identities and activities of political communities. Hence compelling stories of the advantages of giving allegiance to their cause are necessary and fundamental to all political leaders' endeavors.

Still, why do I term those accounts "stories"? Leaders sometimes, after all, present hardheaded, reasoned "cause and effect" arguments in favor of certain conceptions of their constituents' core allegiances and interests. At other times they offer what they hope to be soaring oratory, but not necessarily in the form of "stories." Explicit reliance on narrative prose or poetry recounting a tale of peoplehood in the manner of the Manas epos or the Pentateuch may seem relatively rare.

Indeed, the use of the term "stories" is of no special importance. Yet the designation seems appropriate for the sorts of implicit and explicit accounts of political membership that I discuss here, because it suggests how they operate politically. To succeed in their mission, doctrines, ideologies, visions of political peoplehood must make a certain sort of case to current and potential members. They must suggest to such constituents that, given their personal origins and history and the way the world is, if they do indeed adhere steadfastly to the community thus depicted, they are likely to experience certain sorts of good things, immediately or eventually. However well reasoned or well documented, those promises can never be more than a plausible conjecture, an imagined scenario of how the future will unfold, made credible by a certain account of the past and present that is usually selectively stylized if not mythical. Hence narratives of peoplehood work essentially as persuasive historical stories that prompt people to embrace the valorized identities, play the stirring roles, and have the fulfilling experiences that political leaders strive to evoke for them, whether through arguments, rhetoric, symbols, or "stories" of a more obvious and familiar sort.[33]

Though many political analysts may not be disturbed by my terminology, a large number may next object that the role of such "stories of peoplehood" is a strictly instrumental one. They presume that, as Gramsci suggested, political associations are formed on some more solid bedrock of real, material interests, and political stories are spun fundamentally to help advance those interests. They are also re-spun or ignored if their utility diminishes, in just the way President Akayev seems to have ignored the assertions of respect for human rights posted at his nation's website. It may therefore seem that in the end political narratives of peoplehood are of slight importance. We may well get further more quickly if we are not distracted by the stories or their content and focus instead on the impelling interests they serve. At most, our concern with those stories should be to determine which truly potent interests they assist and how they do so.

My assumptions harbor a contrary notion: that stories of peoplehood do not merely serve interests, they also help to constitute them, for aspiring leaders and potential constituents alike. As suggested above, here I side with those who argue that, though human beings have biological needs that must be met if they are to live, the forms of what people take to be adequate satisfactions of those needs, and indeed their answers to whether they should continue to live at all, vary greatly (see, e.g., Wendt, 1999, 113–130). Some people may think it right to starve rather than to eat pork. Most human beings think it better to starve than to eat their children or mates (even though other species do so). The interests people

---

[33] As discussed below, though all stories of peoplehood are in a broad sense historical, certain ones are more purely "historical" in that they see political peoples as created essentially by contingent human historical actions, rather than as the working out of some underlying providential, biological, or other predestining "deep structure" of human identity. Wald, 1995, is a stimulating work by a literary scholar that understands the role of stories in the construction of political identities much as I do here; but she concentrates on the efforts of various writers to narrate their own stories in ways that resist the "official stories" that they know to have partly "constituted them" nonetheless (3). An influential collection of literary perspectives on narratives and nation-building is Bhabha, ed., 1990.

pursue, then, are constituted as much or more by their ideas of who they are and what they value as by sheer biological or material realities. Akayev may not govern the Kyrgyz people in ways that fully comply with his own official story of Kyrgyz peoplehood; and his history shows that he has been willing to govern Kyrgyzstan both under Soviet Communist rule and as an independent, titularly democratic republic. Even so, if both his own identity and those of his constituents were not extensively defined by shared conceptions of Kyrgyz membership, it is far less likely that he would seek to govern that particular population or have any chance to do so.

This claim is entirely consistent with the presumption that elite desires for power, in alliance with other concerns, form the main engines of the politics of people-making: again, power is the common denominator to the goals of all and the ultimate goal for some. It is similarly compatible with the belief that among such concerns, the economic interests of elites' core constituencies are especially important in shaping the ideologies and institutions that structure political life. In the examples of people-making explored here, we will see power-seeking and economic interests playing such roles over and over again. But it will also be evident that notions of these interests are constituted in diverse ways in different contexts, partly due to varying available ideas of human identity and value that successful political actors incorporate into their programs, policies, and personal identities and ambitions. That is why I view an understanding of prevalent traditions or ideologies of political and cultural belief as essential for grasping the construction of stories and institutions of peoplehood in different contexts.

Yet one might still ask, just what do we mean by saying that political stories, policies, and institutions partly "constitute" persons' interests? If people are socialized into certain stories of, for example, their religious duties, can we say these stories "cause" them to eat chicken rather than pork, in the same way that heat and spices can cause the chicken to taste different? Without wading far into some rather deep waters of philosophical debates over causality, let me employ a distinction here between "determinative" and "generative" causality. "Determinative" causality includes physical operations that, all things being equal, generate an outcome as a result of mechanical, chemical, or other natural forces. When flame is placed under the chicken, the resulting heat inevitably causes the chicken to grill or burn unless other physical forces intervene.

"Generative" causality, in contrast, occurs when an actor is provided with a capacity to do certain things but not others – making it more probable, but not inevitable, that the actor will do those things and less likely, though not impossible, that the actor will do something else entirely. Providing a chef with matches; a gas grill; a chicken; and the belief that God approves consumption of chicken but not pork are all acts of "generative" causality. They make it possible, perhaps likely, that the chef will then grill the chicken; and certainly this action cannot occur in the absence of all such things. Conversely, a chef who possesses only this equipment and belief system does not have any immediate option to microwave the chicken and probably has a disinclination to grill pork. Still, endowing the chef with these empowering elements and not others does not "determinatively" cause the chicken to grill.[34] A rather unconventional chef may decide to pursue acquisition of a microwave before cooking, whatever the risks to the chicken's freshness. An iconoclastic one might defiantly choose to grill pork.

Under these circumstances, then, we can only make a probabilistic prediction that chicken grilling will occur, along with an explanation for why and how this might take place. That explanation will invoke the presence of certain biological needs, material resources, *and* human beliefs. Both this probabilistic prediction and this explanation will fall short of fully determinate knowledge of the chef's behavior, but they represent well-founded and useful knowledge nonetheless. Most of the time, we will be right about what the chef will do, how she will do it, and why. Because I think that we must operate by assuming the reality of meaningful human agency, moreover, I believe that "determinative" causal relations can account for only a portion of human conduct.[35] On many important questions, this sort of probabilistic knowledge of human affairs is the best knowledge we can have.

One such important question is the issue addressed here: how shared senses of political membership are created and sustained. Force, obviously, often has "determinative causality" in making people members of one political community rather than another for at least most intents and purposes. When Roman soldiers occupied much of what is now Western Europe, when conquering knights imposed a new lord over a body of peasants, when modern border guards physically compel would-be immigrants to remain in their homelands, the choices of political membership available to those so treated have plainly been severely constrained if not

---

[34] Wendt therefore distinguishes "causal" operations from "constitutive" ones (1999, 77). I have resisted his terminology because for many, myself included, it is counterintuitive to regard non-causal forces as meaningfully efficacious. Hence I think it clearer to speak of two kinds of causality, "determinative" and "generative." The concept of causality has been parsed many other ways, some compatible with this distinction and indeed more nuanced, some quite different; but it would take us too far afield to explore those variations and nuances here.

[35] I certainly do not, however, claim to be able to provide a definitive account of such agency. For some reflections see Smith, 1992.

decisively determined. The prospect of force, moreover, undoubtedly also restricts the forms of political community people perceive as available to them in myriad ways.

In contrast, stories of peoplehood have only "generative causality" in the politics of people-building; but this role is nonetheless crucial. Even when people's statuses are being imposed by direct coercive power, those wielding that power inevitably rely on some sorts of stories or accounts of how their political society should be constituted. Because most leaders do not want to fight more dangerous battles than they have to, they seek through these stories to make their imposed form of political community more palatable to at least some of their new subjects, as well as to potentially antagonistic outsiders. They also need such stories to clarify and justify to themselves who is to be conquered, who is to be turned away or expelled, who is to be segregated or killed, and who is instead to be fully included as an equal. There cannot be "imagined communities" without mental images of what those communities should be and who should be in them. And as for force, so for stories: the "stronger" and more demanding the form of political peoplehood being propagated, the greater the need for compelling support.

Even so, it might be said that these circumstances fail to show that stories of peoplehood are meaningfully *causal*, that political actors are significantly *constrained* or *impelled* by the tasks of persuasive story-telling. After all, most human beings learn many quite varying images of possible communities to which they might belong in the course of their lives. With the explosive advances in global communication technologies, the prevalence of such contrasting multiple images is probably rapidly on the increase in the world today. As aspirants to political power struggle with the obstacles and opportunities that life affords them, these plentiful alternatives might seem to give them great discretion to try to reshape the mental self-images of the "people" from whom they are seeking to enlist loyalty. Similarly, many of those whom they hope to lead seem to have genuine choices over who they will give their allegiances and how far, choices that are not really constrained by the great variety of political stories being spun around them.

I believe to the contrary that the forms of political peoplehood that leaders and constituents can imagine are largely generated by, motivated by, and also meaningfully limited by the particular range of stories of possible political identity that they have inherited and long valued. The complexity and the multiplicity of even deeply entrenched, profoundly cherished narratives of peoplehood generally do make them malleable to some degree. Still, in many regards and under many circumstances human attachments to their established senses of identity, interest, and ideals often prove to be quite tenacious. For example, both psychologically and politically, it is probably harder for Akayev to form genuine alliances with his ethnically Uzbek, radical Islamic Kyrgyz citizens than to arrest or expel them, given the multiple gaps between them. The contrasting ethnic, religious, and political power stories that Akayev, his Kyrgyz constituents, and the Uzbek Islamics embrace have "generative causality" in shaping *and constraining* their beliefs, both tactical and sincere, concerning what their vital political interests and identities are and can be. Those beliefs, in turn, do much to define the forms of peoplehood that they are likely to support or oppose.

Let me emphasize strongly, moreover, that I see the generative causality of stories of peoplehood as operating not only at the level of political *imaginations*. To construct and sustain any type of human association, there must be some sorts of *institutions* that define fairly concretely who is in, who is out, who is a full member, and who is not. In the case of any fairly large-scale political community, this usually means some array of rules and some sets of rule-making and rule-applying officials, backed by coercive power, who seek to enforce the dominant conceptions of membership. Those officials and rules draw on and institutionalize the politically prevailing stories or combinations of stories of peoplehood that rule-makers and rule-appliers see as somehow defining their authorized duties and expressing at least some of their identities, values, and interests. These institutionalizations of stories of peoplehood then become realities that contribute materially to the constitution of the political identities of all whom they affect.

A body of immigration and naturalization laws might, for example, say that a person of Asian descent cannot become an Australian (to take an only recently hypothetical example).[36] Effectively enforced, such rules not only prevent most if not all would-be Asian immigrants from becoming part of a political people they might otherwise join. They also make it far more likely that many Australians will conceive of their own identities and Australia's as intrinsically "white," or at least non-Asian. To be sure, the prevalence of racialized or anti-Asian stories of Australian identity could never alone determine that Australia's laws would have that form. The existence of those laws, moreover, could not by itself insure that no Australian would ever identify himself most with Asians, or that no Asian would ever come to see herself as actually deeply "Australian." But the laws would not exist without some sort of anti-Asian account justifying them. And the subsequent legal institutionalization of such stories

---

[36] For an account that stresses how deeply Australian citizenship has been shaped historically by concerns about racial exclusions, see Rubenstein, 2000.

of peoplehood long made it very likely that contrary senses of political identity (as Asian Australians) would not occur even on an individual level. They all but guaranteed that any such self-conceptions would be widely regarded as idiosyncratic.

There are, moreover, a great many rules and policies that express certain conceptions of political membership and thereby help to constitute the identities of persons in accordance with those conceptions – far more than may first be apparent. When educational institutions educate different ethnic groups and genders differently out of the expectation that they will play distinctive roles in the economy and in politics; when some religiously inspired practices are seen as socially valuable and given tax exemptions and others are instead forbidden; when social policies treat certain sorts of workers as meriting governmental underwriting in the form of pension and unemployment insurance, and other sorts of workers as undeserving of any sort of public assistance, these measure work to constitute separate and unequal forms of political identity and status in quite concrete ways (Spinner, 1994; Lieberman, 1998; Mettler, 1998). The ultimate significance of "stories of peoplehood" thus cannot be adequately gauged unless their role in generating a broad variety of identity-constructing laws and policies is recognized.

In fact, the institutionalization of stories of peoplehood introduces another level of analysis that, some might say, should be the real center of our inquiry, both because of its importance and because of its relative autonomy from the kinds of political propagation of stories of peoplehood I am stressing. Given the complexities of power, interest, and identities prevalent in the populations with whom they deal, it is rare for leaders to be able to create laws, policies, and institutions that express their own vision of the community in pure, straightforward, undiluted fashion. Instead, laws, policies, and other institutions usually are the results of compromises negotiated among competing leaders and parties advancing significantly different conceptions.[37] These political products of compromise then go on to shape the interests and the very identities of those defined and affected by them in ways that may well depart from many of the desires and expectations of virtually all those who participated in their creation. Those departures from legislative aspirations can occur either because of unanticipated consequences, or because all

[37] In this spirit, Patrick Weil has recently authored a definitive history of French nationality laws that convincingly treats this body of law as not simply a reflection of conceptions of French nationhood or citizenship; though I think his evidence justifies the claim that those laws cannot be understood apart from an evolving politics in which conceptions of nationhood and citizenship play significant roles (Weil, 2002, 13). Cf. Smith, 1997, 35.

parties felt compelled to give up something of great importance to them to get some key portion of what they wanted. Thus it can make sense for many purposes to treat these laws, policies, and institutions as social science's "independent variables," as the proximate determinative and generative causes of much subsequent political behavior and political identities, as many contemporary "historical institutionalists" do.[38] But though those analyses are unquestionably worthwhile, it is still essential to understand the kinds of accounts of peoplehood that compete in the politics that produces such laws and institutions. Although those accounts may not be blueprints for how the laws and institutions they have shaped will operate, they still help us grasp both why the laws and institutions have been built as they are, and they can help us forecast political responses to subsequent institutional failures and successes in pursuing the goals that brought together the coalitions enacting them. Stories of peoplehood do not explain everything, but they do help explain much that is politically important.

This discussion of the wide-ranging institutionalization of such stories also raises the important further question of the relationship of "people-building" to "state-building," to the construction and legitimation of governing institutions generally. Many scholars are likely to think that "people-building" is simply an unhelpful, indirect way of talking about what should really be seen as "state-building." I instead regard "people-building" and "state-building" as linked but distinguishable dimensions of processes of constructing stable systems of political power (processes that may, again, be driven by many aims beyond pure power-seeking; but all such aims require power for their effective pursuit). The links are, however, not inevitable: though every enduring people must have some sort of leadership and institutional structure, it is possible for leaders to foster, institutionalize, and sustain a conception of shared peoplehood without possessing a titularly sovereign "state" or an independent government, as Jews showed for two millennia. To be sure, their example

---

[38] Excellent recent "institutionalist" accounts of nationality include Brubaker, 1996, 23–54; King, 2000; Tichenor, 2002; Weil, 2002. To clarify some issues of how this positions law in "historical institutional" analysis that readers have raised about my earlier treatments of citizenship laws (1992, 1997): the "relative autonomy" of law that results from law's origin in political compromises, leaving laws irreducible to expressions of any single political agenda, also creates distinct tasks for legal reasoning. Judges and lawyers face both pressures and opportunities to resolve coherently the logical and normative tensions created by these compromises through creative legal interpretations. Laws then play a "constitutive" role in shaping persons' identities, interests, and values through the manner in which they assign resources, impose constraints, and structure statuses – again, for example, by making some "Australian" or "French," with access to certain resources and protections, and others not, as amply documented in the works of Rubenstein (2000) and Weil (2002), respectively.

also suggests that under many circumstances, senses of political people-hood are likely to work to support aspirations to the possession of a state, or at least institutions providing a significant measure of self-governance for that people. And it seems impossible for any state or government to sustain governance over populations for very long without fostering a sense among at least some of those within their jurisdiction that they are that state's "people" and it is their state. That sense of peoplehood may be vertical and dichotomous, as in colonial and aristocratic regimes, but "state-building" still will not be effective in the long run unless "the state" engages in some successful "people-building."[39]

Even so, "state-building" and "people-building" remain distinguish-able dimensions of processes of constructing systems of power, because the interests of elites in building states, in constructing effective in-stitutions of governmental power, cannot be wholly reduced to the requirements of people-making. As James C. Scott (1998) has elo-quently argued, state-builders have concerns about matters such as ad-ministrative manageability and resource acquisition for their own ends that shape their policies along with, but sometimes in tension with, their desires to inspire loyalty from key constituencies. I do not, how-ever, explore those tensions thematically here. My concern is to sketch the elements of political people-building, and I address government-building and "state-building" only insofar as they are linked to those processes.[40]

If, then, none of these understandable objections to the project of at-tending closely to stories of peoplehood and the roles they play in the politics of people-forming seem so formidable as to doom the enterprise,

[39] John Breuilly (1982) has argued in fact that nationalism arises only in the context of mod-ern state-building; but his argument is dependent on *defining* nationalism as involving the attainment of independent statehood (3), so it does not apply to the broader notion of political peoplehood I am employing here. Even so, it is certainly true that those who occupy or seek to occupy positions of governmental power (in any era) necessarily must engage in a politics of people-building conducive to their governance. Breuilly's con-tention that nationalism is about politics, because it asserts the priority of one group's interests and values over all others and seeks power sufficient to vindicate that priority, is moreover in the same spirit as the analysis here. And though I believe he focuses too narrowly on power as concerned with "control of the state," clearly in the modern world all political "peoples" must struggle with states even if they do not seek to establish their own (Breuilly, 1982, 2–3, 352–356, 365–373).

[40] Anthony Marx (1998) provides an excellent analysis of the construction of racial and national identities that takes its inspiration from Weber and, though parallel in many respects, is more state-centered than the account here. If we instead view all systems of governance, such as the officials of churches or radical labor movements, as types of "states," then "people-making" and "state-building" become effectively identical. I agree with Marx, however, that for many purposes there is a value in preserving the conventional, narrower, Weberian usage of the term "state" for formal structures of political governance claiming prime authority for the legitimate use of force.

we can proceed to draw some other basic points about that politics out of the assumptions that I have delineated.

(2) Because of the asymmetry of the political processes of people-making, the accounts or stories of political peoplehood that would-be leaders advance are always likely to be crafted with two goals. Leaders seek both to prompt constituents to embrace membership in the community or people they depict, and to persuade them to accept as leaders the very sorts of persons who are advancing these people-building accounts. That is why even the most "horizontal" stories of peoplehood are likely to have certain dichotomous elements; and "vertical" accounts that define a ruling class in opposition to various lower ranks will display internal divisions even in their depictions of the ruling class. All these stories of peoplehood will stress themes that speak to the values, aspirations, and interests of political constituents, but they will also advance themes expressive of the somewhat distinctive values, aspirations, and interests of the would-be leaders who propagate them. Thus the leaders' stories, however truthful and however sincere, will always be partly self-serving or partisan. It is often in the interest of modern leaders, especially, to minimize or deny that partisan character, to blend the elements designed to gain constituent support as fully as possible with those that express the leaders' own distinct agendas. Analysts of stories of peoplehood should, however, be aware of these ever-present internal tensions.

(3) Because no political community is simply natural and all are products of contestation and compromises, the politics of people-making, involving both force and stories, is always an ongoing as well as a competitive politics, even within apparently well-established and unified political communities. The "ongoing" and "competitive" features are two sides of the same coin. Inside and outside every political community, in rival political parties, in civil associations, in ethnic minorities, and in neighboring regimes, there are always rival would-be leaders. Such leaders will often seek to win support by advancing views of shared peoplehood featuring deeply held interests, values, and identities that are neglected or relegated to secondary status in the prevailing order of a particular community. Those engaged in the politics of people-building, whether in government or out, must take even possible conversions by their constituents to support for such rivals into account. Hence an ever-present theme in every would-be leader's exhortations, sometimes implicit, sometimes explicit, is this: you should embrace the sense of political community and peoplehood that I advocate as your primary political identity. In so doing, you should also recognize that my leadership, my allies, and my policies are best for that community and for you – not those favored by anyone else. Rather than treating stories of peoplehood as only episodically important,

then, we need to appreciate the "people-making" dimensions that infuse a startling variety of routine political communications and actions, sometimes self-consciously, sometimes not.

(4) This ongoing, competitive politics and the stories through which it is partly pursued require analyses that routinely encompass both "domestic" and "international" politics. Those boundaries are, again, human creations, and it is this politics that creates them, never with finality. Unsurprisingly, then, rivals to any particular set of governing elites are usually to be found both within their government's current jurisdiction and borders and outside them. Sometimes it is the vision of peoplehood advanced by internal opponents that seems most threatening and must be countered, as for example when "Court" and "Country" partisans struggled in the late seventeenth and early eighteenth centuries to define the direction of the system resulting from the "Glorious Revolution" of 1688 – though even those debates cannot be analyzed apart from controversies over the expanding empire and the conversion of the "English" into "Britons."[41] At other times the ambitions of external challengers and their accounts of why they deserve to govern are most pressing, as was the case for the Soviet Union and many other governments during World War II and the tensest phases of the Cold War. It is striking, for example, how John F. Kennedy's Inaugural Address recasts all the familiar tropes of American political identity as traits that define American superiority in relation to the "iron tyranny" of Communist regimes.[42] But in every time and place, any adequate account of the politics of people-building and the stories rivals deploy must always consider the roles that both "foreign" and "domestic" contenders for power play in shaping the positions advanced.

(5) Because this point has been a chronic issue among scholars of nationalism, in particular, it is necessary to stress that the constraints present in the politics of people-making mean that stories of peoplehood always partly maintain and partly modify preexisting senses of political identity, though in greatly differing proportions. In most contexts, elements contributing to maintenance are far more prominent, particularly when a political community is well established. Most community members are firmly attached to their basic political identities, so rival leaders within such societies compete mostly over what particular sense of that community, its interests, values, and proper policies shall prevail. But in some contexts modifications, even radical modifications, in established political identities will predominate – because existing political communities

---

[41] For useful discussions see Pocock, 1975, 423–461; Burtt, 1992; Colley, 1992.
[42] Hofstadter and Hofstadter, eds., 1981, 545–549.

are coming apart and new societies with new regimes must be formed.[43] Yet both elements are always present.

Leaders are never likely to win support, even in periods of revolution, if they are not speaking on behalf of at least some vital interests and identities their constituents already possess. Otherwise, who would listen? That is one reason why King Josiah had his scribes reinterpret longstanding Jewish traditions; why President Akayev found it prudent to launch a new regime in part by reviving an ancient political narrative; and why the most transformative US Presidents claim to be returning to the principles of the American founding.[44] The Soviets themselves used the Manas epos to bolster patriotic feelings, if never so centrally as the leaders of the new Kyrgyz Republic have sought to do. Similar elements of "maintenance" partly structure and constrain all stories of peoplehood. Indeed, this omnipresent necessity to connect with some of the entrenched senses of political identities and interests that always confront political actors may explain why the tasks of people-making, as opposed to simply acquiring power among existing peoples, have not been more elaborately addressed in the history of political thought. Since the dawn of human history, no one has ever engaged in "people-building" using completely raw wood.

But because would-be leaders have rivals, domestic and international, and because conditions change, even within well-established political communities, successful leaders must always advance senses of peoplehood that modify preexisting conceptions of political community and political identity in ways that justify their distinctive leadership and policies. Whereas for Stephen Douglas the American Revolution was a crusade to secure popular self-governance for all white men, for Abraham Lincoln it was the launching of a nation dedicated to the proposition that, in terms of basic rights, all humans are created equal. Whereas for Pierre Trudeau, Canada was at heart a multilingual federal union, for Joe Clark it was an English-speaking decentralized nation.[45] And while for Margaret

---

[43] Mallon puts this point in more explicitly Gramscian terms: "In this constant, complex interaction among spaces of conflict and alliance, there are moments of greater change or transformation. These moments can be explained by analyzing the historical articulation of different hegemonic processes into a broader coalition or political movement . . . The leaders of a particular movement or coalition achieve hegemony as an endpoint only when they effectively garner to themselves ongoing legitimacy and support. They are successful in doing so if they partially incorporate the political aspirations or discourses of the movement's supporters. Only then can they rule through a combination of coercion and consent and effectively bring about a 'cultural revolution.'"

[44] On US Presidents, see Skowronek, 1993. Again, there is a long tradition of recognizing the political need to claim a "return to first principles" that traces back to Machiavelli (1950, e.g. 182–183).

[45] On the Canadian debates see generally Cairns, Courtney, MacKinnon, Michelmann, and Smith, eds., 1999.

Thatcher Great Britain was (and is!) fundamentally a sovereign nation, for John Major and then Tony Blair it would ultimately be fundamentally part of Europe.[46] All these leaders have had to ignore or alter certain features in their inherited national stories to advance the particular vision that they regarded as desirable.

(6) Finally and perhaps most controversially, the politics of people-making inevitably centers on stories of peoplehood that are to a significant degree exclusionary. That is necessarily true philosophically: to embrace one sense of peoplehood and shared way of life, however free and inclusive, is to reject at least some others. That reality is not altered by the fact that those others might be more restrictive yet; and it explains why stories of peoplehood are likely always to be contested and often to be contested with enormous passion and intensity.

For that philosophic reality has very tangible political expressions. Most aspiring leaders may well aspire to lead as many people as possible. Most try to forge the broadest coalitions they can, and often the largest coalition will be the most powerful. Yet though some people-building coalitions are broader than others are, all will involve important exclusions. Because the entrenched interests and identities of their potential constituents are diverse and often at odds with each other, even the most ambitious leaders must decide who their core constituents are. They then cannot afford to alienate those core constituents by including too many others whom the constituents perceive as threatening to their fundamental economic interests, political beliefs, religious or cultural norms, or other values. Moreover, leaders will realize that some groups are likely to be supporters of their present or potential rivals no matter what the leaders say or do. Leaders thus have incentives to advance accounts of peoplehood and forge coalitions that render such groups outnumbered, disempowered, subordinated, or excluded altogether. The politics of people-making, then, involves continual, partisan, conflictual, often invidious, and always exclusionary processes centered on stories and force. These processes also do much to make us who we are and to make it possible for us to flourish on this earth.

Stories of trust and worth

With the aid of this general picture of the politics of people-making, let me now focus on stories of peoplehood, seeking to specify their main varieties, the distinctive contributions they can make to that politics, and the problems and opportunities they pose for constructing political

---

[46] Pilkington, 2001, 18–19, 40, 44, 98, 184–188, 192, 212.

communities in morally defensible forms. Though political scientists have not sought a general "theory of people-building," there is a wide range of scholarship in many fields – on nationalism, on race and ethnicity, on gender, on identity politics, on coalition-building, and related themes – that reveals much about the sorts of people-building accounts that can prevail and endure in our politically competitive, constantly community-constructing world. Since one goal here is to be brief, I do not seek to do justice to those literatures. But I suggest that they can be usefully organized according to what they implicitly or explicitly take to be the most difficult challenge facing the architects of sustainable senses of political community. Speaking broadly, two linked but distinguishable conceptions of what successful people-builders must achieve emerge: senses of trust and senses of worth.

The "trust" camp includes political theorists like John Dunn (1984), David Miller (1995) and Ben Barber (1995); rational choice-oriented political scientists like Margaret Levi and Valerie Braithwaite (1998), James Fearon (1996) and David Laitin (1998); many economists; sociologists like Anthony Giddens (1985) concerned with coordination problems in complex societies; and also many scholars influenced by Robert Putnam's arguments about civil society (Putnam, 1995, 2000). These writers all suggest that the problem of political people-making is fundamentally a problem of finding ways to generate political trust, understood as including two different things: both trust among the fellow members of a particular political community and trust between its members and their leaders. But it is especially the latter concern, the conditions under which potential members might trust potential leaders enough to invest in the sense of community and leadership those elites offer, that much of this literature features. Many writers treat political trust as a grand variant of problems of principal–agent relations and credible commitments. Accounts of peoplehood then become stories of trust, stories told by leaders to persuade constituents that if they adhere to the political community thus defined, they can trust their compatriots, and particularly their governors, to respect and perhaps to advance their own interests, values, and identities. Such stories may feature warm feelings of civic solidarity and shared values, but they need not. Thomas Hobbes's famed governmental "Leviathan," for instance, is supposed to use absolute sovereign power to persuade subjects that they can trust their citizens to obey the laws, and that they should do so themselves, because they can trust their government to crush anyone who does not (Hobbes, 1968).

In contrast to these "trust" scholars are older intellectual historians of nationalism like Elie Kedourie (1961) and Hans Kohn (1957), recent political theorists like Michael Walzer (1983) and Norma Thompson

(1996), and comparative political sociologists and political scientists like Rogers Brubaker (1992), Liah Greenfeld (1992), Anthony D. Smith (1991, 1995), and Benedict Anderson (1983). They all stress the normative and psychological appeal that accounts of political community have for potential members, given their particular histories and cultural and intellectual traditions. They are joined in my analysis by some Marxian scholars like Etienne Balibar and Immanuel Wallerstein (1991), Eric Hobsbawm (1990), and writers on political economy from Adam Smith (1776) through Ernest Gellner (1965, 1983) to the present. These scholars stress the economic worth, the wealth and prosperity that membership in a particular political community promises to provide, at least for some. I link these writers into a broad "worth" camp because for all of them, the basic task facing the proponents of a particular conception of peoplehood is to persuade its would-be citizenry of the distinctive worth or value that can be realized by loyalty to the community thus understood. As previously indicated, I see material wealth as a particularly important form of worth that people pursue through their political memberships and activities; but it is far from the only one.

Congenially, I believe that both the "trust" and the "worth" camps are correct. The creation of relatively enduring senses of political community requires accounts, narratives, or stories of peoplehood that successfully inspire senses of both trust and worth. Indeed, I think that to engage in successful people-building, it is necessary and *sufficient* to have a story or stories of peoplehood that meets each of these broad challenges on an enduring basis. I say a "story or stories," because coalitions sufficiently powerful to govern over time usually have to be put together by blending together as much as possible distinctive stories that appeal to different portions of the coalition. We may view the result as the governing coalition's "story," but we should not lose sight of the fact that it has multiple, distinct components that are often in logical tension, even if they work collectively as powerful political cement. But precisely because the different parts of a multivalent story of peoplehood may matter to different constituencies, precisely because the story may actually mean different things to different constituencies, it can work politically, inspiring in a critical mass of constituents a sense of trust in their political community's leaders and members and a sense of the relative worth of giving allegiance to the dominant coalition's vision of their community, rather than to rival visions, leaders, or communities. Bear in mind, however, that if economic, military, law enforcement, or other policies achieve far less than what the reigning account of the community has led constituents to expect, that account is likely to lose its capacity to persuade. Success does not depend on having a good story alone, or rather, sustaining a good story depends on results as well as rhetoric.

One might object that "trust" and "worth" are not really two different categories, and certainly they are linked. But I stress their analytical distinctiveness because so much recent literature emphasizes trust and therefore neglects the irreplaceable and unique roles that stories of worth play in the politics of people-building. Again, "worth" in the form of material goods generally seems essential to people, so much so that hopes of wealth may tempt many to follow even leaders whom they do not really trust. Stories affirming the normative worth of political memberships, moreover, can be seen to serve political functions that no other accounts can really provide. That is why my subsequent discussions pay particular attention to what I term "ethically constitutive" stories, for they have special capacities to inspire senses of normative worth.

To be able to highlight such distinctive qualities, let me define "trust" here as the belief that the leaders and members of a particular community are relatively likely to *seek* to advance some of one's important values or interests. They might be likely to do so because they share those values or interests, because their own differing interests are thus well served, because they have a sense of duty, because they have structural incentives to do so, or for some other reason. Whatever its basis, trust is simply the belief that they are likely to try to do the right things, from one's own point of view.

Worth, in contrast, I define as the belief that a community's leaders and members have the capacity to *succeed* in advancing some of one's important values or interests, if they should try to do so. This capacity may stem from those leaders and members' own special competencies; the great material or cultural resources that the community being formed or sustained will possess; divine assistance; or some other circumstance. Accounts of membership in a particular community might foster in us a strong sense of trust without a strong sense of worth, and vice versa. Many Puerto Ricans trust that independence advocates will pursue their island's good devotedly, while doubting that their strategy can best achieve it. Many also believe that they can enhance their wealth by remaining under US sovereignty, even though they do not trust Congress to weigh Puerto Rican interests fairly.

What types of stories of peoplehood can quell such doubts, meeting the challenges of inspiring convictions of both communal trust and worth? Examination of many examples leads me to suggest that there are at least three types of stories that can all help to accomplish each of these tasks. But they do so in different ways; and perhaps as a result, actual narratives of peoplehood seem always to involve complex blends of all three, though in very different combinations and with very different degrees of emphasis. These three types are "economic" stories, "political power" stories, and "ethically constitutive" stories.[47] All three sorts of stories, let me stress, are deployed as means to gain political power, among other ends; but only the second sort cultivates constituent support primarily by *stressing* the power consequences of accepting or rejecting the proffered vision of membership.

Economic stories, in contrast, promote trust by arguing that it is in the interests, usually the economic interests, of particular groups of leaders and their constituents to advance each constituent's economic well-being. And again, they offer worth in the very tangible and tempting form of increased wealth for all, individually and collectively. When the American revolutionaries described in the Declaration of Independence how the colonists' common economic interests were being thwarted by King George, and when Tom Paine wrote in "Common Sense" that "Our plan is commerce," they were trying to inspire both trust and a belief in the worth of their proposed new political community partly in economic terms (Ver Steeg and Hofstadter, eds., 1969, 470–471; Paine, 1967, 423). Similarly, when the Fifth All-Russia Congress of Soviets adopted a Fundamental Law for the Russian Socialist Federative Soviet Republic on July 10, 1918, they sought to promote economic trust by promising the "abolition of all exploitation of man by man" and economic worth via the socialist extension of "the prosperity of the exploiters" to the whole of the "working people."[48]

In so arguing, both sets of political leaders were contributing to what appears to be an important modern development in stories of peoplehood: the placing of special emphasis on how support for a particular form of political community will produce expanding economic benefits for its members. Promises of prosperity are certainly not new in human political life. Still, in the last several centuries political leaders have seemed more often to assert or imply that economic concerns and aspirations form the bedrock of their community's activities and shared interests.[49] How far this apparent development suggests a fundamental transformation in the character of the politics of people-making is a question to which we will return. But in any case, because of the great importance of economic welfare to most persons, few stories of peoplehood are

---

[47] All three types of stories can be advanced in the form of "selective incentives" attracting active partisans, but I will focus here on versions that seek to inspire widespread allegiance among relatively politically inactive as well as active constituents. I am grateful to Andrew Polsky for prompting this clarification.

[48] Available at http://coral.bucknell.edu/departments/russian/const/18cons01.html.

[49] A justly influential discussion of this development is Hirschman, 1977.

likely to inspire widespread senses of trust and worth if they do not assert that members will be made well off economically by living as the stories suggest.

As I have indicated, all three types of people-making stories are likely to include themes that speak to the interests and values of core constituents, along with elements expressing the distinctive concerns of aspiring leaders. In regard to economic stories, we might try to catalogue the great variety of economic interests that people possess and pursue in most reasonably large societies. But appropriate as such a catalogue might be for many purposes, it is more useful here to group economic interests into two categories corresponding to the basic contrast between "leaders and followers."

It is plausible to assume that the great bulk of people are predominantly concerned with achieving a measure of economic security, a level of basic comfort and protection against material privation, whatever their forms of work. In contrast stand a comparative few who are most driven by desires to amass great riches, again whatever their forms of economic activity. Though many people undoubtedly would welcome Midas-like fortunes, only some people make it their life goal to acquire extraordinary wealth. Because their intensely pursued economic goals are so affected by government and because they have unusual capacities to shape policies, those few are far more likely to be politically active and influential than most people are, and sometimes they will be political leaders themselves. When they are, then effective economic stories of peoplehood can be expected both to promise the economic security that most people seek and to justify the leaders' drive to acquire and retain riches for themselves. Sometimes, however, political leaders are not themselves much motivated by wealth. Even so, they usually still have to craft stories of peoplehood that can gain support from both economic security-seekers and from ambitious wealth-seekers, for the former group is often numerous and the latter group is often disproportionately powerful. They include, after all, most of the rich.[50]

Indeed, after Marx, if not Rousseau, and amid the sharply inegalitarian conditions of the early twenty-first century, the question immediately arises: don't stories of peoplehood often really only work to advance the economic interests of some elite members of communities at the direct expense of many, perhaps most, other members? This question challenges the notion that economic stories ever really express the interests of most members, and it also implies that inegalitarian economic aims are in fact at the heart of virtually all stories of peoplehood.

[50] For one classic analysis of this theme, see Lindblom, 1977.

And it is true that these stories often do such work. But again, many leaders have goals that go beyond and sometimes against those of wealth-seeking elites; presumably this was true of many of the priests who led peasant revolts in France. Leaders also often seek to maintain the support of substantial constituencies who are not rich, as modern-day peasant leaders like Fidel Castro and Mao Tse-Tung seem to have succeeded in doing for very long periods. In response it may be said that Castro and Mao have simply sought to advance the economic interests of some, however numerous, at the expense of others; and it is also true that even such mass leaders can prove over time to be pawns of avaricious wealth-seekers, or to be so motivated themselves. But think also of those who form ecovillages or militantly activist environmental groups like Greenpeace. These leaders do advance economic stories. They promise their constituents that the activities and ways of life they advocate will serve human economic interests by helping to avert environmental catastrophes. Even so, it is unlikely that most such leaders are chiefly concerned to improve their own economic statuses or those of wealthy constituents. It thus seems far too simplistic to assume that all stories of political peoplehood are essentially tools of the greedy rich, even though all will have economic themes. It is more likely that, however optimistically, many leaders and followers sincerely "buy" stories promising that certain forms of political membership will produce secure, perhaps growing material well-being for most or all.

But these sorts of economic themes have never wholly displaced the second type of narrative of peoplehood, ones stressing personal and collective political power. The various sorts of "political power" stories all promise that governors, especially, and other members of a political community as well, will exercise their powers through institutions and policies that give significant power to each member, often via some system of alleged virtual or actual representation that can inspire trust. Even monarchs and totalitarian dictators have usually claimed to be the true representatives as well as the great champions of their people. Leaders of smaller, more localized forms of political community such as provinces and townships often claim that their sheer proximity makes them more representative of their constituents and hence more trustworthy repositories of the powers the constituents can bestow.

Political stories further promise that membership in the political community will enhance the power of members of the community, either as individuals, as a people, or most often both. That sense of heightened power can imbue the political membership with considerable worth in the eyes of citizens. When local leaders have claimed greater representativeness and trustworthiness for themselves, rival leaders atop large federal systems have often replied by insisting that only governance at the more encompassing level can provide the power that can enable a government truly to protect the governed against their enemies.

Thus to inspire trust, the American revolutionaries' Declaration advocated government by the consent of the governed (Paine, 1967, 469); and to inspire a sense of the worth of a new confederated regime, Paine argued that if Americans united as an independent nation, they "need fear no external enemy" (440). Again similarly, the Preamble to the 1982 Constitution of the People's Republic of China rehearses China's long history and concludes that with the founding of the People's Republic, "the Chinese people have taken control of state power and become masters of the country." The Chinese people are said to have since "safeguarded China's national independence and security," and Article 2 of the Constitution asserts that "All power in the People's Republic of China belongs to the people."[51] By such contentions, both early American and modern Chinese leaders have sought to foster trust and faith in the worth of their nations partly in "political power" terms.

In keeping with my expectation of dualistic themes expressive of the different interests of leaders and constituents, it is plausible to presume that political leaders are most likely to be attracted to "political power" stories that promise power for the community as a collectivity. Many will see such heightened communal prominence as a basis for their own personal power and glory. Some may, indeed, be motivated at bottom simply by a thirst to achieve active domination over large numbers of other people. Others may seek to make their community sufficiently potent to accomplish what they regard as inherently praiseworthy services for all their members, or even for all humanity. Given the enormous difficulty of providing for human flourishing without the organization of people into thriving political communities, the latter sorts of aims may often be quite compelling. All of these as well as other possible motives of leaders may prompt them to urge the community's construction of an ever-wider political stage.

Constituents, in contrast, may often not share such dreams of greatness to any considerable extent, recognizing them to be beyond their realistic personal aspirations. Thus they may respond most favorably to political power stories that promise personal physical security for all members – protection from domination both by other private parties and by public authorities. That is why, at the extreme, Hobbesian threats to obey a conqueror or else face annihilation are political power stories which, if believed, are likely to produce the conduct the conqueror desires, if not

[51] Available at http://www.europeaninternet.com/china/constit/.

true allegiance. If, however, a leader actively seeks heartfelt allegiance, rather than suspicious and fearful obedience, then just as in the case of economic stories, here too the differences in the ambitions of leaders and followers may pose a serious challenge for successful "political power" story-telling. The quest to be a great power as a people often involves risking the lives of many ordinary people in military adventures, rather than providing them with the physical security they desire.

This difficulty may help explain, for example, the patterns of partisan success in the early American republic. Most late eighteenth-century American voters favored Jefferson's championing of a rather isolationist, pacific nation of agrarian republican yeomen, rather than Hamilton's calls for national economic and military greatness, to be achieved via the concentration of political and economic power in elite hands and by extensive engagement with Europe. For much of the electorate, the security against both abusive elite power at home and wars abroad that Jefferson promised was more attractive than the national glory Hamilton championed.[52] Still, the success of Jefferson and later Andrew Jackson in winning mass support for a westward expanding "empire of liberty," won by economic and military means, suggests that political power stories furthering the concerns of both elites and mass constituents can be crafted. Indeed, we will see many examples indicating that "political power" stories stressing both personal protection and security and the potentially inconsistent pursuit of collective imperial glory have been quite common in human history.[53] It is not so obvious whether these stories have ultimately served the interests of elites or their constituents better.[54] A better question might be whether more benign sorts of successful people-building stories can be found.

That issue is raised all the more pointedly by my third category, ethically constitutive stories. The meaning of this term may be less intuitively clear than in the first two cases. It refers to a wide variety of accounts that present membership in a particular people as somehow intrinsic to who its members really are, because of traits that are imbued with ethical significance. Such stories proclaim that members' culture, religion, language, race, ethnicity, ancestry, history, or other such factors are

[52] I am grateful to Erik Wright for suggesting this distinction in political power stories to me. For the Hamilton/Jefferson contrast, see e.g. Cunningham, 2000; Read, 2000.

[53] See e.g. Rogin, 1975.

[54] The question is raised dramatically by Shakespeare's hero king, Henry V, who crafts a sense of common English identity ("we band of brothers") to inspire support for his successful invasion of France. One night during the campaign a sleepless, doubt-racked Henry wonders whether the glory or "ceremony" that is his reward is anywhere equal to his burdens, or to the benefits his efforts bestow upon those who are now his countrymen as well as his subjects.

constitutive of their very identities as persons, in ways that both affirm their worth and delineate their obligations. These stories are almost always intergenerational, implying that the ethically constitutive identity espoused not only defines who a person is, but who her ancestors have been and who her children can be.

Some writers suggest, in fact, that most if not all senses of nationhood or peoplehood invoke an account of unchosen, inherited, usually quasi-ethnic identity (Smith, 1987; Canovan, 2000). Such a conception need not, however, be biological. Some "ethically constitutive stories" are purely historical, in that they present the communities and forms of membership existing in the world into which we are born as the contingent products of past human historical actions. Such accounts can still suggest that these preexisting historical entities have profound importance in shaping our identities.

Indeed, all ethically constitutive stories, biological, religious, historical, cultural, can be read to imply that those who share a common heritage cannot properly choose to belong to any other political community, at least for the foreseeable future. It is often in the interest of people-building elites to advance such readings. If they are accepted, these ethically constitutive stories may well be able to inspire trust. Sometimes they may do so because people will think that their fellow religious believers, ethnic kinsmen, historical compatriots, or linguistic and cultural partners have values and interests similar to theirs. Sometimes they may do so because, as Fearon and Laitin (1996) and others suggest about ethnicity, people are more certain that they can identify untrustworthy conduct in those whose customs and social networks they know best.

Such stories are also able to inspire senses of worth, moreover, because the shared constitutive traits are generally depicted as inherently valuable. Jewish leaders' invocation of the Mosaic story of the "chosen" character of the Jewish people is, of course, a historically seminal example; and as I have already suggested, such claims are by no means confined to ancient epochs. Paine wrote that "Europe and not England is the parent country of America," so that Americans were a people who could claim "brotherhood with every European Christian," thereby both presuming and implying an ethnic, religious, and also gendered ethically constitutive story of this sort (1967, 421). He also suggested that Americans were a new "chosen people" much like the ancient Israelites, and that it was the plan of Providence to establish a New World nation that would be an asylum for this blessed, liberty-loving people (409–413, 423–24). He thereby advanced a more specifically religious constitutive story of America's special providential destiny that has echoed through the rhetoric of American leaders ever since.

Paine's ancestral and religious stories each served well to promote trust in the members and leaders of the incipient American people, as well as faith in the prospective nation's divinely sanctioned worth. When the Declaration's authors spoke of their "Consanguinity" with their "British brethren" and chose to denounce the "merciless Indian savages" instead of treating them as fellow tyrannized subjects, they implied a similar ethically constitutive story of who Americans really were and would be. An independent American people would not include Indians, but only citizens who could be trusted to strive to protect the interests of European-descended colonists against Indians; and the American people would not be savages, but rather bearers of a civilization of superior worth. Again like Paine, moreover, even though the Declaration does not explicitly disavow gender equality, it focuses on the "consent of the governed" to governments "instituted among men," and only "men" are overtly said to be "created equal" by the "Creator" on whose "divine providence" they firmly rely (471–472).

Ethically constitutive stories can take a fascinating variety of forms, but they display strong tendencies to include three elements visible in the Pentateuch, in Paine, and in the Declaration. First, as Margaret Canovan suggests, they tend to be religious or at least quasi-religious. There simply is no stronger basis for making a membership seem both unquestionably intrinsic and morally worthwhile than to have it assigned by God or the gods. No purely biological, ancestral, cultural, linguistic, or historical account can provide quite the same degree of sanctification that divine authorship bestows. Religious justifications are, indeed, so potent if accepted that religions can in many cases treat "converts" as members just as fully and truly as those born into the faith.

Second, as just noted, ethically constitutive stories have a weaker but still powerful tendency to include "ethnic myths" of common descent, whether descent from the patriarch Abraham or from Mother Europe. After divine authorship, the most straightforward way to make a membership seem natural is to portray it as an expression of actual physical kinship or shared ancestry.[55] These kinds of doctrines have more logical difficulty extending fully equal status to those "naturalized" into

---

[55] This is true even though, as Bonnie Honig instructively details, myths of founding and refounding often feature foreigners, like the Bible's Ruth and the Russian founder Riurik (Honig, 2001, 3–7, 41–72). Very special foreigners can be interpreted both as divine agents and as sources of reinvigoration for a lineage, as Ruth has been; and if they are not so portrayed, either their foreignness or their founding role may be disputed, as in the case of Riurik. Sometimes, moreover, foreign-founders may be made the scapegoat for the violences involved in the people's founding, as in Thomas Jefferson's effort to assign the British responsibility for slavery in the first draft of his Declaration of Independence (Wills, 1978, 66–75).

membership despite birth outside the group, but when they suit the interests of the group's core constituents and leaders, such "naturalizations"
generally prove politically feasible, though some lingering shadows of
"outsider" status often remain.

Third, this genealogical strain has frequently combined with entrenched economic and social arrangements to support the elaboration
of gendered, often patriarchal themes within narratives of peoplehood.
Ancestral constitutive stories, particularly – ethnic, racial, religious – can
prompt official concern with the roles of men and women not simply as
members of the political community but as reproductive agents, as parents. They provide political incentives for community leaders to adopt
rules that inhibit "their" people from openly bearing children with mates
whose "foreign" origins would threaten the credibility of claims of shared
biological origins. As Nancy Cott has written, "laws of marriage must
play a large part in forming 'the people.' They sculpt the body politic"
(Cott, 2000, 5).[56] And enforcement of marriage laws is inevitably bound
up with the entire construction of gender identities, statuses, and powers. Accordingly, bans on religious intermarriage have been prominent
in Jewish traditions, and bans on interracial marriages were widespread
in the early American states, in ways that did much to define sexual,
racial, and religious identities as dimensions of distinct forms of peoplehood. Even in the "vertical, differentiated" form of peoplehood that
constituted medieval serfdom the notion that lords and serfs might be
biologically related was abhorrent, at least to the lordly class. Nobles did
not marry serfs, and a serf was "not allowed to marry outside the group
of serfs dependent on his lord. This provision was necessary to ensure
that the lord kept control of the children."[57]

While such bans have generally applied in principle to both sexes, moreover, they have often been implemented with particular concern to police
the behavior of women. That unequal implementation is probably bound
up with the ways in which, in many human societies, men have valued
and enforced certain sorts of economic divisions of labor. Women have

---

[56] Cott notes that "Typically, founders of new political societies in the Western tradition
have inaugurated their regimes with marriage regulations, to foster households conducive
to their aims and to symbolize a new era – whether in colonial Virginia, revolutionary
France, the breakaway republic of Texas, or the unprecedented Bolshevik system in the
Soviet Union" (2000, 6). I would go further and say that it is not simply in the western
tradition but in virtually all societies, and not in regard simply to marriage laws but to
policies defining gender roles more generally, that changes are often instituted as part of
the founding of new political peoples.

[57] Bloch, 1970, 88. Armstrong, 1982, maintains that before the eleventh century, severe
Christian restrictions on endogamous marriages meant that peasants were sometimes
forced to seek spouses in distant villages, though this did not alter their dependency
(44).

often borne primary responsibility not only for biological reproduction but also for the time- and energy-consuming tasks of child-rearing. Those arrangements have given many men economic incentives to espouse visions of peoplehood in which women are portrayed as essentially wives and mothers, and in which men are legally and physically empowered to make sure they stay so.

Those roles, in turn, have often meant that women have been assigned special roles not only in the biological reproduction of various peoples, but also in their cultural reproduction. Political elites have often charged the women of "their" political society with primary responsibilities for rearing children who would be "true" members of that society in their identities, values, and commitments. And elites have therefore often claimed they were entitled to regulate not just female reproductive behavior but their morality more broadly, to make sure that the right lessons were being passed on to the next generation. George Mosse has argued, for example, that even as industrialization wrought disruptive economic, class strife, and social transformations in the nineteenth century, making the future uncertain, emerging nationalist doctrines in many western societies incorporated images of virile but "respectable," sexually self-controlled men and passive, domestic women in both their iconography and their social policies. Those women were supposed to maintain the senses of "honor" that would provide the moral underpinnings for correct conduct in changing times.[58] Hence the politics of people-making can foster political pressures to regulate women, especially their sexual conduct but also their behavior more generally, in ways that often reinforce men's economic interests in confining women to male-governed "domestic" roles, even as they also institutionalize patriarchal ethically constitutive accounts of peoplehood.

It is nonetheless true that in some times and places, efforts to build modern nations have been led in part by women and have included calls for female emancipation as part of the quest to achieve freer and more just institutions (Moghadam, ed., 1994, 3–6). It is also true that in different times and places, the economic roles treated as suitable for women have varied greatly, including jobs out of the home such as sewing in garment factories, nursing, social work, elementary school teaching, and many others, as well as domestic work and child-rearing. And obviously, the specific content of the political, cultural, and religious senses of the peoplehood women are expected to convey also have ranged widely. Still, the construction of gender roles in ways that can be understood to express and also concretely reproduce certain conceptions of political

[58] Mosse, 1985, 9–14, 191.

peoplehood is, though certainly not universal, historically pervasive. And some scholars believe that, far from declining, in many parts of the world today nationalist projects "increasingly" assign to women "rather onerous responsibility for the reproduction of the group – through family attachment, domesticity, and maternal roles" (Moghadam, ed., 1994, 3).

The resulting gender identities are ones to which many people become profoundly psychologically attached, making them very difficult to alter even if they prove less advantageous under changing economic and political conditions (Wade, 2001, 852–853). The economic motivations for gender inequities and their role in fostering psychological conceptions of sexuality, both mean that gender relations cannot be understood *simply* as instruments of the politics of people-making. Often male support for particular conceptions of peoplehood has seemed unthinkable unless they incorporated distinct and unequal gender roles. Yet those roles may still be significantly reinforced in some ways, modified in others in order to construct gender identities that can advance other racial, religious, economic, cultural, or political features of those visions of peoplehood. As with most political pressures, these circumstances favoring patriarchal stories of peoplehood are at most generative, not determinative; but they help explain why historically so many conceptions of political community have featured inegalitarian conceptions of gender identities.

Ethically constitutive stories, then, are more likely to be religious or quasi-religious, kinship-like, and gendered than economic or political power stories. They are similar to these other stories, however, in also tending to differ in the appeal they hold for leaders and followers, though that dichotomous character is frequently less obvious. All members of a community valorized in an ethically constitutive story are offered a secure sense of self-worth or self-respect because of their innate participation in a valuable common identity, as one of "God's chosen people," a "master race," a great culture or historic people. But precisely because this community is presented as intrinsically valuable, its leaders, those who help fend off its enemies, guide it to prosperity, enhance its special greatness, often claim to be entitled to special esteem from all who believe in the community's ethically constitutive story. They are God's ministers, the wise "founding fathers," the "race men" who deserve special honor among their "people" because they have enabled it to fulfill its distinctive potential. Their constituents are their wards, children, flock; not their peers.

In sum, I contend that enduring successful accounts of peoplehood inspire senses of trust and worth among the members of a people by weaving together economic, political power, and ethically constitutive stories tailored to persuade a critical mass of constituents while also advancing partisan elite interests. All three types of stories are likely to be present, because needs for some minimal sense of material sustenance, physical security, and personal worth are so fundamental to human existence, while longings to achieve abundance in one or more of these regards are very common. Viable stories of peoplehood thus inevitably include some sorts of responses to all these felt needs and longings. The weaving and tailoring of stories of peoplehood must also take into account the more specific established interests and identities of core constituents and the particular economic, military, and political contexts in which the people-building is occurring. Hence accounts of peoplehood can take many forms, including the varieties of modern nationalism but also "pre-" and "post-national" conceptions of community. Particular narratives might give more explicit attention to economic or political power themes rather than ethically constitutive ones, as may seem true of the Declaration. Others might feature an ethically constitutive story of a people's providentially endowed duties and destiny over mundane economic and political power concerns, as King Josiah's scribes apparently chose to do. Some stories might stress themes of economic security or instead the promise of abundance; they might stress the collective power of the community thus envisioned, or they might emphasize guarantees of sufficient personal power for individuals to feel secure. They might emphasize provision of trust over worth. They might focus on enemies within or without existing borders.

There is one further option that may seem quite fundamental, though regrettably, I do not think it is quite as consequential as might first appear. Leaders can also advance stories that are primarily positive about their proffered sense of community, or they can instead stress negative themes about the rival conceptions of community, rival leaders, and rival groups they oppose. From the standpoint of constructing more benign and morally defensible forms of political life, it can seem tremendously important to encourage more positive stories. The history of genocides in the twentieth century makes it abundantly clear that negative stories can indeed help fuel and justify great atrocities. It is certainly preferable to foster forms of politics, if we can, in which leaders instead praise their own people and traditions while pledging respect and esteem for others, as the Kyrgyz website does. Still, it is analytically true that any story valorizing what is especially estimable about one group logically implies a comparative derogation of others. And in practice, policies advanced simply in the name of positive visions of one community may work in very harsh ways against the interests of many outsiders, even if they are not specifically denigrated. When more prosperous nations design immigration policies and multinational trade agreements to strengthen their economies, for example, they may do so only with their own interests in view, not with any conscious intent of harming others; but the costs to those excluded can be high indeed. In a diverse, divided, conflictual world, it is hard to be positive without being negative.

Even so, with all these options at their disposal, creative leaders can sometimes find accounts that can make a shared peoplehood seem trustworthy and valuable even to many members of groups that have long seen themselves as opposed in certain ways. Some of those political visions, moreover, genuinely can foster forms of political life that are more beneficial for their members and more defensible toward outsiders than many alternatives. But to build any sort of enduring community, leaders are likely to have to offer stories of peoplehood containing some version of all these themes. These three types of stories, along with force, comprise the basic elements of the politics of people-making.

2   The role of ethically constitutive stories

The framework I have sketched is deliberately elementary. As in much social science, my hope is to gain substantial clarification by working out the implications of a few simple but plausible ideas. This framework generates a great many questions that may prove useful for analyzing the political processes through which forms of peoplehood are created and sustained. For example, I have already suggested that when people-building proceeds through dangerous exertions of violent force, it is likely that leaders will need to deploy stories that can inspire great sacrifices and risk-taking by at least some who fight for their side. More broadly, a whole range of issues concerning the interrelationships of force and stories are obviously crucially important. Whatever the disadvantages of people-building via certain sorts of stories – however much they may represent more subtle yet more totalizing forms of domination, as some postmodernists forcefully contend – still, they are in vital respects less brutally oppressive than the forging of political memberships through slaughter and physical coercion. It would therefore be tremendously valuable to understand the circumstances under which reliance on stories becomes impossible and resort is made to force. It would also be valuable to know more about the sorts of stories that can make the use of force seem appropriate or even desirable, and about the kinds that can minimize reliance on violence. Again, once these questions are posed, we can quickly perceive a wealth of literatures from which pertinent insights might be synthesized.

But because I wish to focus on peoplehood stories here, I do not pursue their connections with coercive force in any detail; though I also seek never to lose sight of the reality that in all politics, however plush the political velvet, sooner or later it is found to glove some iron fists. A sobering illustration: the Mennonite religious communities in the United States and Canada have long been devout pacificists, and these principles have left them to some degree "a people apart" even today. Yet they would not possess their lands at all if the political regimes under which they dwell had not cleared away most of the continent's original inhabitants, often through violence.[1] Even setting the thorny inescapability of violence aside, the typology of stories and their political contributions laid out so far raises more questions than I can explore here. Must stories of peoplehood always promote *both* a sense of trust and a sense of worth? If so, under what circumstances is "trust" or "worth" likely to matter most? Is it generally more important that stories foster a sense of trust, as the emphasis in much recent literature would suggest, or are senses of worth just as frequently significant, perhaps more so? Is it, moreover, really true empirically that all three types of stories are always present? If so, why? What are the distinctive and irreplaceable contributions each type of story makes to sustaining both trust and worth? Are some (perhaps political power stories promising security and accountability) more essential to trust, some (perhaps economic stories, perhaps ethically constitutive stories) to worth? Or, to put the same issue differently, what forms of trust are generally most essential, or most essential in definable circumstances – economic, political, or ethical trust? What forms of worth? More generally, if it is true that all three types of stories are always all present, but in very different combinations, under what circumstances is one type of story likely to be more dominant in prevailing projects of people-making than the others? Are there particular types of stories or combinations of stories that seem more enduring and more normatively desirable?

These questions are listed, alas, only in the hope of persuading readers that my framework generates a range of intriguing inquiries. Most of these issues are not pursued in this book, though the discussion leads to some arguments and suggestions in regard to many of them. Here I seek simply to show the potential of the framework by developing the implications of its most novel element: its emphasis on the role of ethically constitutive stories. The chief goal is to vindicate my claims that political scientists, especially, must attend more closely to such stories in order to have adequate explanatory theories of political identity, and to have better informed normative theories of how we should seek to construct political memberships. In line with my original aims in undertaking these analyses, I pay special attention to racial ethically constitutive stories, though the arguments are illustrated with many other sorts as well.

---

[1] MacMaster, 1985, 242, 280; Driedger, 1988, 49. As discussed below, traditional Mennonite theology not only permitted but required giving allegiance to "Caesar" – to whatever political authorities happened to be reigning – so long as those authorities permitted the Mennonites to practice their faith, which included pacifism. Benefiting from, as opposed to contributing to, political violence was not sinful.

These claims put me in opposition to two strains in contemporary scholarship. I first side with the growing chorus of critics of efforts to distinguish empirically between "civic" and "ethnic" nations. Such efforts were revived in the early part of the 1990s, only to be met with weighty empirical and theoretical objections. Even so, the distinction persists, largely because whatever its empirical limitations, many scholars agree with those normative theorists who urge us to seek to make our political communities more "civic," less "ethnic." Many add that, though purely "civic" regimes may not have been possible in past human history, several long-term trends are making them far more feasible today. Though I am in agreement with these advocates on many political particulars, the account of the politics of people-making developed here nonetheless leads me to see their basic quest as misguided in fundamental ways. It is a quest that seeks to avoid the dangers of ethically constitutive stories by marginalizing them in ways that are neither practical nor desirable. In this chapter I explain why I think ethically constitutive stories have not only always been part of the politics of people-making but always will be. I also lay the groundwork for the controversial claim I will defend later, that this is not only the way things must be. It is the way things should be.

"Civic" v. "ethnic" nations

At least since Hans Kohn's 1944 classic, *The Idea of Nationalism*, it has been common for both historians and social scientists to distinguish between "civic" and "ethnic" conceptions of nations and to classify many existing societies as primarily if not essentially one or the other. Until recently, Germany and Japan have often been termed "ethnic" nations, with senses of national identity that have rested on notions of shared kinship and ancestry that are broadly ethnic or racial. France and the United States, especially, have long been said instead to exhibit "civic" nationhood. In "civic" nations members are bound together by voluntary, shared allegiance to political principles and procedures. In theory those principles might stem from any purely "political" notion of membership, such as the sorts of pragmatic beliefs in constitutional monarchy that can still be found in modern Britain and Belgium, among other places. But "civic" nations have most often been identified with systems of democracy or popular government, in which, in theory, the nation is comprised of free and equal self-governing citizens. Still there are variations. France's historical "civic" principles are usually termed forms of "republicanism," while the "civic" precepts attributed to the United States are today more often called "liberalism," "liberal democracy," or, at most, "liberal republicanism" (though the American revolutionaries spoke of "republicanism" as often and as ardently as the French).[2] Though its roots are much older, this civic/ethnic distinction gained new prevalence in the early 1990s. The fall of the Soviet Union and the rise of the European Union, among other events, led to revisions in citizenship laws, new projects of nation-building, and some violent conflicts in Europe and Asia. The contrast between the two conceptions of nationhood seemed to clarify the alternatives that were arising and provide guidance as to which was preferable. Michael Ignatieff's book and television series, both entitled *Blood and Belonging*, probably did the most to popularize the distinction. Still, he was riding a scholarly wave: a number of significant sociological and historical works of the early 90s also relied on it for their foundational empirical classifications.[3]

And because "civic" principles are usually deemed to be liberal, democratic, or republican, these empirically centered works have only reinforced the manner in which contemporary normative theorists tend to categorize many modern societies as constituted by agreements on "liberal," "republican," "liberal republican," "republican liberal," "liberal democratic," or "social democratic" principles and processes. Such theorists generally trace what they term "liberalism" back to the seventeenth-century political tracts through which John Locke and others shaped the English and later the American revolutions. "Liberals" are said to present citizens as persons who have somehow contracted with each other to create a government that will make their individual human rights to life, liberty, property, and the pursuit of happiness more secure. Civic membership is thus understood basically as an artificially, consensually created instrument of a diverse range of self-interested personal life plans, with the emphasis generally on seeking economic, religious, and familial fulfillment. Theorists generally derive "republican" models instead from the eighteenth-century writings through which Jean-Jacques Rousseau had his much-debated impact on the French Revolution, and they sometimes look beyond him to Machiavelli and Aristotle. "Republicanism" is said to present citizens as persons who have contracted with those whom they can regard as civic siblings to create institutions of collective self-governance. Civic membership is then understood as a means of realizing common goods, perhaps even a shared kind of collective immortality. When those

---

[2] See e.g. Kohn, 1944, 329–333; Kohn, 1955; Plamenatz, 1976; for summations of the distinction's intellectual history see e.g. Brubaker, 1992; O'Leary, 1998, 83n37; Schnapper, 1998, 137.

[3] Along with Ignatieff, 1994, important examples include Brubaker, 1992, Greenfeld, 1992, and Hollinger, 1995 (arguing at 192n1 that the "distinction is proving more useful than ever to students of nationalism, past and present").

common goods are thought to include substantial guarantees of redistributive social assistance, as they have often been in the philosophies
of socialist thinkers and labor-led political movements, modern visions
of "social democracy" also emerge. Out of these basic notions and with
many additions and subtractions, contemporary writers have sculpted
most of the prescriptive images of "liberal," "republican," and "democratic" citizenship that predominate in "mainstream" western political
theory. All these represent visions of "civic" nations, held to be preferable to "ethnic" nations.[4]

No sooner was the civic/ethnic distinction reemphasized by both empirical and normative writers in the early 90s, however, than criticisms of
its adequacy appeared. The distinguished French sociologist Dominique
Schnapper in her 1994 book, *Communauté des Citoyens* (translated in 1998
as *Community of Citizens*), advanced some of the most influential arguments. Part of Schnapper's critique was a bit idiosyncratic: she chose to
define the modern idea of the "nation" as an essentially democratic "community of citizens," so that "ethnic" nations could not logically be called
"nations" at all. But when she moved from ideas to history, it turned out
that she thought there were not really any "civic" nations and probably
could not be. She maintained that the "political projects" through which
putatively "civic" nations have been built have always relied on "elements
of ethnic order." Those elements were logically inconsistent with their
"ideal type," but they were politically unavoidable: rationalist, voluntarist
civic accounts were in her view simply incapable of inspiring the senses
of belonging and commitment that the imperatives of collective political
life have always demanded (60–62, 91, 112, 138–139, 149–150). In different ways political theorists like Brian Singer (1995), Nicholas Xenos
(1996), and Bernard Yack (1996) soon all similarly contended that all
actual nations have been built on particular, distinctive inheritances and
identities, so that they cannot be described as based on rational consent
to "civic" political principles alone. Like Schnapper, these writers see
perhaps unavoidable political pressures at work, especially pressures to
identify a somehow preexisting, bounded and grounded "people" who
can consent to their "civic" nation and share concrete senses of patriotism toward it. These writers also affirm, however, that it is hard to find
modern nations that are devoid of conceptions of membership that stress
allegiance to at least some "civic" principles. Hence the critics generally
believe that as an empirical matter, we can see both "civic" and "ethnic"
elements in virtually every modern nation, if not indeed all of them.

---

[4] The range can be suggested by e.g. Barber, 1984; Habermas, 1996; Dagger, 1997; van
Gunsteren, 1998; Hutchings and Dannreuther, eds., 1999.

This claim is made all the more plausible by the fact that in truth, almost no one disputes it. From Kohn on, most writers have stressed that distinctions between "civic" and "ethnic" nations are at most matters of degree. All actual political communities are enormously complex entities in which multiple conceptions of membership can be found. In Liah Greenfeld's influential 1992 study of nationalisms, for example, she added after making the civic/ethnic distinction that "In reality, obviously, the most common type is a mixed one," but with compositions that varied significantly enough to make the classification a "useful analytical tool" (1992, 11–12). Similarly, Michael Ignatieff has recently written that "The difficulty with the distinction is that most 'civic' nationalist societies depend on certain 'ethnic' elements to sustain nationalist commitment; while most 'ethnic' societies ostensibly safeguard a host of 'civic' principles... Most allegiances fuse the two" (1999, 145). David Hollinger concedes that in any case, over time "civic" affiliations "help to create those that are eventually recognized as ethnic," as inherited, constitutive, but significantly unchosen identities (2000, 214).

Yet these analysts still employ the distinction, partly because they think it empirically useful, chiefly because they see it as normatively essential. It provides "ideal types" of forms of nationhood that human beings should seek to build, even if they have not yet done so fully in any particular context. Especially influential here has been the example of modern Germany's leading social theorist, Jürgen Habermas. He agrees emphatically that modern nationalisms have been built on inherited ethnocultural notions of shared identity, used to provide initially crucial "social-psychological" reinforcement for national political allegiances (1996, 494–495; 1998, 112–113). But he contends that the task today is to seek to transcend the more ethnic conceptions that historically served as a political "catalyst" for modern nation-building. We can and should seek to make modern republicanism "stand on its own two feet," inspiring allegiance in essentially "civic" terms (1996, 494–97; 1998, 115–118). It is this assertedly more "benign" form of nationalism that most proponents of the "civic/ethnic" distinction urge us to pursue (Ignatieff, 1999, 147; Hollinger, 1995, 132).

The problems of notions of "civic" nations

And why not? We have only to think of the horrors of racial nationalism in the pre-World War II United States, Nazi Germany, imperial Japan, and modern South Africa, the mutual atrocities inflicted by Palestinian and Israeli militants, along with the bitter ethnic and religious conflicts in the former Yugoslavia, Rwanda, Northern Ireland, and all too many other places, to see that "ethnic" nations often, perhaps always, pose terrible dangers to human well-being. Just why can we not build politically communities that are essentially "liberal," "republican," "democratic," or at most some combination of these essentially "civic" traditions? Even if we have been unable to do so in the past, are there not many historical trends and current realities that support confidence that we can do so in the future?

These questions are all the more pressing because, as we have already seen, modern democratic liberalism and republicanism are in many respects superbly equipped to inspire the senses of trust and worth that, I have contended, successful stories of peoplehood must foster. The liberal doctrines of economic rights to own the fruits of one's productive labors and to exchange them in fair markets are "economic stories" that promise to generate expanding wealth for all through mutually beneficial competitive efforts. Liberal guarantees of personal rights against violations of one's life and liberty, by other individuals or by government agents, are "political power" stories that promise power in the form of personal security, the form most valued by most people. And insofar as liberal visions of peoplehood are also democratic, they offer further valuable political powers: powers to keep rulers reigned in, and powers to share in the political authority of a sovereign people.

Since the days when modern republican stories were invoked to oppose King George III and King Louis XVI, such narratives have stressed the latter forms of political power even more emphatically. Many types of republicanism, especially contemporary social democratic descendants, also include "economic stories" promising to shelter all members against material hardships and massive economic inequalities, much more strongly than "liberal" capitalist societies have done. The potency of these economic and political power stories today is such that, even if we are not at the liberal democratic end of history, it is extraordinarily difficult to craft popularly acceptable forms of political community around the world without trumpeting some sort of commitments to liberal doctrines of personal and market economic rights, republican self-governance, and public concern for the economic welfare of all. When African leaders transformed the anti-colonialist Organization of African Unity into a new African Union in July 2002, for example, its first chair, President Thabo Mbeki of South Africa, promised that the Union would promote "democracy" and "human rights" as well as "good governance" that could "raise living standards" and provide "peace" and "stability."[5]

---

[5] Rachel L. Swarms, "African Leaders Drop Old Group for One that Has Power," *New York Times,* July 9, 2002: A3; Associated Press, "Key Principles of the African Union," *New York Times on the Web,* July 9, 2002, http://www.nytimes.com/aponline/international/AP-African-Union.

Those aims were proclaimed despite the fact that unelected Libyan leader Colonel Muammar el-Qaddafi was an equally prominent founder of the new Union. Like the Kyrgyz website, the African Union's emphasis on these themes probably is a response both to domestic and regional political pressures and to the foreign policies of powerful modern states with liberal republican elements, for they generally wish to see a world filled with regimes professing values like their own.[6]

Whether the overwhelming predominance of promises of economic progress, democracy, and human rights in political discourse today is due to the intrinsic appeal of those elements of economic and political power stories, to the influence of regimes that legitimate themselves in such terms, or more likely to both, it clearly exists. That predominance extends, moreover, historical trends that many insightful thinkers have long perceived as basic, perhaps irreversible transformations in human life. These include the heightened modern emphasis on the provision of economic goods as the centerpiece of social life; the now almost global embrace of beliefs that legitimate systems of political power must somehow be democratic; and the related spread of more universalistic and egalitarian "ethically constitutive" stories of human moral identity. To many today, those trends suggest that even if particularistic ethically constitutive stories have been politically necessary in the past, today at last we can have truly "civic" forms of political life that will in fact be able to "stand on their own two feet." I do not think that is the case, but the trends are all real enough to make the contention worth taking seriously.

Perhaps the most undeniable of these historical changes is the rise of economic concerns to far greater prominence in the political aspirations expressed around the globe today than they had in the west's ancient era of Greek and Roman city-states, in the Roman Empire, and in the Christian "Middle Ages." To many, the Enlightenment and the spread of modern commerce and industry seem to have produced "a world where the market is absolutely transcendental," globally interconnecting a species of "*homo oeconomicus*" (Schnapper, 1998, 4, 121; Ong, 1999, 7, 129). If economic goods are now what people care most about, then it may be possible to base enduring forms of political community essentially on the economic benefits they offer.

One can question how new this possibility is. Accounts designed to inspire political loyalty have always included promises of enhanced material welfare, in keeping with my claim that we can always find all three types of stories present in every time and place, though in different combinations. For example, in Thucydides's famed presentation of Pericles's

---

[6] Rachel L. Swarms, "Role in Group Enhances Mbeki's Image," *New York Times on the Web*, July 10, 2002, http://www.nytimes.com/2002/17/10/international/africa.

funeral oration, Athens's most powerful leader sought to inspire and in-struct his auditors, both "citizens and foreigners," by defining his city's "spirit...constitution and the way of life which has made us great." In so doing he indicated that "the greatness of our city brings it about that all the good things from all over the world flow in to us, so that it seems just as natural to enjoy foreign goods as our own local products." But despite this enticing promise of an exotic abundance of worldly goods, Pericles identified the true "greatness of Athens," with which he wanted his fellow citizens to "fall in love," as consisting not in "money making." Wealth was merely "something to be properly used," not "something to boast about." Athens's greatness was found instead in citizens' coura-geous achievement of "honor" and "the respect of one's fellow men" through law-abiding, public-spirited contributions to the democratic in-ternal life and international empire that he depicted as at the heart of the Athenian regime (1954, 145–147, 150).

Thus while there was certainly an economic theme present in his con-fident indication that Athenians could trust their regime to produce ma-terial prosperity, Pericles's story of peoplehood placed far more stress on the honorable worth of the political power that Athenians possessed, both as equal, dutiful democratic participants and as citizens of a glorious em-pire. Regardless of how accurately Thucydides depicted Pericles's words, this speech is a celebrated ancient example of the blending of a demo-cratic republican promise of personal power for each citizen with collec-tive imperial glory that modern leaders like Andrew Jackson, Theodore Roosevelt, Winston Churchill, and Charles de Gaulle would later exhibit in otherwise distinct forms.[7]

Although Pericles's oration does not ground Athenian membership on shared economic concerns, its emphasis on political power themes might still be thought to express a fundamentally "civic" conception of political community. Thucydides does not portray Pericles as explicitly invoking the Athenian ethically constitutive myth that we know to have been a favorite of the city's orators: the story of how all true Athenians were a superior stock, for their ancestors had sprung from seeds planted in the soil of Attica by the goddess Athena. That cherished myth had practical consequences. Though Athenian laws technically permitted marriages to

---

[7] See e.g. Rogin, 1975 (Jackson); Gerstle, 2001, 8–9 (Roosevelt); Blake and Louis, eds., 1996, 7–8 (Churchill). Jennifer Pitts (2000) has shown that even Alexis de Tocqueville, the great student of American Jacksonian Democracy, recommended imperialism in Algeria as a means to buttress liberal republicanism in France. Though de Gaulle came to accept an end to formal colonial empire, notably in Algeria, his similar ardent support both for a republican France (with a strong executive) and, especially, a France that still maintained "grandeur" on the world stage are legendary (e.g., Williams and Harrison, 1973, 103–104, 203–204, 424).

outsiders and naturalization, both were strongly discouraged. Perhaps the most concrete discouragement was a law proposed by Pericles himself in 451, requiring Athenian citizens to be sons of Athenians on their mother's as well as their father's side. The aim was to insure that all Athenian men could continue to be said to be "born of their own land and sharing in common a lineage of unsurpassed nobility," as Hyperides asserted in his own "Funeral Oration" (Ober, 1989, 80–81, 261–266). Thus not even Aristotle, a resident alien (or metic) from the Greek colony of Stagira, ever became a naturalized Athenian citizen (Barker, ed., 1968, xi).

And in the oration Thucydides presents, Pericles did articulate one vital corollary of this ethically constitutive myth. Like many modern champions of republican empires, he linked his imperial republican sense of honor to a patriarchal account of gender identities. In fact, Pericles contended that gallant civic service displayed the very "meaning of manliness" (1954, 148). His peroration made clear that this was no throw-away line. There he informed women that their "great glory is not to be inferior to what God has made you, and the greatest glory of a woman is to be least talked about by men, whether they are praising you or criticizing you" (151). An Athenian woman who rejected Athenian manly leadership by daring to marry outside the citizenry, contrary to the goal of Pericles' citizenship law, would surely be intensely criticized. Here, then, is a clear instance of how subordination of women to men, and attendant views of "manliness" as involving domination of women and martial virtue, helped to maintain a politically potent myth of kinship. Though Pericles' vision of peoplehood did contain an economic promise, its emphasis was plainly on a republican political power story, joined to a masculinist ethically constitutive story of honor and glory that served to reinforce a traditional "ethnic" conception of Athenian identity. That combination would have a long history in political thought and practice.[8]

As many recent writers have detailed, this blending of patriarchal conceptions of masculinity with republican nationalism has been especially visible in nineteenth- and early twentieth-century Europe, North America, and South America, nor is it absent today. In some ways, as George Mosse has argued, the disruptions wrought by the nineteenth-century industrial revolution as well as the spread of democracy may have led to heightened assertions of such gendered nationalism.[9] Still, there has indeed been a fundamental shift in western political thought away from a Periclean and Renaissance republican emphasis on male glory, and also away from the medieval emphasis on Christian virtue, as the

---

[8] For pertinent analyses see e.g. Kerber, 1980; Pitkin, 1984; Pateman, 1988.
[9] See e.g. Mosse, 1985; Bederman, 1995; Radcliffe and Westwood, 1996, 145–147.

reigning accounts of human worth. Since the eighteenth century, many modern republicans have increasingly given the role of political communities in promoting economic prosperity, usually via commerce, center stage in their civic visions. Albert Hirschman has suggested that this shift was produced in part as a conscious effort by seventeenth- and eighteenth-century elites to channel human passions into endeavors that were both materially productive and politically non-threatening. They did so, in his view, because commerce was already on the rise, but also because aristocratic preoccupations with male honor and glory had come to seem too politically disruptive, while religious notions of moral conduct seemed less able than commercial republicanism to restrain either aristocratic or economic vices (Hirschman, 1977).

Even if all this is correct, however, my framework is not challenged by conceding that economic promises have become far more prominent in most modern forms of the politics of people-making than they were in the rhetoric of Pericles. The pertinent question is whether political life has become so overwhelmingly a matter of economic calculations that political leaders can forego any substantial reliance on ethically constitutive appeals. There is little reason and less evidence to suggest that such is the case. For purposes of people-building, even modern economic stories have great drawbacks as well as great attractions.

From the standpoint of leaders, it remains risky to attempt to "sell" a vision of political community strictly in terms of its economic benefits. Inevitably, economic bad times will come, to some or many of their core constituents. If there appear to be better economic opportunities elsewhere, then those who have joined for material benefits alone will literally have no reason not to change allegiances. And from the standpoint of many constituents, in modern market societies there will always be some, and at times there may be many, who find a membership understood essentially as a matter of economic convenience not very satisfying, much less compelling. It is a familiar but fundamental fact that markets intrinsically generate substantially economic inequalities, even if everyone is willing to work hard (and never more so than today) (Ong, 1999, 11). This fact means that within a market society and across market societies, there will always be many living under economic conditions of comparative poverty, and often there are many who struggle to meet basic subsistence needs. Generally those conditions will do little to make less prosperous members feel worthy or to inspire in them great trust in their economic and political order. Instead, those on the lower rungs of liberal economic ladders may experience their market societies as cruel, lonely arenas of competitive self-seeking in which they are branded losers, the "unfit." Even more affluent members may find life in such societies crassly

materialistic and alienating. Its lionizing of economic acquisition can foster a destructive ethos of unbridled greed among elites and constituents
alike. Yet efforts to combat market inequalities through redistributive
forms of social assistance can only go so far before they are perceived,
quite reasonably, to threaten overall prosperity, growth, and economic
freedoms (Smith, 1994, 635–639, 660; 1997, 37).

   For these reasons and more, innumerable social analysts have long
doubted that economic benefits alone can be enough to bond political
societies. Just as aristocracy was beginning to give way to modern commercial republicanism, Edmund Burke famously argued that a political
community "ought not to be considered as nothing better than a partnership agreement in a trade of pepper and coffee, callico or tobacco, or some
other such low concern . . . it is not a partnership in things subservient
only to the gross animal existence of a temporary and perishable nature"
(Burke, 1968, 194). In a similar spirit, today Dominique Schnapper insists that "Mere participation in the same economic and social system is
not sufficient to unite men" (1998, 166). These are, moreover, not only
the complaints of intellectuals. However great the shift in the direction of
making economic values central to political life, it is difficult to find even
recent examples of successful efforts to craft enduring forms of political
community based solely on economic appeals.

   Yitzhak Brudny argues, for instance, that as the Soviet Union fell,
Russian liberals sought to gain power by relying too exclusively on
a narrative devoted to "the power of market economy to raise living
standards." That strategy left them with little recourse when economic
reforms wrought hardships, and when their rivals were offering more stirring ethnically tinged, imperial, and nationalist visions of Russia's future
(2001, 19–20). Florencia Mallon similarly contends that nineteenth-
century nation-building elites in Mexico and Peru devoted themselves too
exclusively to economically "liberal" agendas, buttressed only by brute
force, instead of embracing compatible aspects of popular culture. As a
result, they could not achieve "consolidation" of their national projects.
Mexican national leaders, she contends, have had more success than
Peruvians in the twentieth century only because they have gone further
in addressing these failings, in still-controversial and incomplete ways
to which we will turn shortly (1995, 247–248). The point here is that,
though economic stories may be more politically central today than when
Thucydides wrote, they still do not appear to be sufficient to sustain a
successful politics of people-building.

   Perhaps, however, their limitations can be overcome simply by com-
bining them with the sorts of political power stories that historical trends
have also brought to prominence – the stirring narratives championing

democracy or egalitarian republicanism as means to provide greater personal security, governmental accountability, and collective power than feudal or monarchical systems did. Again, the reality of those trends cannot be disputed. When Sir Edward Coke, Chief Justice of the Court of Common Pleas, defined the allegiance of the subject of King James I of England in *Calvin's Case* in 1608, for instance, he could employ accounts of peoplehood not so dramatically different from those of ancient Judah's King Josiah. Coke, too, defined political memberships and statuses chiefly in terms of divine as well as natural laws, "written with the finger of God in the heart of man," and first reported, he asserted, by Moses in his books. Coke's opinion suggested that these laws, if obeyed, would surely lead to peace, security, and prosperity – but regardless of whether they conferred such benefits, they had to be obeyed.

The pageantry at James's recent coronation as king of England and Wales as well as Scotland had also celebrated a further ethically constitutive story, although in *Calvin's Case* Coke barely alluded to this account. James was said to be the direct heir of King Arthur, mythologized by Geoffrey of Monmouth in the twelfth century as England's greatest king, supposedly descended from the Trojan founder of Britain, Brutus, and most importantly for James's purposes, a previous unifier of all Britain under one throne. James, then, was a "second Arthur." Coke said little about this beloved royalist historical legend, because though he supported James's claim to a unified monarchy, he also favored legal limits on royal authority, which his court would define. He did note the existence of a form of "legal ligeance" expressed in a leet oath "first instituted by King Arthur"; but he made clear that this oath only articulated the more fundamental kind of allegiance, "ligeance natural, absolute . . . due by nature and birth-right," made law by God but interpreted by Edward Coke.[10] No king, much less any "people," could alter these obligations.

It was these sorts of ethically constitutive stories, used to sanctify repressive monarchies, with which the American and French revolutionaries broke so dramatically when they proclaimed that legitimate governments derived their just powers not from natural or divine birthrights but from the consent of the governed. They thereby sought to substitute a democratic political power story, along with other elements, in place of the sorts of religious and naturalistic constitutive accounts that had underwritten absolutist monarchies.[11] By the 1830s, Alexis de Tocqueville

---

[10] *Calvin's Case*, 7 Coke's Reports 1a, 7b, 13a (1697; orig. 1608); Pocock, 1967, 40–41, 56; MacDougall, 1982, 22–24.

[11] As previously noted, Paine invoked a different view of the law of nature as well as the Old Testament to insist that God preferred republican governments to monarchy; and Thomas Jefferson, the author of the Declaration's interpretation of the law of "nature's God," also insisted that true Americans were descended from republican Saxons, not monarchist sons of some Trojan Brutus (Smith, 1997, 40–48, 73–75).

saw the trend toward democracy thus inaugurated as an "irresistible revolution," already "too strong to be halted," though it could still be constructively channeled (1969, 12). Today many scholars believe that, as Ian Shapiro has contended, "democracy has won the day in the sense that it has no serious political competitor in the modern world" (1996, 2). It seems possible to hope, then, that this widespread consensus on the propriety of reasonably egalitarian political processes can now make essentially civic "political power" stories of democratic or republican citizenship sufficient to sustain political communities, especially if they are reinforced by attractive economic appeals.

But here again, both theoretical analyses and historical evidence give us ample room for doubts. From the standpoint of leaders, democratic republicanism imposes demands to win popular approval over one's opponents that can often be burdensome. Those burdens create great temptations to manipulate or ignore democratic procedures while winning support on other grounds. And often, foregoing any genuine reliance on democracy has worked. From First Consul Bonaparte to Louisiana's Governor Huey Long to President Robert Mugabe in Zimbabwe today, it has often been possible for ambitious leaders to achieve near-absolute power in titularly republican or democratic societies, at least for a time, by extending plausible promises to secure glory, wealth, or cultural pride for their supporters. The 2000 American presidential election also showed that "even" in America, contemporary democratic electorates may not be particularly disturbed by revelations that their machinery for accurate democratic decision-making is substantially faulty, and that a candidate not preferred by most voters can still be elected.

From the standpoint of the citizenry, this willingness not to insist too strongly on conformity to democratic republicanism is in many ways understandable. As Rousseau's esteem for Sparta and Geneva showed, republican principles can in theory inspire excessive regimentation of the citizenry along with contemptuous hostility toward non-citizens. Critics contend that French culturally assimilationist "republican" policies have long done just that in practice.[12] In any case, republican civic precepts often impose rather high expectations on people for intense civic participation and sacrifices for the community. And especially in large-scale modern democratic republics, most people find the costs of trying to gain real political efficacy too great to pay; yet they quite reasonably doubt that the routine exercise of their republican voting rights really does much to direct their governments. As a result of this "democratic deficit," few modern citizens gain really strong senses of either security or

---

[12] Maxim Silverman (1992) has gone so far as to deem French "cultural absolutism" a form of racism.

pride from engaging in republican activities of self-governance. Instead, laments about mounting civic apathy abound.[13] Probably the most that we can say about democracy today is that the political and bureaucratic elites who effectively govern most of the time do so under institution-alized influences of popular opinion that make them more constrained than despots (Dahl, 1989, 113–114). That is certainly worthwhile; but it is evidently, and understandably, not enough to sustain political societies on the basis of commitments to their "civic" democratic principles alone.

And in fact, even the most ardent advocates of modern economic and political power stories of "civic" membership have never really treated them as sufficient, either in themselves or in combination. The truth is that, even when economic and political power themes have been more prominent, certain sorts of ethically constitutive stories of humanity's intrinsic moral identity have always been used to provide philosophic underpinnings for liberal, republican, and social democratic political visions. John Locke argued that human rights stemmed from the fact that we are God's property; Immanuel Kant, that liberal rights and republicanism flowed from our characteristics as intrinsically rational creatures. According to Hannah Arendt and J. G. A. Pocock, other republican theorists since Aristotle have often suggested that through civic political participation, human beings realize essential aspects of their identities and may have their best chance for a kind of immortality. That is why both the American and French revolutionaries could proclaim that their quest to create new republics was also "the cause of all mankind." For more than a century, moreover, at least some democratic socialists have seen themselves as advancing a Marxian vision in which human beings become what they are through their relationships to the means of production, which can be made freely and consciously self-productive. And though modern liberals have generally followed John Rawls in asserting that moral commitments to seeing ourselves as free and equal persons are simply imbedded in our community values, no one denies that it is from such historical religious and philosophic sources that they came to be so imbedded.[14]

But while modern liberalism, republicanism, and socialism have all rested on various sorts of "ethically constitutive" narratives, so that even conceptions of "civic" nationhood must be seen as always embodying

---

[13] See e.g. Barbara Crossette, "U.N. Report Says New Democracies Falter," *The New York Times on the Web*, http://www.nytimes.com/2002/07/24/international, July 24, 2002; Dahl, 1992, 47–51; Sandel, 1996; Schnapper, 1998, 1, 4, 159, 169.

[14] Arendt, 1958; Mendel, ed., 1961, 13–44; Kant, 1965, 21–30, 111–14; Locke, 1965, 311; Paine, 1967, 402; Pocock, 1975; Brubaker, 1992, 44; Rawls, 1993a. These issues are thoughtfully probed in Berkowitz, 2002. See also Smith, 1999, 22–26.

economic, political power, *and* ethically constitutive stories, it is still not clear that actual nations must be "ethnic" as well as "civic." The religious, rationalist, republican, and socialist ethically constitutive stories of thinkers like Locke, Kant, Rousseau, and Marx are all often termed "universalistic." They present themselves, at least initially, as applying to all human beings. All are God's children; all are entitled to basic human rights; all have the moral worth that at least minimally rational nature bestows; all have the potential to achieve self-realization through republican participation or the free, collective production of each and all. And since, in principle, these stories encompass all humanity, they do not have the divisive particularism of "ethnic" political conceptions.

Here, moreover, "civic" advocates might find hope in the fact that these universalistic ethically constitutive stories represent a major change from ancient western cultures, a transformation perhaps even more fundamental than the other types of stories have undergone. Probably most significant has been the spread of constitutive accounts that are not only universalistic but also more egalitarian, first in the form of universalistic, monotheistic religions like Judaism, Christianity, and Islam, then in more secular philosophic and scientific accounts of human existence, from Kant's noumena to Sartre's self-defining existential beings. These more egalitarian, universalistic perspectives may seem, again individually or in combination, to provide a basis for more inclusive, indeed cosmopolitan forms of politics that do not center on particularistic identities, ideologies, or communities.

To be sure, today even the willingness to include all humanity is insufficient to justify a claim to true "universalism." Philosophers and political activists alike make cogent cases that we need to justify giving preference to humanity over, at least, the more sentient species of animals, if not all the other living members of our ecosystems. Depending on whether and how we can do so, a "species-ist" attachment to humanity may still appear to be only our preferred "ethnicity" among living things. It is likely that such moral challenges to "homo-centric" thinking will increase in the years ahead.

Even for those who do not find those challenges compelling, it remains true that, analytically, the distinction between more "universalistic" and "particularistic" narratives is a thin one. All doctrines defining and valorizing membership in a particular political community or "people" are implicitly also "universalistic." They all suggest characterizations of everyone who is not seen as part of that "people," even if their account amounts to little more than saying that all outsiders are "barbarians" or "savages" or "primitives" or the "unchosen" (Wade, 2001, 848–849). And despite the very real rise of more egalitarian forms of moral universalism, we will see that such hierarchical doctrines are still alive today in many forms, including racial, cultural, and religious ones.

But if the distinction between "universalistic" and "particularistic" conceptions can be disputed, there remains a crucial substantive difference between "universalistic" doctrines that are egalitarian, that deem all human beings to have some real worth, and doctrines that deny any real value to many millions of people. Yet even this distinction only goes so far in practice, because all types of "universalistic" stories often operate politically as partisan ones. The main reason that proponents of conceptions of "civic" nationhood do not explicitly endorse any single supporting ethically constitutive story is that they cannot agree on one. The proponents of Locke's universalistic, individualistic natural rights obviously clashed sharply with early twentieth-century Communist advocates of collective self-realization through dictatorship by an international proletariat. Political projects shaped by two equally "universalistic" religions, Christianity and Islam, have sparked violent struggles for more than a millennium (Armstrong, 1982, 90–91, 165). Many such contrasts could be drawn. Due to these conflicts, even such "universalistic" political visions have had to be pursued in practice through particular communities, distinctive coalitions of constituencies who can be brought to embrace the basic ways of life and endeavors the vision valorizes. And this need to have *particular* communities who serve as bearers of more "universalistic" ideologies has always created, in turn, a need for leaders to incorporate into their visions of peoplehood accounts or stories explaining why it is ethically right for those particular communities and their constituents to play that role.

Once even a morally egalitarian and universalistic ethically constitutive story becomes embroiled in the politics of people-building, then, once it becomes an argument for membership in one political people and not others, that story tends to become a more particularistic one capable of justifying certain subordinations and exclusions that can be quite vicious. We may all be children of God or moral agents, but still there may seem to be something dramatically wrong with those who are not with us. That something may give us less reason to trust them or to believe in their genuinely equal intrinsic worth. Even if we accept their moral equality, their intense, perhaps militant opposition to what we believe in most may still make us feel that, sadly, we are morally compelled to make them conform to what we genuinely believe to be right. Many would-be leaders remain likely to exploit such reasoning, employing universalistic stories to try to win support for certain forceful courses of action against their rivals. Others may share the sense that the moral imperatives of their community demand violent resistance to those who threaten it or otherwise stand in its way. These leaders, to be sure, may present the particular form of political community they are advocating, whether it is a religious organization, a social movement, a state, or some other body, as only instrumental to the realization of values that are ultimately appropriate for all humanity; and they may in fact devoutly believe this to be true. I will also suggest later that such instrumental views of the value of particular memberships may well be normatively desirable in several respects. It is, however, no guarantee that these religious groups, social movements, or states will not display all the ills associated with "ethnic" nations.

I do not mean to deny that egalitarian religious and moral themes can be used to challenge the invidious potential of particularistic senses of membership. We should prize this potential highly. Yet in light of the political policies of religious persecution, racial and gender subjugation, and genocide that long prevailed in modern societies with monotheistic religious and Enlightenment-influenced moral traditions, especially in the twentieth century, it is hard to place full faith in this potential. It does not seem plausible to assert that the dangers of the politics of people-building are inevitably muted by the rise of more universalistic and more egalitarian ethically constitutive doctrines in western religious and political thought. It instead seems incontrovertibly true that political leaders and potential constituents will often still seek to define grounds for holding that allegiance should really go to more particular, often substantively disturbing forms of political community, whatever broader or even universal purposes those communities are felt to serve.

And precisely because they are abstract theories that present memberships as matters of contract or other forms of choice, theoretically "pure" forms of liberalism, republicanism, and social democracy are too voluntaristic and "universalistic" to be able to provide such particularistic accounts. Their inner logic tends strongly to point to the creation of some global, cosmopolitan form of political community; for it is difficult to find grounds in them to exclude any who can claim human rights or capacities for democratic self-governance (Ackerman, 1980, 88; Scheffler, 2001, 70–76). In any case, liberal, republican, and democratic theories do not by themselves define the "people" who are to self-govern consensually. They also do not indicate where that people should live and why. And if there should be many regimes with strong "civic" elements, they cannot provide anything more than instrumental arguments as to why individuals should prefer one liberal society, republic, or social democracy over another. Finally, they do not provide much guidance on the proper political processes for deciding such questions.[15]

[15] See e.g. Gray, 1992, 1995; Smith, 1994, 662; Singer, 1995; Yack, 1996.

To be sure, most contemporary civic conceptions treat democratic processes as ultimately authoritative. Yet however much we esteem democratic ideals, they do not help us much with the problem of defining who gets to participate in those processes (Dahl, 1989, 139, 146–147; Yack, 2001, 522–524, 529). Ian Shapiro and others have suggested an intuitively plausible "principle of affected interests" for decision-making, according to which all persons who have significant stakes in the issues in question, but no one else, would be entitled to participation in their resolution (Shapiro, 1999, 38–39). But in an increasingly interconnected world, what issues are really in question, and who really has stakes in them, are often terribly difficult to determine. We are quickly led into controversies over who gets to participate in making *those* determinations. These circumstances set up a problem of infinite regress in which we can always challenge the breadth of participation in whatever decision-making procedure has defined a particular electorate. In response, at the logical cosmopolitan extreme, one can imagine a democratic solution to the problems of political boundaries through some sort of recurring worldwide referendum in which people would choose their political communities in the way university students sometimes choose their housing. But if such a system were ever to exist, it undoubtedly would not be itself the product of democratic processes, nor could it realize anything more than the most minimal form of democratic decision-making. The scale would be too vast. As a practical matter, then, appeals to democratic principles to resolve boundary questions are not as likely to provide clear answers as they are to spur a politics of people-building that will be contested extensively via different means and different ideological themes, not by democratic procedures and values alone.

The fact that liberalism, republicanism, and social democratic perspectives cannot generate answers to these questions that are purely internal to their theories need not be and has not been politically paralyzing. Even as theories, all these viewpoints can coherently support certain *alliances* with more motivating particularistic notions of peoplehood under some conditions. The "civic" contentions that memberships and governments are in fact artificial, and that they should somehow originate in the revocable consent of the governed, do not preclude choosing to construct "civic" nations among groups to which people feel allegiance for a variety of reasons that do not stem from liberalism, republican, or social democratic principles directly (Schuck and Smith, 1985, 9–41). If persons wish to join with those with whom they share kinship ties, religious traditions, a particular language, history, culture, or territory, such embraces of more particularistic conceptions of peoplehood are perfectly permissible – so long, that is, as violations of human rights or democratic precepts do not result.

This crucial proviso is, admittedly, a huge one, rarely if ever met in practice, for reasons that include the exclusionary and subordinating pressures
generated by the politics of people-making. It is in fact unclear whether
we can avoid constructing a world divided into particular societies in ways
that do not involve unjust global inequalities. Still, at the level of theory,
one can imagine liberal republican societies that are linked to particular
historical identities, but that constantly endeavor to respect the personal
and political rights of all. If we could construct a world consisting of many
such societies living in peaceful, non-exploitative relations with each other
(admittedly a very open question), it might well be defensibly just. Moreover, Will Kymlicka has argued powerfully in recent years that liberal and
republican conceptions of deliberative self-governance logically presuppose the existence of particular cultural identities that endow people with
the cognitive resources and psychological motivations for such deliberation. Hence egalitarian liberal and republican theories provide grounds
for giving moral weight to the preservation of such identities, again so long
as they operate in ways that are not sharply illiberal or anti-republican
(Kymlicka, 1989, 1995).

And far more than modern liberals, who have prized opportunities for
the development of distinctive forms of individuality, republican theorists have long added that viable democratic republics need considerable homogeneity among their citizens. In the era of the French and
American Revolutions, widely read works by writers such as Montesquieu
and Rousseau argued that similarity in ethnicity, gender, economic status, and cultural traditions all fostered the sense of "common interest"
among the citizenry that republics need to sustain an ethic of civic virtue.
Most versions of republicanism prior to the late twentieth century particularly stressed, like Pericles, that republican citizenship demanded martial virtues and civic spiritedness of a sort that only men displayed, so
that women could be appropriately confined to the republic's domestic
spheres. Those arguments have been so deeply imbedded in the rise of
modern republics that, though it is possible to disentangle them from
egalitarian republicanism as an "ideal type," in practice the maintenance
of republican virtues has most often been tied to highly inegalitarian,
patriarchal understandings of masculinity and femininity.[16]

I have argued that in the American context, republican arguments for
homogeneity also helped foster an alliance between republicanism and
racial, nativist, and religious exclusionary impulses throughout US history (Smith, 1997, 84–85). As previously noted, this potential of republican arguments is visible in French political development as well, including

---

[16] Montesquieu, 1949, I, 20–21, 37, 69, 96, 138, II, 30–31, 52; Rousseau, 1973, 40,
358–63; Kerber, 1980.

recent debates over nationality reforms, even if French abuses have fallen short of the extremes of American racism (Nicolet, 1982; Silverman, 1992; Favell, 1998; Feldblum, 1999, 71–76; Weil, 2002). Thus it has always been easy in theory as well as in practice to combine republicanism, even more than "liberalism," with more particularistic conceptions of constitutive identities; though the results have rarely been fully consistent with principles of human rights.

Both liberalism and republicanism, then, not only presuppose more universalistic ethically constitutive stories, but they also can be and have been allied, politically if not always logically, with other ethically constitutive stories advancing particularistic conceptions of political identity. Yet profound, vital, and indeed inescapable as those particularistic political alliances have been, at the level of theoretical principle they still remain merely instrumental. Advocates of liberal and republican principles in different times and places must connect their causes with some prevalent senses of local identity, religious, ethnic, cultural, or others; but those senses will vary, whereas the essential liberal and republican precepts are supposed to stay the same. Hence the historical associations of liberalism, republicanism, and democracy with different national identities do not prove the sufficiency of consensual "civic" principles for peoplehood. Instead, they underline again the need to combine liberal and democratic elements with stories of peoplehood that are not fundamentally "civic" at all.

Admittedly, these more particularistic ethically constitutive stories still need not be "ethnic" in the narrow sense of involving doctrines of shared kinship, though a great many will be. Linguistic, historical, religious, or cultural accounts that make no claim of shared ancestry may sometimes suffice, as in Quebec today, which seeks to make French-speaking, but not French descent, central to Quebec identity (Kymlicka, 1998, 96). Still, most writers who have employed the "civic/ethnic" distinction emphatically place linguistic, cultural, and all other particularistic identities that do not simply express principles of political procedure on the "ethnic" side (e.g. Greenfeld, 1992, 12; Ignatieff, 1994, 6–7, 249; Hollinger, 1995, 137). If it is correct that politics continues to pressure all leaders to advance particularistic ethically constitutive stories as dimensions of their visions of peoplehood, then, it also remains true that we will be able to see what many term "ethnic" elements in virtually all, if not all, political societies. That is why it seems advisable to eschew categorizing existing political communities as fundamentally "civic" or "ethnic," "liberal" or "republican" or "democratic." We should instead adopt alternative frameworks that can provide a place for all the dimensions of peoplehood that we can expect to find empirically, as I seek to do here.

The distinctive contributions of ethically constitutive stories

I nonetheless wish to underline that, even if economic and political power stories are not sufficient to promote enduring senses of trust and worth in visions of peoplehood, any such alternative framework must give a primary place to the many ways they contribute to doing so. I simply cannot give them the attention they merit here. A short book cannot do everything, and I assume that not much elaboration is required to indicate why successful political stories need to assure constituents that, at a minimum, their basic economic needs will be met, and that they will have sufficient power to be relatively safe from violence and arbitrary rule. It should also not be hard to see how and why people have so often responded passionately to efforts to mobilize them against economic exploitation and political subjugation. Still, a careful analysis of the role of such endeavors must be central in any full-scale analysis of projects of people-formation. I hope the narrower focus here on ethically constitutive narratives will not obscure the reality that those stories never form the whole substance of any widely embraced ideology of political membership, and only sometimes are they predominant. Whatever the limitations of civic conceptions like liberalism, republicanism, and social democracy, economic and political power stories of these and other kinds are still often the most visible components of quite successful people-building endeavors.

For example, as the discussion in Chapter 1 suggested, the accounts of American peoplehood in Thomas Paine's "Common Sense" and the Declaration of Independence do indeed stress the sorts of economic and political power themes that have tempted scholars to classify the US as a "civic" nation. Both "Common Sense" and the Declaration primarily offer negative stories fomenting economic and political distrust of Britain. They detail grievances over the heinous misdeeds of King George, accused of "scarcely paralleled" acts of "Tyranny . . . Cruelty and Perfidy" in the Declaration (Ver Steeg and Hofstadter, eds., 1969, 471), labeled "the Royal Brute" by Paine (1967, 418). But both also offer inviting, positive stories of economic and political worth, in several ways. Each suggests prominently that Americans will prosper far more economically and possess more political power, as citizens and as a people, if they gain independence and establish a liberal republic, a commercial regime with protections for individual rights and government by consent of the governed. Similarly, the Soviet Union was obviously founded both by force and by appeals to an ideology that made ending economic injustices, enhancing prosperity on an egalitarian basis, and extending political power to the proletariat the dominant themes. Though I do not think the US, the USSR, or any other society should be viewed as a fundamentally "civic" nation, I agree wholeheartedly that to a considerable degree, the Declaration and Paine offered accounts of peoplehood that inspired trust and worth primarily in liberal republican economic and political power terms, while Lenin and his comrades emphasized Marxist socialist economic and political power themes.

The fact remains, however, that those terms did not appear sufficient and almost certainly could not have been sufficient to enable either political project to succeed. That is why the Declaration of Independence's authors, like Paine, invoked other standards for legitimacy, promising that Americans would win recognition for their "sacred honor" by seeking independence, and that "divine Providence" would sustain American efforts (Ver Steeg and Hofstadter, eds., 1969, 472; Paine, 1967, 424). These promises invoked older martial and, especially, Protestant Christian stories of worth that were probably needed to fire up support for such a dangerous enterprise. Yet there was still more to their accounts of peoplehood. Each also depicted, albeit more briefly, who Americans were by blood and descent, making clear that they were not, in Paine's words, either "the Indians" or "the Negroes" (435), but rather the kinsmen of Europeans.

True, these exclusions were not trumpeted in either text; and some free blacks as well as former tribesmembers were recognized as citizens in some of the colonies. Those facts only make our question more pointed, however: why did these early American leaders need to deploy such exclusionary language at all? After all, the revolutionaries hoped to get as broad a base of support as possible. That is one reason why Paine insisted that all of Europe, not just England, was parent to America, and why the Declaration complained of King George obstructing "the Naturalization of Foreigners" (Paine, 1967, 421; Ver Steeg and Hofstadter, eds., 1969, 470). They were, moreover, defining and defending their revolution partly in terms of its service to greater recognition of basic rights for all humanity. Why exclude some humans who were also potential constituents?

The obvious answer is that the revolutionaries had to take both the economic interests and the cultural identities of their core constituents into account. They would have lost far more support than they would have gained if they did not clearly indicate their partisanship to the colonists in their many disputes with the native tribes whose lands Europeans coveted. Though both Paine and Jefferson elsewhere opposed chattel servitude, Paine's pamphlet and the Declaration also could not have succeeded in their work if they had directly challenged slavery. Hence an ethically constitutive story of true Americans as European-descended men formed a crucial, if not an especially highlighted, part of their people-building enterprise, intertwined with contrasting if not contradictory narratives that portrayed Americans as champions of self-government and human rights. Then, muted though they were in these seminal documents, these particulars of American people-building – the need to define membership in some ways expansively, as including all of European descent and serving the rights of all mankind, and in other ways narrowly, as excluding tribespeople and Africans whose lands and labors Europeans wanted and whose religions and cultures they disdained – mattered enormously. They provided the context for the elaboration of explicitly racial constitutive stories in the new nation, and also for their contestation. As a result, the US has been not only the land of commerce and dollar bills and not only the cradle of democracy and personal liberties, profound as those features are. It has also been a patriarchal land, an overwhelming Christian land, and perhaps most of all, the land of some of the world's most epic struggles over slavery and white supremacy.

In the case of the Soviet Union, Lenin was bitterly disappointed during World War I when workers in the "oppressing nations" displayed on the whole more loyalty to those countries than to the emerging international socialist movement; but he also came to accept the political potency of ethnic nationalism. It became one of the "basic principles of Leninism," as the Fifth Comintern Congress of the Executive Committee of the Communist International proclaimed in 1924, that Communists engage in "resolute and constant advocacy" of "the right of national self-determination (secession and the formation of an independent State)."[17] Lenin himself seems to have hoped that these concessions to ethnic nationalism would be transcended in time, but instead the political blending of Communist economic stories with ethnic conceptions only deepened.

Within the Soviet Union itself, the alliance of Communism with nationalism eventually took the form of an elaborate four-tiered structure of national territories, headed by the fifteen "Union Republics," each of which was named for what was conceived to be its "rooted" or "titular" ethnic nationality (like Kyrgyzstan). Most had policies of preferential treatment for members of that nationality. By 1989, below those units were twenty less powerful "autonomous republics," eight "autonomous regions," and ten "autonomous districts," creating fifty-three distinct national territories. Soviet citizens also were assigned personal nationalities, stated on their internal passports, which usually corresponded with the nationality of the territory in which they resided but which was based on descent (regardless of a person's self-identification, as the passports

---

[17] Connor, 1994, 156–158, citing Degras, ed., 1960, II, 106; Laitin, 1998, 45–49.

were instruments of centralized control). Despite the overwhelmingly economic character of its state ideology, then, the Union of Soviet Socialist Republics was also institutionalized, stabilized, and in the eyes of some analysts, eventually eroded extensively through alliances with cultural, historical, linguistic, and often overtly ethnic conceptions of sub-state national identities.[18]

If we accept, then, that economic and political power stories are always necessary and often dominant but never sufficient to sustain a political community – not even in the capitalist constitutional democracy of the US, not even in the Communist, vanguard-led USSR – just what is it that ethically constitutive stories provide that the other stories do not? The analysis so far has suggested two answers that merit some elaboration, and those elaborations lead to a third.

The first answer is that ethically constitutive stories can support claims of particularistic community memberships more effectively than economic or political power accounts, such as liberal commercial or democratic republican stories. Particularistic stories are often attractive to leaders and constituents alike, because everyone in both categories is endowed with economic and power interests, inherited identities, and religious, cultural, and political ideologies that put them in tension, often stark and bitter opposition, to many others, just as many American colonists felt themselves to be in opposition to British ruling authorities, French Catholics in Canada, their own slaves, and the native tribes. Most people are therefore likely to perceive real advantages in conceptions of political membership that promise to protect and promote their distinctive interests, identities, and values against their rivals. Even leaders without enthusiasm for those conceptions may feel compelled to incorporate them into their political projects, as both Paine and Lenin did in different ways.

It is not immediately obvious, however, that ethically constitutive stories can play this "particularizing" role so much better than economic and political power ones. The American revolutionaries used a commercial vision of greater mobility in a new American society to make it seem more compelling than the more stagnant class structure of Britain. Fidel Castro, in turn, has long advanced a Communist vision for Cuba promising greater economic equity and security than capitalist America provides, and at least some Americans as well as Cubans have embraced it. Similarly, North and South Korea today, North and South Vietnam and East and West Germany in the past, have partly used political power stories of either rule via a proletarian party or via a liberal democratic system to defend the legitimacy and desirability of their particular political

---

[18] Brubaker, 1996, 26–35; Laitin, 1998, xiv, 45–49; Brudny, 2002, 5.

communities against their co-ethnic national rivals. And even if I am right to suggest that liberal and republican theories give us no intrinsic reason to prefer one true liberal republic over another, in practice both differences in resources and relatively minor differences in institutional structures can make some communities comparatively choiceworthy on purely economic or political power grounds.[19] For example, though their origins are linked to very different choices made by North American colonists concerning whether or not to remain part of the British Empire, for several decades now the United States and Canada have both been fundamentally liberal democracies with market economies. Even so, America's much greater economic resources and opportunities have long attracted many immigrants from Canada, while Canada's more extensive social support systems, lesser racial violence, and comparatively less militant republicanism have at times drawn Americans north. Economic and political power stories, then, can in certain times and places articulate the particularistic visions that both leaders and constituents often seek.

It is also true that ethically constitutive stories are not necessarily "particularistic" in ways that can easily serve the purposes of, especially, power-seeking elites. Some, as I have noted, are universalistic, or at least applicable to all humanity. That means they must be elaborated in particularistic ways if such stories are to explain why membership in a specific people is justified. Why did faith in the Protestant God, for example, imply that of all Protestant peoples, the British of the seventeenth, eighteenth, and nineteenth centuries were entitled to celebrate themselves as "another and a better Israel" (Colley, 1992, 30)? Britons had to strain to "find" answers within Protestantism alone. And even more overtly particularistic ideologies, like racial ones, can present similar difficulties. They rarely map precisely on to the sorts of political boundaries leaders can feasibly seek to draw. Why did membership in the "people" of the "yellow" race support allegiance to a sovereign China, as many early twentieth-century anti-imperialist intellectuals and reformers like Sun Yat-sen and Zhang Binglin argued, rather than to a broader regional identity encompassing much of East Asia? Why did it justify overthrowing the Manchu in favor of the more "pure yellow" Hanzu population, while still including other non-Hanzu groups (Dikötter, 1997, 4, 6, 9, 13; Chow, 2001, 54–63, 74–76)? Again, aspiring elites had to modify prevalent racial doctrines before they could be used to support their preferred

---

[19] Rawls, 1999, argues similarly: "Even when two or more peoples have liberal constitutional regimes, their conceptions of constitutionalism may diverge and express different variations of liberalism" (11) – though Rawls does not discuss the possibility that at times these differences can play into political competitions for the allegiance of at least some constituents.

political conclusions. They did so, but in the process they often provided nettlesome openings for adversaries to turn these racial ethically constitutive stories to their own rhetorical advantage.

Even so, ethically constitutive accounts remain better suited to promote particularistic senses of membership than economic or political power themes, for they alone present membership in a particular community as somehow intrinsic to who a person is. A membership that is presented as appropriate because it confers certain economic advantages and political powers remains something that is essentially outside a person's identity. Rationally, it remains a membership that should be embraced only insofar and so long as it confers the economic and power benefits it promises more abundantly than any concretely available alternative. In contrast, an ethically constitutive story presents membership as profoundly expressive of something very basic to the members' identities – their heritage and place in a meaningful larger order, whether divine, natural, historical, or cultural. However much ethically constitutive accounts may have to be manipulated to support particularistic memberships, once these stories are accepted, they make that specific political identity something that cannot easily be abandoned unless its members radically reject and revise their understandings of who they are. For most people, it is much harder to make those kinds of changes than it is to conclude that there is more money to be made or rights to be had by redefining their allegiances. Hence as long as human beings find themselves wishing to define, embrace, and defend compelling particularistic identities – even their identities as a special species – they are likely to construct ethically constitutive stories.

But the question still nags: just what provides the "compelling" character of these accounts, if it is not wealth or power or both? It cannot be *simply* that constitutive stories express core features of personal identities. Our identities usually contain many deeply rooted features that we do not particularly value or that we actively dislike. That may be true even of the characteristics depicted in ethically constitutive narratives. But it is not likely to be – precisely because those stories have ethical content. This is the second reason that such stories play distinctive political roles: they present the traits they emphasize as things having tremendous, often priceless ethical worth. To believe one's self to be a beloved child of God or a member of a superior race or the descendant of heroic ancestors or the bearer of a brilliant culture is to have a firm basis for a sense of meaning, place, purpose, and pride.

Many people do, of course, derive such senses from riches and from possessing political dominion over others. But in and of themselves, personal wealth and political power are rarely depicted as ethically or morally good; even in pre-Christian eras their pursuit was often depicted as corrupting or destructive, as in the fable of Midas's golden touch. In any case, most people simply cannot claim that they have obtained great riches or high political status. It doubtless is and should be disturbing to many contemporary sensibilities to hear some constitutive stories, particularly accounts claiming racial superiority, described as "ethical." Straightforward thirst for lucre may seem comparatively desirable, especially if we believe that in market systems, "greed is good." Yet however perverse it may seem, the reality is that those who have deployed racialist theories for purposes of political people-building have always portrayed their preferred races as morally meritorious, as playing primary roles in advancing the purposes of God, nature, reason, history, and often the interests of all humanity.

For example, Edward Wilmot Blyden, the Liberian educator who was a founder of black nationalist and Afrocentric thought, contended in the late nineteenth century that if the distinctive "African personality" of the "Negro" race were fully developed in all its "God-given" individuality, it would contribute more communal, cooperative, and profoundly spiritual qualities than humanity would otherwise achieve (Conyers, 1999, 82–84, 197–98). José Vasconcelos, the Mexican philosopher who headed his country's new Ministry of Education in the early 1920s, similarly contended that the *mestizaje* or mixed race population of Mexico could make distinctively valuable contributions to the "species," because "hybridism in man, as well as in plants, tends to produce better types and tends to rejuvenate types that have become static" (Vasconcelos, 1926, 20, 85). Chinese intellectuals like Zhang Binglin and the Japanese *toyoshi* historians of the early twentieth century all claimed that their peoples had been destined by evolution and divine providence to lead the struggle of the yellow races against white imperialism and save true civilization (Chow, 2001, 67–74). And many late nineteenth-century American advocates of imperial expansion and immigration restriction, like Senator Henry Cabot Lodge, contended that "our race," the Anglo-Saxon, had superior "mental and moral qualities" which could be lost only if "a lower race mixes with a higher in sufficient numbers" (Smith, 1997, 364–365). In the ethically constitutive accounts of all these figures, racial identity was intrinsic to moral identity and worth, and all members of the higher race could claim this distinction automatically.

Ethically constitutive stories thus put forth very strong claims. How can people tell if they are true? The answer is that we really cannot; and that answer reveals the third and perhaps least obvious source of the unique role that ethically constitutive accounts play in the politics of people-building. By and large, ethically constitutive narratives are less subject to tangible evidence than economic or political power stories, particularly in regard to the forms of moral worth that they promise to provide. This characteristic makes them frustrating to many social scientists, but alluring to many aspiring political leaders and potential constituents.

Admittedly, people are often ignorant of the larger economic structures of their society and their places in them, and comparisons with their immediate peers may lead them to believe they are relatively better off than in fact they are. Even so, most of the time they can still judge whether their basic material needs are being met or not. People can tell if they are homeless and facing starvation; and even without severe privations, they know when they cannot pay their bills. Similarly, power relations are so complex that scholars have debated endlessly who has "real" power to determine the agenda and policies of various societies. But at the extremes of power deprivation, it is not hard to recognize that one is legally a slave, or legally disfranchised, or a member of a community that has been conquered by another regime, or of a group denied the formal representation accorded other groups, or of a sect or ethnicity relegated by sheer numbers to persistent minority status. There are many elements in economic and political power stories that can be reliably confirmed or disconfirmed, at least in most eyes.

But what counts as solid evidence that our community is especially favored by God, or that evolution has made us a morally superior race, or that we have developed an especially valuable civilization or culture, or even that our language has distinctive worth meriting sacrifices to maintain it? There are certainly many "authorities" who make these kinds of claims, and some sorts of evidence seem relevant. Assertions involving measurable abilities or particular historical events for which records are available can be falsified. But many contentions are not easily measurable: does one group really have more empathetic souls, another more courage in the face of danger, another, more analytical detachment? And often, historical events are said to have occurred so far in the past that skeptics can say only that no evidence has been found for them.

In any case, the invalidation of particular claims does not prevent adherents of an ethically constitutive story from insisting that it expresses, perhaps metaphorically, a larger binding truth. The gods or God may not have actually sent a descendant to found our people, but in the story that they did, we may perceive symbolic representations of genuine historical events, or a moral parable about how we ought to live, or both. It is, to put it mildly, much harder to contend that our poverty metaphorically reveals to us that we possess material riches, or that disfranchisement bestows on us superior power, than it is to "spin" our allegedly ethically constitutive conditions in these ways. In regard to this third kind of story, our judgments often turn on our aesthetic tastes, our strongly felt emotions, and our senses of faith. This difference contributes greatly to the capacity of ethically constitutive stories to play an irreplaceable role in people-building. As a result of their hard-to-verify, hard-to-falsify qualities, such accounts are likely to be in some ways less politically reliable but also in some ways more politically reliable than the other sorts of stories. They are less reliable not only because it is harder for constituents to judge their credibility via concrete evidence but also because the core benefits they offer are less tangible. Political actors are undoubtedly well advised always to include credible economic and political power appeals in their narratives of peoplehood and to fulfill the promises thus conveyed as fully as possible; and in many circumstances it will make sense to put those stories center stage.

Yet ethically constitutive stories are in some ways more politically reliable than these alternatives, because once they are accepted, it is very hard for rivals to mount relevant evidence against them. It may not be easy to prove to the satisfaction of all doubters that God is on our side, that our ethnicity is especially noble, or that our cultural achievements, past, present, and future, are humanity's most magnificent; but it is also tremendously difficult to dissuade believers that these things are not so. And most people have profound philosophical and psychological needs to believe some sustaining ethically constitutive story. Most of us do need communities that endure and identities that feel secure if we are to be happy. Precisely because no forms of human social life are simply natural, because none are constant and unchanging, because none are long free from contestation, criticism, and doubt, the reassuring work that ethically constitutive stories can do is often crucial in these regards. They provide sturdy anchors of morally compelling identity and worth amidst the roiling seas of competitive community construction. They give us a sense of belonging, a sense of place in the world, a sense of partnership in a larger, meaningful collective existence and its shared endeavors. They help us make sense of our lives, intellectually and morally. And in so doing, they help to cement and sustain the communities that sustain us. Many people are in fact so deeply invested in the ethically constitutive stories that have given definition and meaning to their communal and personal lives that the very notion of conceiving of themselves or their affiliations very differently seems alien, unnatural, immoral.[20]

Neither economic nor political power stories are nearly so capable of defining and grounding our identities in satisfying, almost irrefutable

---

[20] Yael Tamir and Will Kymlicka make similar arguments for the importance of cultural identities: see e.g. Kymlicka, 2001, 250–251 (reviewing Tamir, 1993).

ways. And again, neither is nearly so able to inspire belief in and allegiance to the intrinsic propriety and goodness of our particular memberships. Ethically constitutive stories are therefore best equipped to help support commitments to our imagined political communities through economic and political bad times, sometimes even long stretches of personal and communal poverty and political subjugation.

This unparalleled capacity to sustain allegiances is the central reason why we should expect to find ethically constitutive stories among the conceptions of political peoplehood prevailing in any long-enduring community, and why we can expect there always to be large numbers of people who are strongly socialized to affirm those stories. From the standpoint of aspiring leaders, these circumstances mean that it is dangerous to neglect or denigrate these ethically constitutive stories, for rivals may use them to mobilize support for their own purposes. It is also almost irresistibly attractive for leaders to seek to turn such stories to their advantage. These sorts of narratives can provide leaders with the best possible insurance policy against losing support amidst the inevitable ups and downs of material fortunes. It also remains true that, because political leaders are first and foremost human beings, such narratives have almost always heavily shaped their own aims and commitments. It follows that we should expect most political leaders to choose to give suitable ethically constitutive stories some place in their people-forming political projects, everywhere and always; and sometimes the primary place. Those who do so in ways that a critical coalition of constituents finds persuasive usually gain power; and those choices in turn further mold constituents and leaders alike in ways that perpetuate the distinctive role of ethically constitutive accounts in processes of political people-building.[21]

The occasions for ethically constitutive stories: some hypotheses

If it is correct that ethically constitutive accounts can provide potent moral affirmations of particular identities, but that economic and political power stories offer more tangible and verifiable benefits, then we can form some reasonable guesses about when political leaders are especially

---

[21] This is why I agree with A. D. Smith's contention (1991) that actual nations are likely to combine "civic" and "ethnic" elements. My category of "ethically constitutive stories" is, however, broader than what is usually invoked by the term "ethnic" (though Smith's definitions of that term are also quite broad). Moreover, I see these elements as blended into all senses of peoplehood, not just nationalism. Like Alexander Motyl (2002, 243–246), I see no sharp, essential distinction between what Smith terms "ethnies" that provide "mythomoteurs" for modern nations and "nations."

likely to feature ethically constitutive narratives and when constituents are most likely to respond to them. Let me suggest three general categories of circumstances conducive to making this peculiar third sort of story prominent, illustrating them with examples meant to suggest the historical and geographical breadth and depth of these phenomena.

The first and most basic category of occasions for stressing ethically constitutive stories includes a wide variety of conditions *when the provision of economic and political power benefits seems uncertain or clearly deficient.* There can be many such circumstances, because judgments of the adequacy of these benefits can always be made comparatively. Potential constituents may measure the economic goods and political powers they perceive themselves as receiving or as likely to receive from their current governors or movement leaders in many ways. They can compare them against those they think they can rightfully expect to obtain; against those they believe they might receive if they supported other elites within their current societies; and against those they perceive as being provided by foreign regimes, with alternative systems and leadership they may wish somehow to have for themselves. When leaders of a regime or an insurgent or separatist political people can be confident of faring well along all these dimensions of comparison, they may overwhelmingly stress economic or political power themes. But whenever and wherever they feel vulnerable, they are likely to emphasize ethically constitutive stories at least as much. If they can craft accounts that attractively reassert widely valued existing identities and beliefs; that express prevailing anxieties, fears, or resentments; that offer constituents a fresh, inspiring self-image; or that do some or all these things, they can hope to win enough support to sustain their governance until they can provide the other sorts of benefits as well.

The themes of the ethically constitutive narratives that leaders advance, and that constituents are likely to embrace, under such circumstances are shaped both by the values, traditions, fears, and antagonisms prevailing in their political contexts, and by the specific sources of insecurity that seem most pressing. Sometimes those sources are chiefly external. To take a fairly benign example, worries about the inferiority of the British throne and its subjects in comparison with the French heirs of Charlemagne seem partly to explain the overwhelming acceptance of Geoffrey of Monmouth's fanciful *History of the Kings of Britain,* published some seventy years after the Norman Conquest. Since the seventh century, various French historians had given their people a glorious past by claiming that the Franks were descended from survivors of ancient Troy (Asher, 1993, 9–21). Geoffrey, a Welsh cleric possibly of Breton descent, won favor with his land's Norman masters by contending similarly that Britain had been founded by Brutus, a banished grandson of Aeneas, the Trojan who founded Rome. Brutus had wandered to ancient Albion, cleared it of a few giants, renamed it for himself, and established a royal dynasty over its three parts, England, Scotland, and Wales. Geoffrey also claimed that a later king, Lucius, was the first in the world to convert his kingdom to Christianity. A treacherous descendant subsequently allowed invading Saxons to take over the domain; but the legendary King Arthur, aided by Trojan-descended Normans, won it back. Geoffrey told the romantic tale of how Arthur was betrayed by Modred and Guinevere and taken wounded to Avalon, allowing the Saxons to regain power. His readers knew that "liberation" had then come via William the Conqueror in 1066 (MacDougall, 1982, 8–12).

This almost purely fictional "history" had acerbic critics from the start, but it was widely accepted for roughly 500 years, even by many continental writers. The Norman and later Angevin British kings embraced it wholeheartedly. Henry II gave aid to those who "discovered" Arthur's body in a monastery at Glastonbury, and he also had his grandson christened "Arthur." Edward I renovated Arthur's tomb at Glastonbury in 1278. Edward II "recreated" Arthur's fabled "Order of the Garter." Many kings used the *History* as legal support for their claims to power over unruly Wales and Scotland. The literary charms of Geoffrey's great work also helped entice many Welsh, Scottish, Saxons, and Normans to see themselves as one "composite people." That political consequence may have been one reason it won royal favor. But it also seems to have pleased these kings for the same reason it pleased many of their subjects: despite their lack of comparative wealth and political power, this ethically constitutive story "proved" the British were not occupants of a backwater to their great French rivals, but rather "inheritors of a kingdom with a proud past and notable achievements" (MacDougall, 1982, 12–14).

The royally instigated "discovery" of King Arthur's noble bones has had many counterparts extending up to the present. When Japan subjugated Korea from 1910 to 1945, Japanese historians portrayed the Koreans prior to 1910 as a backward, stagnant people, with a culture entirely derived from the Chinese and Japanese, and a history that included prior rule by the Japanese in ancient times. Korean historians such as Ch'oe Namson and Sin Ch'aeho responded by reviving and reinterpreting the myth of Tan' gun, said to have been the historical founder of the first Korean nation, Ko Choson. According to this myth, long ago the God of All, Hwanin, sent his son, Hwanung, to Earth to provide humans with happiness. Hwanung descended to the T'aebaek Mountains, on the border of what is now Manchuria and North Korea, with 3,000 subjects. A tiger and bear prayed to him to make them into human beings, and he instructed them to eat mugwort and garlic, and avoid the sunlight. The tiger faltered but the bear complied for twenty-one days, whereupon Hwanung made her a woman, married her, and she gave birth to Tan' gun. He then established the Choson Kingdom and ruled it for 1,500 years. Ch'oe Namson argued that this tale was constructed out of known symbols of ancient East Asian shamanism. It was therefore evidence that there had indeed been a great ancient Korean nation, possibly formed by the union of two tribes, with Tan' gun as its first prince (Allen, 1990, 788, 791–796; Palais, 1995, 409–411).

The political motives for Ch'oe Namson's rehabilitation of the Tan' gun myth as evidence of an actual historical greatness were and are obvious: he went on to assert that in a variety of ways Korea, not Japan or China, was the true source of spiritual and cultural greatness in East Asia. The colorful story of Tan' gun remains well known in South Korea today, and the notion that it may be based on an actual historical figure appears in history textbooks, though few South Korean scholars defend that view (Allen, 1990, 796, 803). Through the 1980s, North Korean officials and academics also tended to ignore the Tan' gun legend as a feudal, religious holdover unsuited to a modern Communist regime. But in 1993, in the wake of the fall of the Soviet Union, the ending of Communism in many nations, and abundant evidence of the incapacity of his regime to provide either material prosperity or personal freedoms, North Korean President Kim Il Sung made a surprising announcement: his researchers had uncovered Tan' gun's mausoleum and remains in Pyongyang. Analysis of Tan' gun's bones provided "scientific" evidence that he had been born 5,011 years ago and had indeed ruled a great ancient Korean state, cradled in what is now North Korea. The mausoleum has since been "restored"; in 1997, a Tan' gun Academy, headed by the President of Korea University, was created to study the founding father; and leaders of the "Committee for the Peaceful Reunification of the Fatherland" have suggested that current Korean leader, Kim Jong Il, was born in the same mountains and so is Tan' gun's heir.[22]

The conclusion seems inescapable that, just as pre-1945 Korean historians gave new credence to the Tan' gun myth in order to inspire loyalty and pride in a sense of peoplehood that could offer few material or political benefits, so North Korean leaders today are stressing this myth to try to garner support, North and South, for their isolated, impoverished regime. They have accused pro-American, Christian South Korean

---

[22] These statements are based on news stories collected at http://www.fortunecity.com/ meltingpot/champion/657tangun.htm. This website is maintained by Leonid A. Petrov, a graduate student in Pacific history at the Australian National University. See also Palais, 1995, 411.

groups of destroying Tan' gun's statues as part of efforts to discredit this endeavor. The Tan' gun myth has, however, also had significant influence in the south. Like most other late nineteenth- and early twentieth-century national mythologists, the historians who revived the Tan' gun legend were infused with Social Darwinist conceptions of racial struggle. They portrayed Koreans as remarkably racially homogeneous throughout history. Those accounts have reinforced Koreans most desirous of national and racial unification, in the south as well as north, in their denigrations of women who marry or consort with non-Koreans as immoral, if not racial traitors. Sheila Miyoshi Jager contends that "Out of the nationalist obsession with a changeless Korean essence came an idealized version of the entire history of Korean culture as a seamless narrative of regenerative fatherhood and ethnic cohesion, preserved intact through the ages by the vigilant virtues of the Korean female" (Allen, 1990, 789, 802–803; Jager, 1996, 16–18). This sense of Korea as properly an ethnically or racially homogeneous people has often worked against gender equity, in South Korea as elsewhere in the world.[23]

Anxieties about external rivals can prompt political promulgation of mythical ancestral narratives even if the competitors do not seem strikingly more successful in the present, so long as they have been threats in the past and antagonisms remain. Though contemporary Ecuador may not come off so badly in comparison with neighboring Peru as Geoffrey's Britain did in relation to France and as North Koreans may well fear they do in contrast to capitalist regimes, it has had ongoing border disputes with Peru since the nineteenth century, including a Peruvian invasion of its Amazonian territory in 1941. Those conflicts have led many Ecuadorians to believe that Peru still possesses lands stolen from Ecuador and would like more. These anxieties are heightened by the fact that Peru can claim to be the home of the now-celebrated Incan empire, which ruled over the territories of modern-day Ecuador for some time before the Spanish Conquest. Indeed, since Ecuador, like much of Latin America, had its basic boundaries assigned to it via the Spanish construction of imperial administrative units, it is not really plausible to say that "Ecuadoreans" as a group have a distinct pre-colonial ancestry at all (Anderson, 1991, 51–53; Radcliffe and Westwood, 1996, 5, 57, 61).

[23] On July 31, 2002, the South Korean National Assembly refused to approve Chang Sung as the nation's first female prime minister. Among the charges against her was the fact that her son, born in the US while she was being educated there, had chosen American rather than Korean citizenship. Rather than deny that women were especially responsible for insuring that the next generation's members were good Koreans, she promised that her son would become a Korean citizen. One of her supporters contended that many male Korean politicians had sons who had moved abroad, and that "These allegations are going on because she is a woman" (Kirk, 2002, A5).

That reality has long not seemed an adequate basis for political peoplehood. In the late eighteenth century Padre Juan de Velasco, a Jesuit priest expelled like all Jesuits from Latin America in 1767, responded by writing his *Historia del Reyno de Quito* (History of the Kingdom of Quito). Somewhat like the Welsh cleric Geoffrey's *History*, this work contended that well before the arrival of the Spanish, Ecuador had once been a great independent kingdom, valiantly resistant to oft-invading Incans. This Quito kingdom, like the Incans, allegedly did not have writing, and other kinds of supporting evidence for its existence have remained sufficiently sparse that many scholars regard de Velasco's tale as a fable. His history did, however, "help create a myth of Ecuadorian Creole nationhood to lend justification to the creation of an Ecuadorian state," and it continues to play that role today (Becker, 1995, 3). Modern Ecuador has a variety of laws and national institutions requiring conservation of what the government terms the Ecuadorean "cultural patrimony." This conservation includes regular reprintings of the *Historia* by the national "Casa de Cultura" (House of Culture), and the teaching of a national history curriculum, required in private as well as public schools, that highlights the kingdom of Quito and its ethnic mixtures, as well as various acts of resistance to encroaching Peruvians. Given its deep internal divisions, scholars suggest that this opposition to Peru, expressed and justified by the Quito myth, is perhaps the most important source of unified political peoplehood in Ecuador today (de Velasco, 1994; Radcliffe and Westwood, 1996, 52–53, 76–79, 171).

But if Ecuadorian national narratives have been massively shaped by efforts to distance their people from Peru, they have also been structured by factors common to Peru and the rest of Latin America. These include broader "external" concerns – how to define their identities in relationship to the US and Europe – and "internal" concerns – how to define their identities in relation to their indigenous, African-descended, and female populations. Since independence the Latin American nations have had to confront American and European beliefs that they were racially and culturally inferior, in many European eyes because of biological and cultural admixture with indigenous peoples and imported Africans, in many North American eyes because they were also Hispanic and Catholic. Chronic problems of political instability and limited economic development in many Latin American countries have long made it difficult to refute these derogatory characterizations in economic or political power terms. In the nineteenth century, in particular, most of the new independent regimes, led by Spanish-descended creole elites, were officially "republican," with "liberal" economic policies meant to foster growing market economies, in conscious emulation of liberalizing and democratizing northern Europe as well as the United States (Helg, 1990, 36–38; Wade, 1993, 9–10). They could not easily claim their economic and political ideologies made them distinctive or superior.

Yet none were faring so well as the large, resource-rich, overbearing republic to their north, with its predominantly northern European origins and conscious privileging of "whites" and Protestants. Many in the US asserted that these racial and religious traits made all the difference. In both the nineteenth and early twentieth centuries US elites regularly invoked ethically constitutive doctrines of their greater innate capacities for governance and their Protestant providential mission to justify the imperialistic Mexican-American and Spanish-American Wars, numerous lesser military and diplomatic interventions into Latin America, and often exploitative public and private economic policies (Stephanson, 1995).

The dominant, if contradictory, response in the first phase of independence was for late nineteenth- and early twentieth-century Latin American governments to proclaim that, unlike in the US, all those native to their soil either were or were eligible to become equal republican citizens, while they also pursued more or less extreme and more or less explicit policies of "whitening." The extreme was Argentina, which became in 1853 a pioneer in constitutionally granting all persons born there not only nationality but formally equal civil rights. But Domingo Sarmiento, President from 1868 to 1874, sought to encourage European and, especially, Anglo-Saxon immigration to make his country more like the United States, and he also authorized military expeditions against "barbarous" indigenous peoples. Those policies were pursued so ardently that by the end of the nineteenth century, Indians were less than 1 percent of the national population, blacks were only 2 percent of Buenos Aires, where most lived, and the country was overwhelmingly populated by European immigrants – though chiefly Italian and Spanish, not Anglo-Saxon. Even so, Argentinians could and did see themselves as "a new variety of European white races" that could play "a tutelary function over the other republics of the continent," as Argentinian sociologist José Ingenieros urged.[24]

More typical was Mexico, where efforts to "whiten" via immigration under the neo-liberal dictator Porfirio Díaz in the late nineteenth century failed, and where indigenous communities were too extensive to make extermination a serious option. Instead the Mexican government sought to "whiten" those communities through compulsory cultural assimilation and the breaking up of communal agriculture, not incidentally

---

[24] Helg, 1990, 39–44; Safford, 1991, 1, 9–12; Guy, 1992, 204–205. Uruguay followed a similar pattern, and Venezuela tried to do so but, like Mexico, failed to attract sufficient European immigrants (Wade, 1993, 12).

promoting creole land acquisition and market economies in the process. Though these policies were often oppressive and exploitative, opportunities for mobility did exist: Díaz himself, who was probably a Mixtec Indian, managed to achieve both power and almost pure "whiteness" in contemporary eyes (Knight, 1990, 73). But though his regime and earlier economically liberal Mexican governments held power largely through force in the second half of the nineteenth century, they succeeded better when they accommodated local indigenous ethnic and religious identities and communal political and property claims than when they sought to eradicate them. The Díaz regime, which came to power on the strength of resistance to French imperialism, initially promised to make such accommodations more than its predecessors, but it seems to have found that road to economic and political prosperity too slow and demanding. Its subsequent reliance instead on coercive domination eventually fueled the Zapatista revolution of 1910, which promised truer republicanism and social justice (Knight, 1990, 76–80; Mallon, 1995, 61, 247–248; Purnell, 2002, 224–225, 229).

Post-revolutionary governments still faced the challenge, however, of defining their worth in relation to the materially more successful North Americans and Europeans. That pressure, greatly reinforced by domestic ones, generated the influential claims of José Vasconcelos, Manuel Gamio, and others that in fact the "mixed race" or "mestizo" character of Mexico made it superior – the "cosmic race," in Vasconcelos's stirring depiction. He accepted late nineteenth-century doctrines holding that humanity was divided into biologically distinct races displaying "spiritual differences," but he thought all the different races had great value. Claims of racial superiority in his view were mere rationalizations of English colonizers. And, he urged, if "all nations then build theories to justify their policies or to strengthen their deeds, let us develop in Mexico our own theories, or, at least, let us . . . choose among the foreign theories . . . those that stimulate our growth." He proposed exchanging the "Darwinism" of racial competition for the "Mendelism" of interbreeding, *mestizaje*: since all races had distinct aptitudes to contribute, it was "a mixture of races, of peoples and cultures," that was always most likely to produce progress (Vasconcelos, 1926, 20–21, 85–86, 96–99).

Thus "the mestizo became the ideological symbol of the new regime," the ethically constitutive countermyth that answered claims of northern European racial purity and supremacy. This racial ideology easily incorporated the conservative form of *indigenismo*, the emphasis on the real if allegedly lesser contributions of the continent's indigenous peoples, advocated by the pioneering Mexican anthropologist Manuel Gamio. This turn to the celebration of mixed race identity found more or less successful counterparts through much of Latin America. All were better than the racial purists of North America; and their varying indigenous peoples also provided a means for mestizo Latin American republics to distinguish themselves from each other. Mexico could say it had blended its Spanish creole stock with the Aztecs; Peru, with the Incas; Colombia, with a special mix of both – though again, to seem sufficiently distinct Ecuador had to invent the Kingdom of Quito (Knight, 1990, 85; Radcliffe and Westwood, 1996, 67–70; Wade, 1993, 12–24; de la Cadena, 2001, 16–19).

Perhaps the most striking turn to celebration of racial mixing came in Brazil, which had been in 1888 the last nation in the hemisphere to abolish slavery and seek to establish a "free labor" economy. Its extensive slave system left Brazil with an exceptionally large Afro-Brazilian population. It remains today "the single largest population of African descent outside of Nigeria," roughly 44 percent of all Brazilians (Hanchard, 1994, 5, 47). But even abolitionist Brazilian elites ardently hoped that interracial reproduction and immigration would produce a "whitening" of their population. Census results were sometimes constructed to provide reassuring evidence that this was occurring (Skidmore, 1990, 7–26; Nobles, 2000, 86–96). At the same time Brazilians, even more than other Latin American nations due to their large Afro-descended population, increasingly stressed during the twentieth century that they were free of the harsh Jim Crow segregation laws and bitter anti-black prejudices that marred the United States. They came to celebrate themselves as the preeminent "racial democracy," offering the "Brazilian solution" to racial animosities. Beginning in the 1930s, anthropologist and then Senator Gilbert Freyre was the leading proponent of this view; but it became "hegemonic" in modern Brazil, the "ideological glue that held together the Brazilian nation" (Hanchard, 1994, 43–67; Marx, 1998, 162–168; Nobles, 2000, 96–110).

That is not to say that the Latin American governments were prepared to recognize fully the claims of their indigenous or black populations or to accept genuine equality among the different "contributing" groups. By emphasizing processes of absorption, *mestizaje* was as much a response to the political challenges posed by indigenous and black communities as it was to the derogations of white supremacist theories. "Racial democracy" masked massive ongoing discrimination and inequality (Knight, 1990, 71, 86; Skidmore, 1990, 27–28; Hanchard, 1994).

But before turning to the role of various governing narratives of peoplehood in relation to "internal" rivals, let me note that, while doctrines celebrating mixed race identity and racial democracy became during the twentieth century the dominant ways most Latin American elites defined their worth in comparison with the imperialistic racism of the United States and Europe, aspiring leaders in other parts of the world responded to that racism in parallel yet differing ways. It would be useful to have a detailed study of this global phenomenon; but some basic contrasts, and the political reasons for them, seem clear. Rarely were the racial theories of the late nineteenth century, given heightened intellectual respectability by the advent of evolutionary theories as well as European imperial success, rejected outright. Instead colonial intellectuals and political leaders modified them, blending them with their own intellectual and cultural traditions, and put them to both anti-colonial and local political purposes.

In China, for example, Kai-wing Chow contends that the term "Han" had long simply been one of several used to refer generally to inhabitants of China, as opposed to "barbarians." It did not clearly connote a particular ethnic lineage. But various works, including Yan Fu's translation of Thomas Huxley's *On Evolution* in 1898, made evolutionary theory "a household phrase" among Chinese readers, by the end of the nineteenth century. Chinese intellectuals then began to portray their resistance to imperialism as part of a world historical struggle between the "yellow and white races." To East Asians, in that contest the yellow race bore the banner of the oldest and highest form of human civilization. Writers like the acclaimed scholar and Sun Yat-sen ally Zhang Binglin then began to use the term "Han" in a more ethnic sense. It referred strictly to members of a distinct line of descent from Huangdi, the "Yellow Emperor" whose name made him well suited to serve as the father of the "yellow race" generally. Today that relatively recent meaning of "Han" is so prevalent that the Chinese governments on the mainland and in Taiwan, as well as most Chinese, regard the "Han" as the largest Chinese ethnic group (Chow, 2001, 47–48, 53–63, 74–76).

And as with North Korea and Tan' gun, if to a lesser degree, the waning of faith in Communist ideology in the modern People's Republic of China has prompted increased stress on China as "the homeland of the Modern Yellow Race," peopled by offspring of the great "Yellow Emperor" (Dikötter, 1997, 10, 25–28). Both mainland Chinese leaders and "overseas" leaders of Chinese descent, like Singapore's Lee Kuan Yew, have sought at times to encourage regional economic cooperation and investment by stressing that fellow children of the "Yellow Emperor" have a "natural empathy" that provides "the trust" that is the foundation of business relations, and that all "ethnic Chinese" should help each other. They have also, however, been careful to insist that shared racial identity should not trump national allegiances (Yew, 1993; Dikötter, 1997, 1, 10, 25–26; Ong, 1999, 59–67).

Similarly, during the Meiji Restoration of imperial power during the late nineteenth century in Japan, the enhanced authority of the emperor was buttressed much as the power of the Norman kings had been: by claiming his divine descent from the legendary first Emperor, Jinmu, whose ancestor was the Sun Goddess. From Jinmu's home, there came the "Yamato spirit" of Japanese harmonious unity, which leads all true Japanese hearts to beat as one. "Nothing besides these myths," enshrined in "state Shinto" nationalistic religious practices, was "available in Japanese political theory for the purpose" of justifying the imperial Meiji Constitution (Brownlee, 1997, 6–7). But as tensions with the west rose, Japanese intellectuals merged these lineage stories with western racial ideas, including those of Comte Arthur de Gobineau, to argue that the Japanese were a "pure," homogeneous "Yamato" race, *Yamato minzoku*. Their divine and evolutionary mission was to lead the weaker "yellow races" in the struggle against "Aryan" imperialism, placing much of East Asia under Japanese imperial rule in order to do so. In the 1920s, Emperor Hirohito's ethics teacher, Sugiura Shigetake, taught his pupil: "Our Japanese empire must be conscious of confronting the various Aryan races by our own power in the future." And though the post-World War II Japanese regime long monopolized by the Liberal Democratic Party has primarily stressed its provision of peace, prosperity, and a more democratic system of government, invocations of the Japanese as a "divine" people blessed with "racial purity" remain persistent, if controversial, elements in the rhetoric of leading political figures, often coming to the fore when the economy falters (Dower, 1993, 272–273, 279; Dikötter, 1997, 4, 6; Buruma, 2001, 26, 28; Doak, 2001, 86, 106).

In Africa, where highly artificial and contested colonial borders overlaid even greater diversity in linguistic, religious, and ancestral identities, modified western racial doctrines probably have played less role in nation-building after independence than in Latin America and parts of East Asia. Whereas East Asians had inherited notions of a "yellow" people that could be merged with western racial theories, and creole Latin American elites inhabited cultures thoroughly imbued with European racial doctrines, Africans generally did not conceive of themselves as having a common "black" identity at all until and unless Europeans so labeled them. Their modern politics have, moreover, been extensively shaped not only by boundaries imposed by various European colonial powers and by economic interests arising from European-influenced forms of development, but also by the widespread colonialist practice of "indirect rule," employment of African intermediaries, often declared "tribal" leaders, especially in rural areas. Those practices and institutions empowered some local elites over others and rigidified more fluid cultural, kinship, linguistic, or religious affiliations in order to administer colonial populations. In much of post-colonial Africa the consequences have involved efforts to craft "national" senses of identity out of former colonial units, often by adapting "tribal" and "ethnic" identities that build on senses of affiliation, economic interest, and shared grievances formed mostly under colonial rule, even if they are sometimes expressed in myths of older identities. At least as often, the post-colonial era has also seen struggles between former intermediary leaders and their local rivals that have most often been defined in ethnic and religious terms. Thus "ethnic," "tribal," and to a lesser degree "nationalist" ethically constitutive stories, along with economic and power ones, are far more visible in post-independence African people-making than specifically "racial" forms of political identity or community.[25]

After the ending of colonialism began to transfer power to native Nigerians, for instance, many aspiring political leaders ceased to stress Pan-African racial identities or even Nigerian identity. Instead they focused on created regional parties that rested on reconstituted senses of ethnicity, religion, and local traditions. Some of these parties came to dominate governance in their regions, even as they contended for power at the relatively weak federal center. In Western Nigeria, Obafemi Awolowo was particularly adept at building support by reviving Yoruba myths of descent from a common ancestor, Oduduwa, and a common place of origin, Ile.Ife. These ethnic, religious, and geographic doctrines of kinship helped him create a coalition of Yoruba elites and traditional chiefs strong enough to make his party, the "Action Group," the leading force in Western Nigeria's "Yorubaland" until his death in 1987 – despite the disruptions of Awolowo's imprisonment by the federal government for three years in the 1960s, military coups at the national level, and the ethnically charged Nigerian civil war from 1967 to 1970 that pitted the Eastern secessionists of "Biafra" against the national regime. Though Awolowo never favored the breakup of Nigeria as Eastern leaders did, he urged formal constitutional assignment of extensive governing powers to four regional governments representing allegedly traditional ethnic "nationalities" (Falola, 2001, 115–119).

Yet despite this post-independence emphasis on ethnic, religious, regional, and "tribal" identities, the pervasive justification of colonialism in racial terms inevitably also had repercussions. In Africa as elsewhere, adapted racial ideas played prominent roles not only in anti-colonial political movements but also in post-colonial foreign policies, even if they

---

[25] See e.g. Vail, ed., 1989, 1–18; Malkki, 1995, 19–38; Burnham, 1996, 1–42; Mamdani, 1996, 16–25, 37–108; Ranger, 1999, 19–20; Jung, 2000, 40–111.

were less central to domestic politics. I have already noted that Edward Blyden, a West Indian who moved to Liberia and became a prominent journalist, educator, and political figure, accepted many imperialist notions of racial difference while rejecting their valorizations. He thought there was an "African personality" that did indeed display "racial peculiarities." Blacks were more spiritual, more communal, more empathetic, more in harmony with nature than whites. That made them capable of making contributions to humanity that whites could not. And though Blyden sometimes stressed that the races were distinct but all of value, he inevitably called attention to the abuses that accompanied what he saw as the less harmonious and more unfeeling white character. He also opposed racial mixing, believing it would prevent Africans from developing their unique traits and potential (he was also scarred by an unhappy marriage to a mulatto Liberian). Blyden achieved more celebrity than political impact during his lifetime, but his ideas have since been invoked by leaders of many West African nations, including Nigeria, Ghana, Guinea, and Sierra Leone, as well as in Liberia itself (Mamdani, 1996, 75–76; Conyers, 1999, 81–91, 99, 200; Falola, 2001, 34–39, 124).

He does not appear to have been a major influence on Léopold Sédar Senghor, the Senegalese poet who became his country's first President and who advocated "negritude" in the late 1940s and 1950s, when decolonization finally began in Africa. Senghor chiefly drew inspiration from European scholars respectful of African cultures and from the essays of W. E. B. Du Bois, though he, too, relied on the racist Comte de Gobineau. From different sources, he arrived at views in many ways similar to Blyden's. He argued that the "physiopsychological" nature of black Africans was sharply distinct from whites, and he too essentially inverted the valorizations given by writers like de Gobineau. It was to their credit that blacks were more attuned to the spirituality of all existence in ways that supported animism, and so they were more communal and caring in ways that, Senghor insisted, argued for an African version of socialism. He further contended, as Blyden and sometimes Du Bois had done, that blacks needed first to cultivate their unique natures so that they could then contribute to the progress of all humanity:

> So that we answer 'present' at the rebirth of the world
> As the leavening needed for the white flour
> For who would teach rhythm to the dead world of machines and cannons?
> Who would loose a cry of joy to wake the dead and the orphans to see the dawn?[26]

[26] Vaillant, 1990, 123, 134, 251–257, 266–267; Falola, 2001, 51, 54–57, 108–109, 124.

In light of their redeployment of European racial theories, it is not surprising that both Blyden, the nineteenth-century "father of black nationalism," and Senghor, the twentieth-century theoretician of "negritude," have been criticized for advocating "anti-racist racisms." Yet both did help supply ethically constitutive stories that advanced their central concern: fostering senses of dignity and resistance in the face of imperialist injustices. And though, understandably, these senses of Pan-African racial identity have not bulked so large in the intra-African politics of the post-colonial decades, they are still often invoked when black African leaders confront European-descended adversaries, at home or abroad, and for both good and ill.

One can still ask, were these ethically constitutive stories really politically important, or simply pleasing window dressing for political projects that elites advanced, and constituents embraced, largely for other reasons? That is a difficult question that no one can as yet answer authoritatively. Yet surely the burden of proof must be placed on those who would deny the significance of these ubiquitous features of political life. For even if the commitments expressed in such stories have been truly motivating only for *some* significant political actors, and even if they have only attracted *some* constituents and shaped *some* policies and institutions at the *margins* of coalition formation and policy-making, it seems inevitable that, in the often closely contested politics of people-building, there have been times when these leaders, these constituents, these policies and institutions have made significant differences in outcomes.

That claim is made all the more plausible by the fact that ethically constitutive stories have played significant roles in conflicts with "internal" rivals as well as "external" ones. In Latin America and Asia, more than in Africa, the adaptations of racial ideas just discussed were often constructed as much or more to serve local political purposes as to combat foreign imperialists. The revolutionaries who eventually founded the first Chinese republic, for example, began by calling for "race war" against white colonialists; but they soon turned to arguing that the imperial Manchu dynasty was illegitimate not only because of its despotism but because it meant governance by a "barbarian" lineage, instead of the Han descent-line. Again, anti-Manchu leaders were engaged in a dangerous revolutionary enterprise, and they could not easily form a sufficiently powerful coalition solely through credible economic and political power promises; so they garnered additional support through racial appeals. But for this strategy to work, that Han lineage (or *Hanzu*) had to be defined quite broadly, as including a great variety of dialect groups. That process of political definition is responsible for the prevailing twentieth-century "common sense" view of the Han as the largest Chinese ethnicity (Chow, 2001, 54–63, 74–76).

A comparable "internal" struggle led to the replacement of Geoffrey's myth of Trojan origins with the succeeding myth of Great Britain's Anglo-Saxon roots. During the exceedingly anxious seventeenth "century of revolution" in England, opponents of Stuart doctrines favoring Catholicism and absolute monarchical power increasingly bolstered their uncertain cause by drawing on the works of "Saxonists," such as John Foxe's *Book of Martyrs* and the writings of Protestant bishop John Bale. They offered a Protestant account of English origins, insisting that the primitive English church in Saxon times had been independent of Rome, and valorizing noble King Alfred as a heroic Saxon alternative to Arthur. Their arguments soon merged with those of German Protestants including Martin Luther himself, who invoked Tacitus's praise of the ancient Teutonic tribes to present all German-descended peoples as manlier, freer, more devout, and possessed of a more beautiful language than southern Europeans. These developing traditions proved extremely useful not only to Protestants but also to champions of parliamentary power and common law restrictions on monarchical authority. They began to argue that the British were heirs of a Saxon "ancient constitution" in which kings had been but elected officials of a people with innate gifts for freedom and self-governance, the same gifts that had led God to choose them as the first Christian kingdom, his anti-papist "new Israel." Normans were on these accounts German-descended also, but they were "the drosse of the Teutonic" peoples. Anglo-Saxons were "the most ancient and noble." Though Sir Edward Coke did not favor tales of Teutonic origins, wishing instead to present English law as self-contained and complete since time immemorial, he played a lead role in contending that the ancient Saxon constitution set limits on the king, in just the way he mythologized Magna Charta as a bulwark of freemen's rights. He also cited the practices of the Saxon kings, along with the contrary Arthur legend, to achieve his ends (Pocock, 1967, 56–58, 64; MacDougall, 1982, 36–62; *Calvin's Case*, 1608, 24a).[27]

With the triumph and consolidation of the parliament-empowering Glorious Revolution of 1688, views of the British as an essentially Germanic-descended, Anglo-Saxon people became so pervasive that in the eighteenth century, both the skeptical David Hume and the radical republican Catherine Macaulay embraced these ideas in their histories. In the nineteenth century, reinforced by evolutionary theories, self-glorifying myths of Anglo-Saxon racial destiny became prime

---

[27] *Calvin's Case*, 7 Coke's Reports 1a (1697; orig. 1608).

justifications for the still-expanding British empire, always blended with predominantly Protestant notions of the British as God's favored people. Views like Rudyard Kipling's smug characterization of imperial rule as the "white man's burden" were the result (MacDougall, 1982, 81–103). From early on, US leaders adapted these racial themes for their own imperial purposes, again never more than in the late nineteenth century, as in Senator Albert Beveridge's notorious sanctification of the Spanish-American War conquests:

God has not been preparing the English-speaking and Teutonic peoples for a thousand years for nothing but vain and idle self-contemplation and self-admiration. No! He has made us the master organizers of the world to establish system where chaos reigns...He has made us adepts in government that we may administer government among savage and senile peoples...And of all our race He has marked the American people as His chosen nation to finally lead in the regeneration of the world.[28]

Such racial doctrines have also been used, of course, to justify domestic systems of subjugation, exploitation, and exclusion as well as imperial conquest. Not only southern Democrats but also Progressive Republicans like Beveridge came to accept that racial limitations justified "tutelary" policies of second-class citizenship for non-white Americans, including blacks, Mexican-Americans, and most Asians. Henry Cabot Lodge's racist proposals for immigration restrictions to keep out the "lower races" also finally prevailed in the United States in the form of the National Origins Quota system that limited admission according to racially defined national statuses from 1924 through 1965 (Tichenor, 2002, 114–149). At the end of World War II, Charles de Gaulle argued that France should deal with the "threat" of being inundated by immigrants from their own colonies by imitating this system (Weil, 2002, 141–150). Though in this regard de Gaulle did not prevail, his concerns still find adherents in European and North American immigration debates. Similar denials of equal rights to indigenous peoples and non-whites generally can be found throughout regimes shaped by European colonialism, and other forms of racialist and ethnic internal discrimination and exclusion can be found elsewhere.

In light of these disturbing examples; the manner in which mid-twentieth century Japanese leaders mixed their doctrines of the divinity of the emperor and the purity of the Yamato race with western conceptions of racial struggle to justify imperialism in East Asia; and above all the spectre of Nazi Germany, among all too many other instances, we can easily identify a second sort of occasion that frequently invokes reliance

[28] This speech is cited and further discussed in Smith, 1997, 430.

on ethically constitutive accounts: *when economic and political power benefits are being obtained, but obtained by questionable means that need moral legitimation.* If the use of racial doctrines to win support for new, more republican regimes, as in the Chinese Revolution and the British Glorious Revolution, may seem pragmatically acceptable to many westerners, they nonetheless justified revolutionary actions that were illegal according to the prevailing legal systems. Theories of racial destiny provided overriding moral defenses for those deeds. When we see how such racial doctrines were used to justify imperial rule established by forcible conquest, as they were by elites in Britain, the United States, Japan, and Germany, it becomes even more apparent that their appeal has come in part from the legitimacy they have bestowed on actions that prevailing legal and moral traditions would otherwise deem morally wrong, both legally criminal and sinfully evil.

And given that distinctions between "external" and "internal" leaders and constituencies are themselves products of people-making projects, there is obviously nothing about this legitimating role that is confined to measures taken against "external" rivals, such as the imposition of colonialism. Ethically constitutive racial, ethnic, and religious accounts, among others, have also been used to justify assigning subordinated, often exploited statuses to a wide variety of "internal" groups in many societies – such as the Jim Crow United States, apartheid South Africa, Protestant-ruled Northern Ireland, the sectors of India ordered by caste, and Hutu-governed Ruwanda, among countless others. I have already suggested that in much of Latin America, even the apparently more inclusive policies of *mestizaje* and *indigenismo* had "internal" targets whose regulation and repression could not easily be defended in terms of democracy and human rights alone. All too often these measures simply represented extensions of European imperialism via continuing cultural and economic policies of "whitening" in more benign form. Generally, the "mixing" of races and the "strengthening" of indigenous and African-descended peoples really meant chiefly assimilating them to Spanish-derived cultural identities and breaking up local communal forms of economic and political life, even while incorporating and celebrating certain indigenous and African cultural elements as part of the national "mestizo" identity. As Florencia Mallon has written of Mexico, starting with the 1920s, "the twin projects of the state vis-à-vis indigenous communities were to excavate the great ancient civilizations and to provide remedial education and services to the 'degenerate' Indians of the present . . . The great mestizo nation of Mexico could emerge in relation to a reorganized and reconstituted Indian past and to the present Indian as 'other'" (Knight, 1990, 80–87; Mallon, 1995, 283).

Thus even as Vasconcelos praised the virtues of hybrid races, he also cautioned against permitting the Hispanic elements of Mexican demography and culture to be "overwhelmed by the wave of the Negro, of the Indian, or of the Asiatic," sentiments that helped support mass expulsions of Chinese immigrants in 1931 (Vasconcelos, 1926, 101; Knight, 1990, 96–97). Similar arguments about the harshly assimilative, repressive, and exclusionary consequences of many strains of *indigenismo* are made about Colombia (Wade, 1993, 25–27), Ecuador (Radcliffe and Westwood, 1996, 68), Peru (de la Cadena, 2001, 17–23), and about the "racial democracy" celebrations in Brazil (Hanchard, 1994; Marx, 1998, 164–168; Nobles, 2000, 96–110), among other Latin American locales. Though *indigenismo* in all its forms still seems preferable to direct genocide, and there have been varieties more respectful of native cultures than others, it has generally represented policies imposed on indigenous peoples rather than advocated by them. Its ethically constitutive themes have simply adorned those measures with moral perfume.

Yet these controversies, still intensely contested in many Latin American locales, exemplify why such perfume is needed, why strictly economic and political power bases of legitimation are insufficient. They also underscore the related reality that the politics of people-making cannot be understood as strictly top-down or as unconstrained: practices of constituent resistance can be powerful enough to win a real place for their ethically constitutive commitments in the forms of peoplehood that prevail. As I have noted, Florencia Mallon and others contend that in both Mexico and Peru, nineteenth-century politicians relying mostly on force and market-promoting economic policies failed to generate a "social and moral project" that included "popular as well as elite notions of popular culture." And because their market economic stories and results were insufficient, they then "entered the twentieth century with state structures built on the violent exclusion of popular constituencies." Like the post-independence federal Nigerian government in relation to its four powerful regions, those structures often lacked effective governing capacity. In various locales, conservatives were able to sustain support by embracing religious traditions that liberal nation-builders rejected. Local populations also often failed to alter traditional forms of communal land ownership and cultural life except insofar as they were continually coerced to do so.

Yet whereas in Peru those patterns persisted through much of the twentieth century, Mexican elites began in some regions to give greater recognition to local communal legitimacy and prevailing cultural and religious traditions – prevailing ethically constitutive narratives of local identity – in ways that helped to modify and legitimate national economic policies and that permitted the development of varying local senses of national identity (Mallon, 1995, 61, 247–248, 311). Those processes of accommodation were and are, to be sure, inherently limited: any project of "nation"-building inevitably means overriding some claims on behalf of local communities. Still, many scholars now argue that, as a result of the need to bolster national economic and political initiatives by allying them with popular cultural elements, local leaders and popular constituencies have had and continue to have genuine, if subordinate, roles in shaping both local and national policies and senses of "peoplehood" in modern Mexico (Purnell, 2002).

The politics of people-making that has resulted is complex and contentious, for conceptions of local identities and their proper relationship to the nation vary widely, within and across local communities and regions. The southern Mexican state of Chiapas, for example, has "a long history of resistance by multiethnic subordinate groups to elite political and economic domination." There, many activists envision the creation of relatively autonomous "multi-ethnic regions as an integral part of the Mexican nation-state" – a position comparable to that of Awolowo in Nigeria, but without his expectation of regional ethnic unity. In Oaxaca, in contrast, the local "sons of the *pueblo*" conceive of themselves as "very particular peoples from very particular places, even as they also imagine themselves to be members, individually and collectively, of the Mexican nation." Many Oaxacan activists support a competing "autonomy project" that envisions greater "communal or village-level autonomy," and ethnic homogeneity, rather than multiethnic regional empowerment (Purnell, 2002, 228–230). At local, regional, and national levels, then, we can see leaders advancing complexly layered conceptions of peoplehood that involve ethically constitutive as well as economic and political power elements. And though these ethically constitutive accounts often express narrow partisan purposes, and though achieving consensus among the quite different conceptions being advanced remains a substantial and only partly met political challenge, their legitimating role does sometimes provide a valuable avenue for multiple constituencies to play meaningful parts in shaping collective destinies.

That is true even though at all levels, the legitimating role of ethically constitutive narratives often includes continued support for gender inequalities. It might seem that the emphasis on the value of racial and ethnic mixing that has prevailed in modern Mexico and much of Latin America should mitigate pressures to control the reproductive roles of women, thereby opening the door to greater gender equality; and certainly it has strengthened egalitarian moral discourses that Latin American feminists can and do use in their behalf. In reality, however, the persistence of goals of "whitening," even if now more tacit, has often still worked to reinforce female subordination. So, too, have many forms of Catholic religiosity; so, too, have many calls for deference to traditional indigenous ways of life; so, too, have republican traditions identifying citizenship with male martial virtues, as well as ongoing male desires to construct economic divisions of labor that free them of many forms of domestic work.

Hence Latin American national identities continue to be constructed in "gendered" terms in many respects, with ethically constitutive accounts often supplying moral rationalizations for these statuses. That remains true even though the picture should be understood as one of ongoing contestation, with historic progress for gender equality, not simply unbroken male hegemony. There are aspects of all these traditions that can be and have been turned by feminists to support of more genuinely equal republican political and economic citizenship; and reinforced by women's successes elsewhere, Latin American champions of gender equity have had some success in shaping national development, just as local, religious, and indigenous community leaders have done. But all too often, a variety of traditional religious, cultural, and biological ethically constitutive accounts continue to provide moral sanctions for discriminations that would otherwise be indefensible.[29]

The example of gendered ethically constitutive stories, even more than racial ones, may make more intuitively clear the third circumstance that can occasion renewed propagation of ethically constitutive stories. Precisely because these stories can be foundational in the development of human identities, human psyches and sense of value and meaning, many people are likely to be made insecure *when the ideas, institutions, and practices expressive of established ethically constitutive stories are threatened*, from whatever source. Even persons whose statuses in prevailing arrangements are far from enviable may feel anxious when their world seems to be undergoing major upheavals and transformations. They are then likely to be responsive to elites who offer refurbished versions of the ideologies, institutions, and ways of life to which they feel allegiance (Turner, 1986, 104). Once institutionalized, then, ethically constitutive stories can become in themselves a basis for their recurrent prominence, whenever events spark an "identity politics" aimed at self-preservation or reassertion.

When we reflect on how psychologically fundamental gender identities are to most people, it is not hard to grasp how even those who suffer from many aspects of traditional male and female gender constructions

---

[29] See e.g. Guy, 1992; Mallon, 1995, 69–79, 86; Chambers, 1999, 189–216; Caulfield, 2000.

may be deeply unsettled by challenges to those senses of themselves, and may be open to calls for their reassertion. Traditionalist women, after all, provided crucial opposition to the unsuccessful Equal Rights Amendment in the United States during the 1970s (Mansbridge, 1986). Many other sorts of ethically constitutive narratives, once institutionalized and psychologically internalized, can serve to motivate and guide subsequent politics in similar fashion. Consider, for instance, the historical choices of the Mennonite communities who came to colonial America for the same reasons as many other colonists: to follow empire and trade in pursuit of economic prosperity and to escape religious persecution and civil disabilities in Europe. In the eighteenth century they established themselves as successful commercial as well as subsistence farmers, and they often sought naturalization to secure their land titles. Many then became somewhat politically active, voting and holding local offices as assessors and unarmed constables. But when the revolution came, most Mennonites were reluctant to support their fellow colonists, in part because of their opposition to force, in part because they believed it was God's place, not theirs, to establish civil rulers. Some went to Canada. More stayed but refused to provide military service or, sometimes, to pay war taxes; and so revolutionary governments initially disfranchised them. After the war, they came again to be tolerated and had their voting rights restored; but henceforth few voted or held public offices in the manner they had previously done. They returned to being "subjects more than citizens" as well as becoming more "a people apart," and their political disengagement long preserved those statuses (MacMaster, 1985, 48–49, 232, 274–287; Driedger, 1988, 10, 16).

How can we account for those decisions? They certainly cannot be explained in straightforward political power terms, since these withdrawals represented abdication of any power in the broader society and, at best, fragile protection against any hostile forces that might emerge. And even though Mennonite farming communities were generally prosperous, it is unlikely that these choices represented the best "wealth-maximizing" or even "wealth-securing" options available to them. It seems more likely that most in these communities genuinely and profoundly embraced their religious tenets of pacifism and acquiescence to civil authorities in all matters that did not violate their core beliefs. The revolution generated pressures to engage in such violations, and in response many Mennonites gave heightened attention to the implications of their ethically constitutive religious senses of themselves. Most of the Mennonite leaders and members chose to reaffirm their religious identities and to accept the increased sense of separate political "peoplehood" it now seemed to entail. The most plausible interpretation of their actions is that they were so committed to their religious conceptions of themselves that they embraced their beliefs all the more fully amidst tumultuous changes, even though this meant foregoing promising new economic and political pursuits and giving up some that they had long enjoyed.

Consider also the case of Quebec. From the colonial Quebec Act of 1774 through the establishment of the Canadian Confederation in 1867 to the Citizenship Law of 1946 on up to the present, Francophone inhabitants of Quebec have been granted formal recognition and various protections for their distinctive linguistic and legal traditions (Morton, 1993, 51–60). But no one denies that up until the 1960s, the French-descended Quebec citizens suffered enormously in comparison to their English counterparts, in the province and outside it. Most Francophone Quebeckers pursued rural, traditionally religious ways of life and were comparatively ill educated, economically poor, and politically impotent. But the "Quiet Revolution" of the 1960s succeeded through a variety of means in erasing most of these inequalities, creating a well-trained, energetic class of Francophone leaders for Quebec's political, economic, and civil institutions, and limiting many of the observable differences between French and English Canadians, apart from language (Carens, 2000, 114–115; Kymlicka, 2001, 256–257).

These very successes have created new political dilemmas. Since, under current arrangements, past inequities have been greatly ameliorated and most other differences between Quebeckers and other Canadians have been attenuated, many Anglophone Canadians ask, what reason is there to support any special political status for Quebec today? Quebec leaders and citizens have asked themselves the same question; but the Parti Québécois has been increasingly successful over time in winning support for an answer that says considerable autonomy, indeed now a declaration of national sovereignty, is necessary to keep Quebec a Francophone society. Quebec leaders regularly affirm their support for a Quebec that has a thriving market economy, cultural and religious diversity, and parliamentary institutions with protections for human rights, as in the rest of Canada. Their claims to distinctiveness rest overwhelmingly on concerns for linguistic preservation alone, even though those concerns also breed support for constitutional arrangements guaranteeing units like Quebec considerable powers of self-determination. But however specific its focus, Quebeckers nonetheless "have developed a strong sense of political identity." They see themselves as "having responsibilities to each other for the ongoing wellbeing" of Quebec, duties that for many far outweigh their commitments to Canada (Carens, 2000, 111–117, 131–137; Kymlicka, 2001, 254–255, 262–263).

Why so? Why have Quebeckers not been content with their increasingly equal shares in the economic and political opportunities and benefits they possess as Canadians? Their insistences on the primacy of French and on autonomous power for Quebec have generated great political tensions and struggles and also cost them productive Anglophone residents and investors. It is, at a minimum, not obvious that their course has been more advantageous in economic and political power terms than acceptance of more standard Canadian provincial status. Yet it is clear that, after generations of seeing themselves as disadvantaged due to the cultural heritage through which others defined them and they defined themselves, many perceive any acceptance of political courses that might lead to the eradication of their distinctive identities as self-immolating betrayals. If the French language is all that is left of their cultural distinctiveness, it must for that very reason be vigorously protected. It is true that its protection involves acquiring special political power; but for most constituents and undoubtedly at least some Quebec leaders, that power appears to be sought more in the service of an intrinsically valued ethically constitutive identity than the reverse.

Finally and most bitterly, consider also the example of mass and elite commitments to systems of white supremacy in US history. Originally racialist doctrines plainly served to justify economically exploitative systems of slavery and native displacement, and they have since often served to buttress different forms of forced labor systems, as in the post-Civil War agricultural South, or to justify neglect of those segments of minority populations for whom productive work cannot be found. Even so, efforts to explain the history of American racial statuses strictly in economic terms have never succeeded. I have argued, for instance, that we cannot make sense of the failure of Reconstruction without accepting that many white Americans felt that not just their economic positions but their social statuses and cherished senses of meaning would be threatened by genuine racial equality. It is hard to see why in 1865 the successor to the assassinated Abraham Lincoln, President Andrew Johnson, alienated his initial overwhelming support in the Radical Republican-led Congress and chose to ally instead with his old enemies, the southern planters. It seems most likely that he was genuinely committed to his openly professed, anti-Radical belief that the "great difference between the two races in physical, mental and moral characteristics" meant that if "the inferior obtains the ascendancy" it would make the country a "wilderness" (Smith, 1997, 287–288, 303–304). As W. E. B. Du Bois recognized, it is also hard to see why so many northern white workers perceived all blacks as threats, even though native whites were willing to join in unions with many European immigrants. It is hard to avoid the conclusion that these senses of threat included anxieties about loss of a long-recognized superior social and moral status, along with fears of competition with low-wage labor (Du Bois, 1992, 674, 700–701). The positions on immigration restriction and imperialism of leading Republicans like Henry Cabot Lodge, Sr., and Albert Beveridge show how extensively white Americans went on to refurbish their ethically constitutive stories of racial identity in the last quarter of the nineteenth century. In part, the very surge of political and legal commitments to greater racial equality that the Civil War had spurred was the disturbing upheaval that led many to reassert visions of "white America" in these ways.

If these are the sorts of occasions when we can expect ethically constitutive stories to become politically prominent – when the provision of economic and political power benefits is deficient or uncertain; when these goods are being provided by seemingly illegitimate means; and when arrangements expressive of entrenched ethically constitutive stories are disrupted – then we can also suggest a variety of circumstances that might render ethically constitutive narratives less central in political life. When valued economic and political power benefits are being reliably provided; when they are being provided through means that are widely accepted as morally legitimate; and when whatever economic, social, demographic, or political changes that are occurring are widely interpreted as prompting modifications but not degradations of established ethically constitutive institutions and practices, we might reasonably expect economic and political power stories to dominate political discourses. Those are potentially quite important possibilities that deserve to be pursued in ways that, once again, I cannot attempt here.

But even if it is true that such conditions can render ethically constitutive discourses less visible in the politics of people-building, everything I have argued so far suggests that they will nonetheless remain present in non-trivial forms and continue to harbor the potential to become far more pivotal. That reality raises the central normative question I wish to pursue in the second part of this book. If ethically constitutive stories are inescapably an integral element of all processes of political people-making, and hence all political life, what do we do about their obvious potential to define and advance viciously unjust political projects? Are there ways we can and should seek to diminish that potential, even if we cannot hope to eliminate it? Though my answers are tentative and controversial, they point to an ultimate "yes."

Part II

Constructing political peoplehood in morally defensible ways

3 Ethically constitutive stories and norms of allegiance

The preceding chapters sketch what I hope is a lifelike portrait of the processes through which shared senses of political peoplehood are generated and sustained. All the great variety of forms of "imagined" political communities are human creations, I have claimed – the products of both coercive force and persuasive stories inspiring a sense of trust and worth among a critical mass of supporters for particular visions of common membership. Those persuasive narratives include not only economic and political power appeals but also "ethically constitutive stories" that claim membership is somehow intrinsic to the core identities of potential constituents. Though their prominence and impact may wax and wane at different times, I have contended that such stories always have important roles in shaping the governing activities, including policies and institutions of inclusion and exclusion, in all long-enduring political societies.

With this chapter the argument takes a normative turn. The guiding question is: if the foregoing arguments are right, what do these political realities suggest for how human beings at the dawn of the twenty-first century should evaluate and attempt to sustain or modify their existing forms of political peoplehood? The claims made so far have been at best reasonable speculations, and to move from any empirical premises, however solid, to specific normative positions always involves many legitimately debatable steps. I believe, however, that much of the rapidly burgeoning normative literature on political memberships and allegiances does not attend sufficiently to the whole topic of the politics through which senses of peoplehood are predictably constructed. Too often, deep basic issues are addressed only in unsatisfying footnotes that, on reflection, undermine key claims in the texts they qualify. If what follows serves as no more than an example of how conscious attention to such politics might help us to address "should" questions of political membership better, it will be a valuable exercise. And, unsurprisingly, I believe the normative positions I defend are in fact more reasonable than available alternatives, although I fully acknowledge that we tread here on slippery and shifting terrain, where we cannot hope for much in the way of solid footing.

Let me also acknowledge that not a great deal in the way of general institutional recommendations can be drawn from the account of the politics of people-making I have provided. The logic of the argument indicates that specific courses of action must always be decided to a large degree contextually, for they will depend on the challenges and opportunities presented by the affiliations and aversions, established institutions, historical traditions, and current material and political circumstances in particular times and places. Even so, reflection on the general picture I have provided does, I think, incline us to pursue certain directions of people-building rather than others in virtually every context. If it is true that political peoples are best understood as valuable yet dangerous human creations, the products of ongoing, competitive politics that can often go awry; and if it is true that many of the worst dangers are associated either with unduly "strong," chauvinistic senses of peoplehood that may be repressive and imperialistic, or with "weak" forms of political community that can do little to help meet the material and psychological needs of their members, then it does not seem too great a leap to suggest that we should seek to create a world of "moderate" political peoples, insofar as we can.

That is a recommendation with some bite. "Moderate" political peoples are communities that assert some significant claims on the loyalties of their constituents and some significant authority over various phases of their lives, and they must be able to inspire corresponding degrees of allegiance. But they do not claim absolute sovereignty over all aspects of their members' lives or primacy over all alternative communities to which their constituents may also belong. Since they do not, they are logically required to accept the legitimacy of multiple political memberships, multiple citizenships, so long as those alternative allegiances do not prevent them from governing in their areas of authority and accomplishing their distinctive purposes. Indeed, moderate political peoples must recognize that in some matters, the claims of other political communities may be more legitimately binding on their members than their own, even in cases of partial conflict. In such situations, it seems advisable for moderate peoples to strive to work out peaceful systems of cooperation among these competing political authorities, perhaps via bilateral or multilateral treaties, perhaps by accepting the authority of "third party" or international commissions, agencies, or tribunals, perhaps, if overlapping interests and conflicts are frequent, by forming some sort of ongoing confederation to deal with shared problems.

Their moderation also means that such political peoples should recognize that their members have *rights* to choose to join more fully with other political associations they value, either individually or collectively, so long as those choices do not violate any existing valid duties or responsibilities within the community in which they have heretofore primarily resided. And that means, in turn, that to the greatest extent that they can while maintaining their viability, moderate political peoples should honor basic human freedoms such as individual rights of expatriation, emigration, and immigration, and also the rights of groups of constituents to redefine their political affiliations, via the establishment of greater political autonomy, participation in transnational groups that make up international civil society, or even at the extreme through secession, aimed either at independence or union with another political people. And because moderate political communities should recognize the rights of individuals and groups to have meaningful choices about their political affiliations and allegiances, it is highly advisable, if not indeed imperative, for these peoples to uphold basic rights of political expression and democratic participation in collective decision-making for all their members (at least). Such rights help make individual and group choices about membership more of a reality, and they also provide means for individuals and groups to shape the collective life of their communities in ways that may make exit a less attractive option.

These points mean that on many contemporary institutional questions, I am in sympathy with the recommendations of "cosmopolitan democrats" like the British philosopher David Held and "liberal nationalists" like the Canadian theorist Will Kymlicka. In only somewhat varying ways, they seek to envision and promote a world that is not structured primarily in terms of nation-states claiming ultimate sovereignty. Instead, they support, at least in principle, the development of international institutions to protect human rights; federated, multinational states when constituent communities desire such arrangements; the devolution of some powers down to subnational communities, to combat "democratic deficits" and to recognize senses of solidarity; the assignment of responsibility "upward" instead, for problems that demand it, to regional or international bodies, which may represent transnational groups such as worker, environmental, human rights, and relief organizations as well as states and multinational corporations; all with ongoing effort to see that all levels of governance are organized as democratically, as openly, and as respectful of basic rights as can be achieved (Held, 1995; 1998, 21–26; Kymlicka, 2001, 229–241, 317–326). This is a world of what I am terming moderate political peoples, with an emphasis on democratic practices and respect for human rights as both expressions and sources of such moderation. Although there remain important differences among these authors about how feasible transnational or even global democratic institutions can ever be, and how desirable it is to sacrifice fluidity of political memberships in order to preserve distinctive particular cultures, their broad brush depictions of desirable forms of political community and institutions are similar to each other and to what I see as some of the main normative implications of the view of people-building I have provided.

Yet if these authors and others provide valuable depictions of what the institutions of a world of moderate political peoples might look like, there are still many questions to be answered. How can we hope to conduct the politics of people-making in ways that can generate such moderate forms of peoplehood and thereby gain support for the proliferation of such institutions? As Kymlicka observes, Held, like most "cosmopolitan democrats," simply says very little about how we are to achieve compelling yet suitably moderate senses of valued "collective identity," of "solidarity and trust," that can inspire allegiance to these sorts of political communities. Nor has Kymlicka himself pursued that topic in depth. He has been more concerned to argue that *states* have historically often built nations, while simultaneously suggesting that some nations simply develop "over long periods of time" as a result of shared territory, history, and language. He then focuses on the problems of conflicts between nation-building states and minority nations within their borders, as well as political groups outside them (e.g. 2001, 229–230, 262). The question of how either states or other political actors are to build sufficiently binding yet sufficiently moderate forms of peoplehood has not been his concern.[1]

Yet the account of the politics of people-building here indicates that this concern is simply not avoidable. The political dynamics generating strong, often intolerant and repressive forms of peoplehood, buttressed by potent ethically constitutive stories, are powerful and enduring. I believe that no prescription for appropriately moderate forms of political memberships can be adequate if it does not explicitly address the need for ethically constitutive stories that indicate why those memberships embody identities that their members should embrace, even as they also support, enduring political moderation. Essential as they are, neither force alone,

---

[1] Though Kymlicka's framework leads him to many useful insights and suggestions, it has three weaknesses. It treats nation-building by states as rather monolithic exercises, understating how this is a highly contested process involving shifting coalitions and visions of nationhood or "peoplehood." It also treats at least some national minorities as if they were somehow more organic and authentic than "state" nationalities, instead of recognizing them as products of similar political processes. Finally, its emphasis on shared language, territory, and history does not sufficiently surface the importance of what I am terming "stories of peoplehood," especially ethically constitutive stories. At various junctures Kymlicka does display keen awareness of all these considerations, but they are not explicit themes of his main lines of analysis and argument.

nor accounts stressing only economic and political power benefits, will be enough to sustain viable and appropriate forms of political peoplehood over time.

Once again, I largely set aside here the inescapable questions of just what forms of force, and what sorts of economic and political power stories and accompanying institutions, are most desirable. Not only must those answers be largely contextual; the issues posed by the necessity of ethically constitutive stories are also complex and far-reaching enough to warrant focused discussion. The necessity for these stories means that virtually all current prescriptions for embracing concepts of a purely "civic nation," a purely "constitutional patriotism," some form of essentially "liberal" or "republican" or "liberal republican" or "neorepublican" or "strong democratic" or "social democratic" or "cosmopolitan citizenship" as conventionally defined, seem insufficient. Although these perspectives provide indispensable elements that can contribute to a more salutary politics of people-making, they recurrently minimize or evade the need for ethically constitutive stories. As a result, none can really work, probably not philosophically, certainly not politically. In contrast, at least some proponents of "communitarian" and "multicultural" conceptions of membership may appear to grasp the place of what I call "ethically constitutive stories" more fully. Many, however, have been reluctant to look closely at the unsettling political processes through which such stories actually come to constitute identities and communities. Insofar as they have done so, it has chiefly been to defend the espousal of ethically constitutive stories by the less powerful, while discouraging their expression on behalf of more powerful communities and regimes.

That will not do. If I am right that the political role of ethically constitutive stories, advanced by more *and* less powerful groups, by state leaders, and by dissidents, cannot be avoided, then their potential for invidious political uses must be understood and resisted in other ways. That potential can and must be opposed in many contexts partly by appeals to democratic values and procedures, by promises of economic benefits that will follow if basic economic liberties and other human rights are respected, and sometimes by resisting vicious coercion by military means. Yet potent but dangerous ethically constitutive stories must often also be met, I believe, by advancing more potent and less dangerous ethically constitutive stories.

A two-part strategy may provide a politically and philosophically feasible way of doing so. First, we should embrace a politics in which particularistic ethically constitutive stories compete against each other for political support, in ways that can check their excesses, encourage moderating modifications, and challenge the claims of all regimes to full sovereignty over those they govern. Second, we should insist that all ethically constitutive stories justifying more particular political memberships must be connected to larger constitutive stories defining the identity and interests of the human species. I further maintain that today the most intellectually defensible versions of such a larger constitutive story must accept that the human species appears to be in an ongoing process of evolution, within a dauntingly mysterious and dangerous cosmos that we did not make and that cannot be relied on to provide for our well-being. Hence, to put it very simply, we are well advised to make sure that we are looking out for each other as fellow members of the human species, as well as for the long-term viability of natural and social environments in which we may survive and perhaps thrive. Our forms of political peoplehood, and the stories that sustain them, must ultimately be measured at the bar set by those standards.

From this species-centered standpoint, particular political communities appear as something empirically and morally akin (though not identical) to political parties within existing societies. They are partisan organizations with distinct visions of humanity's development that clearly benefit their members, or at least some of them, first and foremost. But like political parties, political communities or peoples are groups who should face ongoing political pressures to show that their existence and activities are also more broadly beneficial, to all their members and to non-members. Often they can make those claims credibly, since it remains hard to see how we can conduct our common lives successfully without organizing ourselves in these ways. It may often be wise to value existing forms of political peoplehood greatly. But all political communities, all "peoples," are clearly imperfect instruments at best – ones in which we should not invest too many of our hopes and loyalties and from which we should not accept claims to be of unchanging and universal value, legitimately resistant to transformation or transcendence.

Such perspectives toward existing forms of political peoplehood are certainly visible in many locations today, forming bases on which it is possible to build. Still, a world in which political communities are widely understood as partial, partisan, and artificial in this way, rather than as complete, sovereign, and somehow natural, and as justifiable only if they contribute to the good of the species as well as their members, is a different world than we have now. And it is a world in which we humans would, I believe, have a much better chance of achieving ongoing, constructive accommodations among the clashing plurality of memberships, interests, and political visions that will inevitably continue to exist. But it is a world we cannot have unless conceptions of political membership incorporate both particularistic and species-wide ethically constitutive stories of appropriate sorts. That is the profound challenge that too few academic advocates of visions of political membership are now recognizing, much less seeking to meet.

Ethically constitutive stories and current citizenship debates

Normative discussions of citizenship and other forms of political membership and identity have proliferated rapidly in recent years and I do not try to review them comprehensively here. I nonetheless wish to show that many current works really are inadequate because they neglect key features of the politics of people-building. Consequently, I review some representative and influential writers and perspectives, fully aware that many readers will not identify with any of the views I examine.

As discussed in Part I, many current writers structure their prescriptions, implicitly or explicitly, in terms of "contrasting liberal and republican ideal types of citizenship," with modern social democratic conceptions elaborated out of elements of each (Hutchings and Dannreuther, eds., 1999, 4–5). I have also argued that, even though these conceptions are frequently discussed as "civic" views of membership that focus only on proper political principles and procedures, they all nonetheless depend philosophically on various sorts of ethically constitutive stories that explain why those procedures and principles are appropriate for human beings. That philosophic dependence is ineradicable, for it is impossible to advocate any course of action as ethically right for human beings without relying, explicitly or implicitly, on some account of humanity that renders those prescriptions sensible. Even though people do not agree on any one such conception and probably never will, no prescriptive argument can be persuasive if it does not appeal to one or more such notions that are accepted by those who are to be persuaded. There is just no reason to follow a prescription that makes sense only for beings fundamentally different than oneself.

Philosophically as well as politically, then, normative arguments need to be associated with some sorts of supportive ethically constitutive stories, preferably a range of such stories that can win wide acceptance. Therein, however, lies a profound intellectual problem that may be manifested as a more or less serious political tension. How do we reconcile the humanity-wide ethically constitutive stories of prevailing "civic" conceptions of peoplehood with more particularistic accounts that can inspire strong identification with memberships in actual, specific political peoples? Admittedly, that philosophic question often does not create any concrete political problems, because people can cheerfully embrace senses of peoplehood that contain deep logical inconsistencies so long as the forms of life that result are working for them in other ways. But sometimes, and certainly today when the evils of chauvinistic particularisms are widely perceived, the task of uniting egalitarian liberal, republican, and democratic or social democratic notions of membership with distinctive ethically constitutive stories can be politically problematic as well as intellectually and morally troubling. Any adequate normative theory of political membership today must acknowledge and confront these challenges.

These are not, however, challenges that are identified or met well in many of the philosophical prescriptions concerning political membership that are currently prominent. Instead, these difficulties are often dealt with essentially by fiat. Like others, I have previously noted that in his most famous works, the most influential American liberal theorist, John Rawls, did not address such questions of political membership at all, beyond making some simplifying assumptions that, if taken literally, would be highly illiberal and impractical. When discussing the proper domestic structure of a "well-ordered society," Rawls long indicated that he prefers to theorize about a "closed society," in which all members enter via birth and stay for life, with none allowed out and no one else allowed in (Rawls, 1993a, 12, 35–36). Yet this assumption is far more devastating to the "ideal theory" constructed in 1971's *A Theory of Justice* and supplemented in 1993's *Political Liberalism* than Rawls has ever recognized.[2]

A "well-ordered" society is, after all, supposed to be one whose "basic structure – that is, its main political and social institutions and how they fit together as one system of cooperation," satisfy basic "principles of justice" (1993a, 35). Institutions of membership are clearly basic to the structures of political societies, and so Rawls has never been able to avoid taking some position on them, however theoretical and provisional. He has plainly wished, however, to bracket membership questions as much as possible, quite understandably. Those questions are complex and vexing. His simplifying "abstract" response in these works is nonetheless deeply problematic, because it reproduces the old common law doctrine of "perpetual allegiance" to one's sovereign at nativity: persons are members of a Rawlsian "well-ordered" society simply because they were born members, and they cannot choose to be anything else. As a result, his "well-ordered"

---

[2] Rawls argues that *A Theory of Justice* laid out a comprehensive view of political morality that all members of a well-ordered society are presumed to accept, while *Political Liberalism* addresses well-ordered societies in which reasonable citizens have different comprehensive views (Rawls, 1999, 179–180). I note the differences where pertinent here, but for the most part they are not.

societies deny the right of expatriation to their citizens and to outsiders, to potential emigrants and immigrants alike.

As Rawls has since tacitly conceded, this denial is no minor step. The American revolutionaries proclaimed the right to dissolve one's political membership to be natural, inalienable, and fundamental to all legitimate governments, and expatriation remains the only right declared to be "natural" by a US statute (Smith, 1997, 80–81, 313). The moral reasons for those special statuses stem not only from the political benefits of moderating claims to absolute sovereignty. They lie deep in the heart of the philosophic conceptions on which Rawls is purportedly relying. If persons are morally free and equal, by nature or some other standard, then no persons are naturally rulers over others, and so legitimate political memberships and governments can result only from the consent of the governed. Membership by consent, in turn, cannot be said to exist unless governments grant members expatriation rights. It also cannot exist meaningfully if governments do not permit at least some opportunities for immigrants to join their societies. Indeed, making membership truly consensual logically points to the propriety of permitting persons to expatriate themselves without leaving their country; toward certain kinds of aid to emigrants and immigrants; and even toward collective expatriation rights. For without real choices, there can be no real consent to membership and governance; without real consent to membership and governance, persons cannot be said to be genuinely free and equal.

One might reply that these are rather theoretical concerns. Even with formal expatriation and immigration rights, most people would not find it practical or desirable to change political societies. Hence, as Rawls once suggested, they do not really do much to make memberships voluntary; so little harm is done in assuming that people do not have these rights (Rawls, 1993a, 136n4). But the more we stress that people do not have real, practical choices to do other than embrace their inherited memberships, the more we undermine the claim that their memberships rest on anything like true consent. If we want to sustain that basis for legitimacy, as Rawls's premises of morally free and equal personhood seem to require, then we are pressed to conceive how we can make membership by choice more a reality.

Admittedly, that direction is deeply disturbing. Policies permitting and even facilitating extensive expatriation and immigration pose many intractable political and moral problems. It is politically difficult to sustain a society in which expatriation, emigration, and immigration are frequent occurrences. The resulting instabilities may make it hard for a political community to fulfill its responsibilities toward its ongoing members, much less outsiders.

Yet it is also impossible to make the basic structure of a liberal democratic society morally coherent without, at the barest minimum, recognizing and supporting meaningful expatriation rights, for one's individual citizens and for members of other political communities. Here, then, is the intractable but inescapable dilemma: it does not seem feasible in practice to construct societies that fully provide rights that it seems our societies must provide to be just. This means, however, that these rights are troubling precisely because they raise issues at the political and moral core of the enterprise of creating a just, "well-ordered" society, grounded on commitments to recognizing all persons as morally free and equal. We cannot responsibly ignore these issues or address them by "provisionally" adopting fundamentally illiberal, inegalitarian "simplifying" assumptions. All reasoning built on such flawed foundations is deeply suspect.

In two 1993 essays, both called "The Law of Peoples" (1993b, 1993c) and his expanded 1999 book of the same title, Rawls says more on these issues; but he still seeks rather desperately to set them to the side, in ways that only reveal how impossible it is to do so. In 1993 he included "the right to emigration" in his list of human rights, rights that must be accepted by all societies with a minimally decent, even if not fully liberal or democratic, political order (1993c, 68). But he said no more about that right and the political problems it might generate. Still, he seems to have been sufficiently concerned with those difficulties that he felt impelled to backpedal from this assertion in his 1999 *Law of Peoples*. There we learn that it is "hierarchical" societies who especially must "allow and provide assistance for the right of emigration." In one of those troubling footnotes that populate this literature, Rawls adds that "liberal societies must also allow for this right," subject to certain "qualifications" that he does not specify (1999, 74n15). In another footnote, he also suggests that every legitimate people "has at least a qualified right to limit immigration," again leaving aside "what these qualifications might be" (1999, 39n48). So instead of emigration being a basic human right in all societies, now it seems that both rights of emigration and immigration are only "qualified" rights in well-ordered liberal societies.

And even as he consigns his limited endorsements of these rights to footnotes, in his text Rawls stresses reasons for giving them narrow scope. He argues that a population must take responsibility for the "asset" of its territory, and he is concerned that large-scale migration might undermine that ethos. He also endorses Michael Walzer's argument that "limiting immigration" can "protect a people's political culture and its constitutional principles," and that failure to provide such protection might produce "a world of deracinated men and women." In fact, Rawls assumes that even "liberal peoples" must be culturally sustained by "common sympathies"; and he cites approvingly John Stuart Mill's view that these sympathies can arise from commonalities of race, descent, language, religion, or history. These kinds of commonalities are important because they help to give each people a sense of *amour-propre*, "self-respect of themselves as a people." Such self-respect rests partly on pride in the "justice and decency of their domestic political and social institutions" and partly from admiration for the "achievements of their public and civic culture," though it does not and must not go so far as to suggest that one people is inherently "superior or inferior to other peoples." Rawls suggests that extensive emigration and immigration are undesirable because they may undermine these common sympathies, a position implying that it may often be wise for policies to discourage such shifts. And Rawls contends that in any case, immigration is often driven by political, religious, and ethnic oppression and by economic hardships, and by population pressures generated in part through the subjection of women. He maintains that if we achieve more decent governments within particular societies, ones that protect minorities, respect women's rights, and promote economic prosperity, few would want to leave their homes, and immigration would be "eliminated as a serious problem" (Rawls, 1999, 8–9, 23n17, 24, 34, 39n48, 47–48).[3]

Yet much of what Rawls says calls that reassuring assertion into question. His analysis actually indicates that many members of many societies might well have powerful economic, political, and cultural reasons to go elsewhere, or to try to bring another regime into power over their territory. Rawls assumes both that a truly cosmopolitan state cannot exist, and that humanity must remain organized into a considerable variety of particular political communities. He also argues that considerable economic inequalities between these various particular societies may well be perfectly just (1999, 36, 41, 43). Even if this argument is correct – a very large if – economic bases for immigration and for competitive, potentially conflictual people-building will clearly persist in such a world.

Rawls also presumes that the world will consist of, at best, both "liberal" and non-liberal but "decent" regimes, and that even among liberal regimes, there will be significant variations in their forms of liberal democratic constitutionalism (1999, 11, 61–67). Hence people who care strongly about their political institutions may also have incentives either

---

[3] Though Rawls suggested in *Political Liberalism* that "immigration is an important question" and should be addressed "in discussing the appropriate relations between peoples" (1993a, 136n4), he uses these arguments to again dismiss any need for extensive discussion in his *Law of Peoples*.

to leave their current regime or perhaps to seek to have it absorbed into some more congenial one.

And perhaps most strikingly, Rawls comes very close to conceding that even well-ordered liberal "peoples" cannot be purely "civic," that they require a sense of distinctive cultural identity that involves "just" institutions but that may also be based on the sorts of feelings of commonality generated by shared "ethnic" traits, broadly defined. He also expresses a strong concern that those feelings of cultural commonality be preserved in all minimally just societies. But again, these variations may provide motives for some members to seek to depart for societies that may be more culturally congenial, even as some outsiders with different cultural backgrounds may seek to enter for economic or political reasons. They may then be perceived as cultural threats.

Under these circumstances, governing and aspiring elites will in many contexts have incentives to maintain and expand their support by making economic, political, and cultural appeals to members of other societies whom they wish to attract, and they will also have incentives to use economic, political, and cultural arguments to fence out persons and groups they or their core constituents find undesirable. Amidst the resulting competitive pressures, many governments even of liberal societies may feel that the goals of preserving a sense of cultural commonality, a prosperous economy, and a functional constitutional system justify limits on rights of expatriation, immigration, and naturalization provided to various groups.

In short, the circumstances Rawls depicts even in his "ideal theory" easily generate the sorts of competitive politics of people-making described here in Part I, a politics in which immigration policies, among others, often remain serious problems, contrary to Rawls's desires. So even the leaders and citizens of a well-ordered liberal society in a world of just societies cannot avoid confronting the issues Rawls refuses to acknowledge or address very openly. They must either illiberally deny or sharply limit rights of expatriation, emigration, and immigration, or they must find ways to build and sustain just and stable political communities while engaging in political contests in which what I am terming "ethically constitutive" stories, prime sources of "common sympathies," will often play prominent parts. It will, in practice, be very hard to pursue that politics without many participants contending strenuously that not only their visions of "peoplehood," but their "people," are indeed superior to the alternative communities that potential constituents might embrace. Yet Rawls has persistently refused to say much about any of these problems, beyond reaching for reasons to limit what he acknowledges to be basic human rights and expressing what his own analysis reveals to be quite unrealistic hopes that all reasons for their exercise, and for invidious contrasts with other peoples, may eventually fade away. In fact, even his account of life *within* "well-ordered" societies is haunted by aspects of these tensions that Rawls does not address. Though his "law of peoples" is supposed to rest on more minimal philosophic grounds, Rawls acknowledges that his prescriptions for a just, liberal domestic society rely on a "normative" and "political" conception of "persons as the basic units of thought, deliberation, and responsibility," with capacities that enable each person "to be a citizen, that is, a normal and fully cooperating member of society over a complete life" (Rawls, 1993a, 18). This notion of all persons as reasoning, responsible thinkers who can act cooperatively if they choose to do so is inspired by the moral vision of Immanuel Kant, even if Rawls eschews invocation of Kant's metaphysical notion of humanity as noumenal rational beings or any other "comprehensive" grounding of these moral conceptions. It is a story of human identity that does indeed support concern and respect for all individual human beings. It can thus serve to resist many of the claims of particular communities to authorize unjust acts toward members and outsiders, which will often include denials of rights of expatriation and immigration. Thus in prescribing for "well-ordered societies," Rawls effectively relies on an ethically constitutive story about the political identity of all humans that all citizens are expected to accept for political purposes; and it is one that points to liberal, indeed cosmopolitan, policies in these regards.

Yet he still assumes, both for "ideal theory" purposes and for his "law of peoples," the propriety of rather rigid, particularistic memberships, even suggesting that they can legitimately be sustained by stories of racial, religious, historical, and cultural distinctiveness (though not superiority). He never fully acknowledges or confronts the moral tensions, indeed contradictions, between his more universalistic ethically constitutive story and his assumptions of more particularistic, fixed forms of peoplehood, or more specifically, between his explicit neo-Kantian account of free and equal human beings and his embrace of policies aimed at preserving distinctive cultures or even "perpetual allegiance by birth."[4] Seminal as it is in other regards, his theory has little to say about either the politics or morals of people-building.

These issues have, however, been more adequately and influentially addressed in various works by perhaps the most prominent modern European liberal thinker, Jürgen Habermas. Especially important is an oft-cited and reprinted 1990 essay, "Citizenship and National Identity,"

---

[4] For a similar critique see Scheffler, 2001, 69–70.

though its arguments have been refined in later writings (repr. Habermas, 1996, 491–515). Habermas agrees with many other scholars that modern republican citizenship originated in the French Revolution in alliance with modern nationalism. And as noted in Chapter 2, he argues that such modern nationalisms relied on inherited ethnocultural notions of shared identity to provide initially crucial "social-psychological" reinforcement for the sacrifices modern republican citizenship involves (1996, 494–495; 1998, 112–113). In my terms, then, these nationalisms often served as ethically constitutive stories inspiring a sense of membership that could compel allegiance even when the costs were high.

But Habermas contends, much as I have done, that republicanism and ethnic nationalism are not conceptually united, however important their historical, political, and social-psychological links have been.[5] At least philosophically, he insists, modern citizenship has come to be understood essentially as an "association of free and equal persons" bound together only by consensus on "the unity of a *procedure*" for conducting common political life "to which all consent." Ascriptive forms of nationalism served only as a historical "catalyst" for the development of this purely civic conception of a nation (1996, 494–497). Habermas has increasingly acknowledged that it nonetheless remains a crucial question whether such naturalistic notions of peoplehood can in fact be abandoned, with modern republicanism really learning to "stand on its own two feet" (1998, 115–118). He concedes that even denaturalized modern citizenship requires support from "a liberal political culture" that accustoms citizens to political freedom and fosters their voluntary participation in civic duties and activities. This shared liberal political culture, Habermas says, can be "the common denominator for a *constitutional* patriotism (*Verfassungspatriotismus*) that heightens an awareness of both the diversity and the integrity of the different forms of life coexisting in a multicultural society." It need not be unduly homogenizing or repressive. Unlike Rawls, when addressing concrete emigration and immigration issues, Habermas explicitly rejects "a chauvinism of affluence" in favor of "a liberal immigration policy" in which immigrants are welcome, subject only to the demand that they become politically acculturated.

To many that demand may still seem too threatening, in light of modern anti-immigrant movements. But Habermas believes that if a liberal

---

[5] This is true even though republican social contract theories presuppose some kind of republic-creating "people," as Bernard Yack argues (Yack, 2001). Again, republicanism per se provides little guidance as to how that "people" comes to be constituted. It probably worked historically to spur the development of modern notions of the "nation," but republican thought did not itself specify those notions.

political culture is rightly understood, a "particularist anchoring of *this kind* would not do away with one iota of the universalist meaning of popular sovereignty and human rights" (1996, 500, 514). It would simply foster a sustaining sense that the realization of those principles in particular forms represents a shared national project. But whatever their diverse historical origins, all societies should converge on essentially the same political principles as their bases for membership, and their shared "liberal political culture" should not contain any "ethical-cultural" elements, any basis for Rawls's "common sympathies," beyond agreement on those principles. Because persons are now increasingly socially integrated by pervasive communication systems and by forms of social security that guarantee material benefits and cultural rights, Habermas is even more optimistic than Rawls that modern democratic polities can eschew reliance on unifying but "dangerous" ethnic myths (1998, 113, 119–120). Indeed, unlike the anti-cosmopolitan Rawls, Habermas thinks those same circumstances can permit the "constitutional patriotism" of modern societies to "pave the way for a *world citizenship*, which is already taking shape today in worldwide political communications" (1996, 514; 1998, 106–107, 153).

Habermas's view has many features that I believe to be normatively appropriate in light of the analysis of the politics of people-building developed here. More than most theorists, Habermas focuses on the sobering reality that the modern political communities we now often call "liberal democracies" or "republics" have won support historically through alliances of republican and liberal precepts with various ascriptive, ethnocultural nationalisms. Habermas also agrees that today, effective practices of free and equal citizenship still require supportive political cultures, and that many will reasonably wish to embrace more distinctive and particular cultural traditions and identities beyond this shared political culture. At the same time he provides explicit normative arguments against upholding membership rules that are hostile to basic human rights. He also points to transformed global conditions that not only work against chauvinistic particularisms but also may actually open the door to gradual development of existing "constitutionally patriotic" national institutions into some form of global citizenship.

Those normative arguments rely on, and elaborate more consistently, the sort of more universalistic "ethically constitutive story" about human beings that Rawls and many other contemporary neo-Kantian philosophers deploy. Habermas invokes a portrait of persons as ideally capable of rational communication and deliberative decision-making, and he contends that the construction of forms of life that stifle rather than facilitate these capacities is unjust (e.g., 1996, 295–302; 1998, 114). It is ultimately this larger ethically constitutive story that works to check the moral claims of particular memberships. It underwrites Habermas's insistence that while a "particular polity" can preserve its identity through exclusion of those who do not share its political culture, to be morally defensible that political culture must embrace "universalistic constitutional principles" of deliberative democracy and human rights. That is why exclusions or subordinations designed to protect the "*ethical-cultural* form of life*" or the broader "majority culture" of a political community, rather than strictly its liberal *political* culture, are in his eyes unjustified (1995, 853; 1996, 513; 1998, 146). To be sure, the people of each community are entitled to see themselves as engaged in a distinctive shared endeavor because they possess "a political culture shaped by a particular history" which provides "the base" for their "constitutional patriotism." But that patriotism is justified only so long as their system's constitutional principles are interpreted "without any harm to their universalist meaning." Hence their particular, distinctive political cultures cannot be *too* distinctive (1995, 851; 1998, 118).

Habermas's articulation of a liberal and deliberatively democratic "constitutional patriotism" may well represent the basic understanding of membership most widely shared by western academics, at least, today.[6] The foregoing analysis of the political role of ethically constitutive stories leads me nonetheless to question this type of view. It still does not sufficiently grasp the ongoing role of ethically constitutive narratives in supporting particular senses of political peoplehood today. And despite the changing global conditions Habermas notes, it may not provide a politically effective ethically constitutive story of all humanity.

Though it is an improvement over Rawls's "closed well-ordered societies" and "law of peoples" discussions, Habermas's "constitutional patriotism" remains essentially another version of standard liberal and republican notions of "civic nations" (Yack, 1996, 198–200). It still bases membership on agreement upon certain political principles and procedures, supported by a universalistic constitutive story of human personhood. Although it authorizes forging alliances with more particularistic conceptions of political identity for the present, it seeks ultimately to overcome any dependence on them. To be sure, like Rawls Habermas

---

[6] It has been explicitly embraced in various modified forms by recent advocates of "cosmopolitan democracy," "transterritorial communities," "cosmopolitan citizenship," and "neo-republican citizenship" like David Held (1995, 155–166, and cf. Falk, 1996, 59), David Jacobson (1996, 134), Andrew Linklatter (1999, 55), and Herman van Gunsteren (1998, 29). Andrew Kuper (2000, 672n55) offers a revised version of Rawls's international arguments that endorses Habermas.

endorses the notion of interpreting universal constitutional principles in terms of different national traditions, thereby sustaining distinctive but liberal political cultures. He also permits still-thicker cultural identities to be maintained among the subgroups of a democratic society, so long as they agree on the universal principles embraced by the shared political culture. Through these means, along with material benefits, he seeks to meet political and psychological pressures for richer senses of belonging that his proceduralist "constitutional patriotism" otherwise does not satisfy. But that "patriotism" remains one in which "a cosmopolitan understanding of the nation of citizens is accorded priority over an ethnocentric interpretation of the nation," because only "a nonnaturalistic concept of the nation can be combined seamlessly with the universalistic self-understanding of the democratic constitutional state" (1998, 115).

These are reasonable but not innovative moves, and Habermas has not done much more than Rawls to address the key problems they leave unresolved. Just how far can a core allegiance to his discursively democratic political principles really be combined, philosophically and politically, with distinctive national traditions and still more comprehensive cultural identities, while preserving a liberal political culture? How far can a liberal society go to make expatriation, emigration, and immigration practical choices for all humanity, as Habermas seems to wish, while at the same time seeking to maintain an at least mildly distinctive form of liberal democratic constitutionalism for its members? Habermas does not really provide any guidance on those issues, beyond repeated sweeping but vague stipulations that positions contrary to popular sovereignty, human rights, and universalist legal principles are not to be allowed (e.g. 1996, 500; 1998, 118). Instead he makes these problems seem less pressing – suggesting rather misleadingly that by the late nineteenth century (before the Holocaust, Jim Crow, and apartheid!) that repressive ascriptive nationalisms were already giving way to purely civic conceptions (1996, 494–495; 1998, 112, 146). He is also hopeful that a common liberal European political culture, indeed even a global liberal political culture, sufficient to support transnational or even cosmopolitan citizenship, can be seen as emerging (1996, 507, 514; 1998, 153). He does argue that those transnational cultures will have to be achieved through the blending by "cultural elites and the mass media" of "various national specific interpretations of the same universalist principles" (1996, 507). But again – how can this blending be done, both philosophically and politically? We need a fuller analysis of the problems than Habermas has provided of the problems that existing national traditions and religious, racial, ethnic, and other cultural identities pose for the political challenge of promoting transnational loyalties while eschewing illiberalism.[7]

And as I suggested in Part I, despite historical developments that seem in some ways more conducive to the establishment of "civic" nations, it remains likely that any effort to check the claims of particular constitutive narratives and memberships by appeal to a more universal story of human identity will need more of an ethically constitutive story than Habermas and other neo-Kantian writers have provided.[8] I do not disagree with Habermas, Bruce Ackerman, and other "dialogic" theorists about the importance of human capacities for rational communication and deliberative cooperation and the desirability of finding political forms that express and develop those capacities. Still, a vision of human beings as fellow participants in rational dialogues, without any account of how they come by those rational capacities or their ontological status, lacks the majesty, mystery, and magic of either the Kantian doctrine of noumena or religious doctrines of divine souls. And philosophic arguments concerning how the preconditions of our conversations and our own autonomy demand recognition of the autonomy of others lack political resonance, however sound academics may think them to be.

Slogans of human rights to freedom and equality in innumerable respects certainly do have political power in the modern world. Yet even Habermas believes that historically, "the dry ideas of popular sovereignty and human rights" were usually insufficient to inspire change without support from ethnic nationalism (1998, 113). I similarly suspect that these precepts gained mass political support more from religious doctrines of universal human worth, and from literary and historical stories

---

[7] Patchen Markell suggests that Habermas is not really so blindly optimistic about this ongoing blending of universalist principles and particular identities, and indeed, Habermas has penned some gloomy passages on the problems of overcoming particularism (e.g. 1998, 118, 127). Hence Markell argues that if "normative principles always depend on supplements of particularity that enable them to become objects of attachment and identification but that also never are quite equivalent to the principles they purport to embody, then perhaps constitutional patriotism is best understood not as a safe and reliable identification with some pure set of already available *universals* but rather as a fragile political culture that habitually insists on and makes manifest this failure of equivalence for the sake of the ongoing, always incomplete, and often unpredictable *project* of *universalization*" (2000, 57–58). This reading is plausible, but it only underlines that Habermas's view does not provide much guidance for dealing with the challenges of these blends.

[8] Martha Nussbaum's much-discussed defense of cosmopolitanism does not invoke Habermas but similarly appeals to Kantian morality (1996, 13, 134). For a related critique of the abstract, rationalistic view of persons underlying what he terms "ethical universalism," see Miller, 1995, 57–58. Kymlicka, 2001, insists like Miller that even "in the most liberal of democracies, nation-building goes beyond the diffusion of political principles. It also involves the diffusion of a common language and national culture," though he sees more points of harmony than Miller does between "cosmopolitanism" and "liberal nationalism" (41, 218–241).

of inspiring political struggles, than they did from the rational philosophic arguments advanced on their behalf. In sum, we probably need both a fuller treatment of particularistic ethically constitutive stories, and more concrete universalistic constitutive stories, than Habermas and kindred writers have provided if we are to promote genuine acceptance that obligations stemming from common humanity deserve to override many claims rooted in more particular memberships.[9]

Perhaps the problem is that Habermas is too much an Enlightenment rationalist universalist. To find normative theorists who focus more on the political role of ethically constitutive stories, it might seem wiser to turn to writers who, in one way or another, stress particular group identities. Two obvious camps are those political analysts who urge us to embrace some form of democratic "difference politics," "multiculturalism," or "identity politics," and those who defend a more firmly communitarian view of democracy or republicanism.

Most of the leading writers in these (mildly overlapping) categories turn out, however, to be not so very different from Habermas on the issues that concern us here. Many have chiefly sought to define the legitimate moral claims that existing groups and political communities may assert. They have generally not tried to analyze or theorize very elaborately the historical and ongoing political processes through which those groups and communities have been formed and are being transformed. Sometimes attention to such historical processes is explicitly disavowed (e.g. Walzer, 1983, 31). Sometimes communitarians are guilty of ignoring or minimizing the harshly undemocratic and illiberal conceptions through which actual communities have been built (e.g. Walzer, 1992, which discusses American identity without considering racial inequalities; Sandel, 1996, which devotes no sustained attention to nativist, racist, and sexist traditions in American life). In earlier writings, Charles Taylor sometimes treated history chiefly as a source of the competing "liberal" and "republican" normative visions of political community that must be appraised philosophically today (e.g. 1989, 166). As he has since reflected, especially, on the issues of Quebec and Canadian identity, he has come to argue that neither vision is sufficient, that modern democratic societies, especially, must politically negotiate and periodically renegotiate "a commonly acceptable political identity between the different personal or group identities that want to or have to live in the polity," much as I

---

[9] Arguing that his "patriotism is not enough," Canovan (2000) trenchantly critiques Habermas and others along these lines. Noting that all regimes, even the emerging European Union, still define membership extensively by birthright rules, she insists that a sense of common peoplehood as a shared and privileged *inherited* identity remains necessary if any particular "democratic body politic is to be able to persist" (426–27, 431).

do here (1999, 286). He acknowledges, however, that he has as yet not said very much about how those identities can best be achieved. Even so, Taylor focuses on this issue more than most. Commonly, normative theorists invoke historical political processes simply to identify the origins of unjust group disadvantages and oppressions that now need to be addressed, without really exploring the dynamics in political life that recurrently generate such patterns of inequality. Instead such writers are concerned to prescribe the proper political arrangements among and within existing groups and communities in light of existing injustices, in ways that are not linked to any very specific analysis of the political sources of those inequities, beyond a detailing of imperialist, racist, nationalist, and patriarchal forms of hegemonic abuses.[10]

At times this approach permits startlingly apolitical accounts of group identity even by intensely political writers. For example, Iris Young, the leading American theorist of "democracy and difference," suggests that social groups defined in terms of gender and race "are more like class than ethnicity . . . inasmuch as they concern structural relations of power, resource allocations, and discursive hegemony" (2000, 14, 82–83). That phrasing verges on a naturalizing ethically constitutive story, for it wrongly implies that ethnic groups are somehow "prepolitical" things that are not in fact equally products of such relations.[11] In most of her work, though, Young joins with radical postmodernist democrats like William Connolly and Chantal Mouffe in decrying the pervasive political tendency of the powerful to impose hegemonic identities that efface legitimate differences. She also joins them in seeking democratic political forms through which difference can instead flourish. These writers all encourage a politics in which diverse ethnic, racial, religious, linguistic,

[10] These characterizations apply to the insightful arguments of James Tully (1995), who is otherwise not easily categorized. Tully calls for forms of post-imperial "contemporary constitutionalism" that can promote popular self-governance via cultural recognition, through the working out of what must be widely varying federated arrangements by means of ongoing dialogues within and across cultural groups. But apart from showing that other modern forms of constitutionalism have served imperialist and nationalist purposes, and that all culture traditions are matters of ongoing construction, Tully does not analyze the politics of people-building; nor does he say much more than most liberal and democratic proceduralists about the sorts of substantive stories of common identity that can best be advanced by different cultural groups that wish to see themselves as part of one polity. Valuable though it is, his focus is simply on the importance of ongoing negotiated agreements defining constitutional processes of self-government that distinct cultural groups can embrace.

[11] Miller, 1995, 130–135, argues that Young's earlier writings wrongly treat both gender and ethnicity as more "genuine" than national identity. His own work, however, similarly verges on treating the "nation" as the most "natural" political identity today, out of his understandable concern to stress that both nationalism and the "nation-state" system remain politically powerful under current, but changing, conditions (183–185).

and cultural communities feel able to articulate their distinctive "ethically constitutive" stories in public life and to try to win support for policies and institutions expressive of them, just as I do here.

Yet precisely because they are most concerned to allow the articulation of different minority group identities, most radically democratic post-modernist writers seem wary of embracing a politics in which different ethically constitutive accounts of larger, encompassing political societies are articulated and institutionalized with similar vigor. Just as they are worried about the potential intolerance of the "universalism" of contemporary rationalistic Kantians, they are also understandably reluctant to suggest that politics ought to include any sort of effort to define a robust sense of the political "whole" of which distinctive minorities might be a part. In urging a politics expressive of a more wide-open democratic "ethos of pluralization," William Connolly argues, for example: "You do not need a wide universal 'we' (a nation, a community, a singular practice of rationality, a particular monotheism) to foster democratic governance of a population. Numerous possibilities of intersection and collaboration between multiple, interdependent constituencies infused by a general ethos of critical responsiveness drawn from several sources suffices very nicely" (1995, xix–xx). Bonnie Honig is even more emphatic: "the denationalization of the state from an affective to an instrumental set of institutions may be a necessary step on the road toward a more vibrant and democratic politics" rich with "alternative sites of affect and identity" (2001, 105, 120). Chantal Mouffe suggests that in a "well-functioning democracy," agonistic politics will actually involve "a vibrant clash of democratic political positions," such as "liberal-conservative, social-democratic, neo-liberal, radical-democratic," rather than any dangerous focus on any form of "identity politics" at all (2000, 104).

As Mouffe recognizes, her view requires "a certain amount of consensus" on democratic values, even though those will always be diversely understood (2000, 103). Connolly also consistently recognizes that his calls for radical pluralization of politics still require broad acceptance of a "culture of democratization" that fosters "critical responsiveness" to a great variety of identities and encourages their "periodic denaturalization" (1995, 154–155). In a footnote, he goes further than Mouffe and concedes that this radically pluralized politics has to have room for "moralities of god, home, and country" to be advanced (1995, 202n13). Similarly, Honig concedes that preaching "mere instrumentalism" as the proper stance toward all nations works against the "passion, involvement, and identification" that are "necessary" for a "vibrant" democratic politics at national levels (2001, 120–121). Yet Connolly devotes little attention to the whole topic of visions of common political identity, as opposed to democratic contestation among different subgroup and transnational group identities. His main thrust has been to persuade us to embrace a "generous ethos of engagement" amidst "multi-dimensional pluralism," rather than "falling right into the black hole of the nation" (2000, 194–195). Honig says nothing about possible bases of passionate attachment to "a nation, a people," instead stressing, as I do, that these attachments can be both powerful and yet ambivalent (2001, 121).

When it comes to the political structuring of the primary public spaces, indeed the broader senses of political community or peoplehood, in which the agonistic encounters of the "politics of difference" take place, Connolly, Mouffe, Honig, Young, and other radical democrats offer practical recommendations that do not really depart far from those of more cosmopolitan, anti-nationalist deliberative democrats like David Held and Habermas himself. All concentrate almost entirely on the desirability of democratic procedures and shared democratic values – what Mouffe calls "the civic bond that should unite a democratic political association" (2000, 96). Most then also stress the importance of transnational as well as decentralized, subnational democratic arrangements and considerable diversity within political memberships. Postmodernists often sound more enthusiastic about the preservation of differences than more Enlightenment-minded social democrats do, but the reliance on democratic political power stories alone as the common ground of larger political memberships is much the same.[12] The problem is that, as Will Kymlicka acknowledges about his own "liberal multiculturalism," even such advocates of "differentiated citizenship" still sooner or later need an account of the "ties that bind," wherever they may seek to locate democratic cooperation. They must suggest some means for fostering "the sense of shared civic identity" required by effective democratic polities at *any* level, and certainly at the level of the more predominant, encompassing larger political society (Kymlicka, 1995, 173–174, 187–192). And as I have argued at length, democratic stories, and indeed activities of democratic participation, are by themselves not likely to be enough in this regard. Kymlicka is probably right that the sort of cooperative spirit

---

[12] For a similar critique, see Kymlicka, 2001, 44. For Young's agreements with Connolly and Mouffe, but also Habermas and Held, see Young, 2000, 41n44, 91n9, 122n2, 222n39, 243n9, 266–267; cf. Connolly, 1991, 198–222; Honig, 2001, 13, 105, 120–121 (endorsing a form of "democratic cosmopolitanism"). Though postmodernist democrats understandably criticize Habermas for threatening to efface differences in the name of rational consensus (e.g., Mouffe, 2000, 84–98), the processes he advocates involve expression of different conceptions of democracy; he has stressed his support for various sorts of cultural rights protective of many of the other salient forms of diversity; and he also argues that existing nation-states must be transcended (1996, 514; 1998, 115, 118, 146).

needed to make democratic politics work "is the product of mutual solidarity, not the basis for it" (1995, 191).

Yet without quite asserting that democratic procedural principles are enough to generate viable political communities in the case of state-governed societies, Connolly, other American "difference democrats" like Young, and European "neo-republicans" like Herman van Gunsteren stress answers that in the end buttress their democratic stories in surprising ways. They turn chiefly to "liberal" espousals of rational reflection, along with "conservative" emphases on inherited circumstances. Most suggest that normatively appropriate senses of common political identity can be achieved if persons who share a "community of fate," whose "lives and actions affect one another in a web of institutions, interactions, and unintended consequences," will but "acknowledge that they are together in such space of mutual effect." They are then likely to "understand themselves as members of a single polity." As a result, they will more readily develop commitments "to work out their conflicts and to solve the problems generated by their collective action through means of peaceful. . . agreed-upon and publicly acknowledged procedures." Democratic citizenship and a democratic political culture will be understood to serve the "metafunction" of defining appropriate relations and mediating differences among those who recognize their unchosen interconnectedness. It can therefore help foster "agonistic respect and critical responsiveness between diverse constituencies" and "*multiply lines of connections through which governing assemblages can be constructed from a variety of intersecting communities*" (Young, 2000, 100; van Gunsteren, 1998, 61, 141–143; Connolly, 1995, xix–xx).

Again, in many respects these views are morally attractive. I share the aspirations of these writers to avoid the hegemonic imposition of narrow particular views of human identity; to promote democratic decision-making; and to make multiple memberships in many sustainable yet only semi-sovereign human political communities more feasible. Yet it is neither politically realistic nor morally desirable to seek to confine "ethically constititutive" themes to visions of "subnational" and "transnational" or "international" group identities, while quieting discussion of ethically constitutive identities for the larger but still particular societies in which most governing is done, as many postmodernist democrats patently wish to do. To take an example I will pursue in the next chapter, it would be neither practical nor right to say that the Nation of Islam is entitled to advance its religious and racial view of the deepest political identities and obligations of blacks in the United States, but that conservative white Protestant leaders must not promulgate their accounts of America as a whole.

The problem is not only that, politically, we probably cannot hope to shape communities that can long endure unless people see them as expressing more than their procedural agreements and senses of abstract justice. That is indeed likely to be the case: in the absence of any very full analysis of the politics of people-building, the assurance that adequate perceptions of shared interests can arise simply from people's reflections on their interlocked circumstances and from democratic participation sounds like optimistic Enlightenment rationalism at its most naïve. On these accounts, so long as one preaches democracy, particular memberships then can be expected to emerge rather organically out of fundamentally extra-political factors. But since those "extra-political" forms of intersection and mutual effect need to be articulated in politics as bases of collaboration, and articulated in what is most often a competitive politics of people-making, the pressures and dangers that impel reliance on ethically constitutive accounts of whole particular political societies cannot be escaped.

Yet equally fundamental is the philosophic reality that all espousals of political procedures, democratic or otherwise, rely on ethically constitutive accounts of human identities that make those procedures morally appropriate, just as much as the views of the Nation of Islam or the New Christian Right do. The views of writers like Rawls and Habermas rest on neo-Kantian and religious roots; those of many "difference democrats" often rely on postmodernist Nietzschean and sometimes religious assumptions; Deweyan democrats like Richard Rorty and Ian Shapiro appeal to pragmatist conceptions of socially constituted selves; and so forth.[13] Even though people may well embrace very similar principles and procedures despite great differences in such underlying ethically constitutive beliefs, as liberals like Rawls and Ackerman stress, citizens are at a minimum morally entitled to understand the commitments of those to whom they are entrusting their political destinies. Only then can they really gauge the significance of the forms of peoplehood they are being asked to embrace. Only then can they gain necessary capacities both for critical distance and genuine loyalty toward their political memberships.[14]

---

[13] See e.g. Connolly, 1999; Rorty, 1998, 4; Shapiro, 1999, 8–11, 26–27 (stressing how shifting technological and political circumstances specify human interests in varying ways).

[14] Charles Taylor has argued similarly that a politics aimed simply at achieving agreement on political procedures "provides no opportunity for people on each side to look into the substance of the other's case," as people both wish to do and deserve to do (Taylor, 1999, 284–285). Rawls himself accepts that it may be appropriate to introduce religious and secular "comprehensive views" into public forum deliberations in order to show that participants have reasons for their proposals that comply with the restraints of "public reason" (Rawls, 1999, 153–156). Still, as discussed in the next chapter, the thrust of his advocacy of "public reason" is more restrictive of such discourse than either Taylor or I would be.

The efforts of many radical democratic theorists to encourage an agonistic politics involving ethically constitutive stories of every political people *except* those identified with a state seem, then, ultimately unrealistic
and morally inappropriate. Other contemporary theorists have provided
moral defenses of certain sorts of larger, yet still particular memberships
that go further than the sorts of writers considered so far. Beginning with
Rousseauian premises, the English philosopher David Miller has argued
most forcefully that egalitarian republican citizenship cannot flourish in
the modern world without the senses of trust, solidarity, and reciprocity
that depend in practice on a shared national identity (Miller, 1995, 1999).
He stresses that this is all the more true if we seek to sustain political communities with extensive social services in which better-off citizens are
willing to sacrifice continually to help their compatriots. Miller recognizes that modern nationalisms usually arose out of "pre-existing ethnic
identities" that were themselves forms of political membership that excluded and subordinated many in unjust fashion, and he acknowledges
strong ethnic elements in some senses of national identity that he finds
acceptable today. He maintains, however, that nationalisms are muta-
ble things and that democratic political movements have succeeded in
making them more inclusive in many modern societies (1995, 127–128;
1999, 68–69). He also sees more benefit than harm, from a republican viewpoint, in encouraging the redrawing of political borders and/or
the adoption of consociational democratic arrangements to channel the
senses of national identity that now exist into discrete, enduring political
communities (1995, 73, 81–89, 188; 1999, 70).

Miller's position is fundamentally an egalitarian republican one that
accepts that considerable homogeneity is necessary to inspire the strong
senses of fellow-feeling needed if people are to rise to the demands of
republican citizenship as well as modern liberal social welfare policies.
He therefore accepts alliances with particularistic national ethically constitutive stories on instrumental grounds, but without Habermas's insistence that such alliances must ultimately be shed or his hope that they
can indeed be overcome. Indeed, though Miller accepts doctrines of basic human rights, he argues that in practice these must be vindicated
and should be vindicated chiefly through reciprocal relations among co-
nationals. Above all, he believes, only such relations can support the sense
of mutual trust demanded to sustain policies expressing ongoing concern
for others (1995, 73–80, 90–98). Hence Miller's position is the most accepting of the political role of ethically constitutive stories encompassing
whole societies of any so far.

Yet Miller must therefore squarely confront the dangers of such stories;
and here his normative stance ceases to be distinctive or especially instruc-
tive. With the other sorts of neo-republican and deliberative democratic

authors I have discussed, he ultimately relies only on engaged democratic politics to check the dangers of such often-invidious narratives of political membership (1995, 39–40, 70, 89, 150–151). Up to a point, this position seems morally appropriate as well as politically hard-headed: political outcomes are determined in the end through political struggles, and democratic struggles are generally preferable to undemocratic ones. But insofar as it is true that both coercive force and persuasive stories play important parts in determining the outcomes of such struggles, I believe we can say more than Miller and other "nationalists" and "particularists" have done about how the dangers of harsh ethically constitutive stories can best be met. In so doing, moreover, I think we can find support for more hope concerning the eventual transcendence of contemporary nationalism and nation-states than Miller and like-minded writers allow.[15] Again, an appeal to democratic processes and principles cannot by itself answer the question of who should get to participate in those processes, and Miller's rigid reliance on nationalism to define the relevant people may well serve to foreclose the achievement of more inclusive responses. At any rate, having recognized how little conscious attention most current normative theorizing pays to the place of constitutive stories in the politics of peoplehood, we are at least in a position to make some relatively novel arguments on how that politics should be pursued today.

Toward constructive ethically constitutive stories

It will by now be abundantly clear that the dangers of strong senses of particularistic political "peoplehood" buttressed by ethically constitutive stories are many. They include demands that all members give total allegiance to a "people's" sovereign authorities; disregard for the basic rights and interests of those dwelling within the bounds of a community, but not regarded as full members of that "people"; and similar disdain, expressed either as aggression or neglect, toward the rights and interests of many of those outside its bounds. If the particular "people" in question is in fact currently a subgroup within the legal bounds of a broader polity, that disdain for outsiders may express itself via disobedience to legal authority and outbreaks of violence, as in the case of some ethnic nationalist and religious groups. If the "people" instead command a state that

---

[15] Gloomier yet is another English theorist, John Gray, who believes Enlightenment universalism has irrevocably lost out to particularistic religious, ethnic, nationalistic, and postmodernist philosophic perspectives. He calls for us simply to seek a modus vivendi among ineradicably different political communities and feel pleased if we happen to be products of societies with relatively liberal traditions (e.g. Gray, 1995). I believe the arguments developed here are responsive to his pessimism as well.

governs many but not only and not all those persons who are putatively its members, then the stage may be set either for colonial rule or "ethnic cleansing," and for aggressive wars of "reunification."

If reliance on ethically constitutive stories of some sort to promote desirable political senses of membership, identity, trust, and worth nonetheless seems politically and philosophically inescapable, what sorts of stories should we twenty-first-century human beings favor in order to lessen these dangers? What, moreover, can we hope to accomplish by "favoring" them in our various modes of political expression?

On the second question, I am not, I hope, unduly sanguine about what academic arguments can achieve. When political actors perceive vital interests to be at stake, they are not easily swayed by words alone. Instead, they are likely to rely on and to respond to threatened and actual uses of force; that much about the world has yet to change fundamentally. Still, recall that human beings are often not clear about what their interests really are or how they can best be realized. I believe academic moral arguments have the greatest potential for enduring impact when they begin with the established understandings, values, and patterns of behavior of those they would persuade. Then the task is to show, as honestly and truthfully as possible, that those values might be better understood and fulfilled if they are conceived and pursued in somewhat different ways. That is the spirit in which I am advancing arguments here both for reconceptualizing ethically constitutive stories in certain regards, and for responding to their role in politics in ways that differ from what many political actors now do and from what many theorists would have us do.

On the first issue, my prescriptions fall under two headings: first, how best to respond to more particularistic ethically constitutive stories of peoplehood, and second, how to reconceive more universalistic stories of humanity's shared identity and interests. Both kinds of response are necessary, I believe, to deal constructively with the often dangerous but inescapable features of the politics of people-building that the previous chapters have explored.

Particularistic ethically constitutive stories

My first set of arguments may seem counterintuitive or at least counterproductive; so let me reaffirm that I agree with many writers that we should seek to promote senses of peoplehood that value and institutionalize human rights and democratic self-governance (along with economic systems providing as many with as much prosperity as possible). In many contexts, especially ones where massive violations of basic rights and democratic principles are commonplace, the need to create institutions that secure basic freedoms and foster greater democratic decision-making must be central themes in any defensible politics of people-making. My argument is not against those themes, but against those who think they alone are usually or always sufficient to support viable and just senses of political community. That difference also leads me to oppose those who believe institutions should somehow permit only democratic, rights-respecting accounts to be advanced.

I favor a more open politics of contestation in which undesirable views are moderated through political engagements, not prior institutional repression or marginalization. This means I differ from those writers, like Habermas and Rawls, who seek to relegate particularistic ethically constitutive stories to social or private realms and to base political peoplehood essentially on agreement to certain decision-making procedures and principles of justice (though, as we have seen, it is unclear that either really adheres to this oft-stated aspiration). I also differ from those, like Young and Connolly, who appear far more receptive to ethically constitutive accounts advanced by long-oppressed minorities or unconventional groups than they are to a politics greatly shaped by competing ethically constitutive accounts of the larger political societies that encompass such groups. Instead, I propose that we welcome a whole range of particularistic ethically constitutive stories, advancing visions of subgroups, national communities, and transnational associations, into political debate, while also encouraging robust and honest criticism of their claims, especially when they threaten democracy and human rights. This means I also differ from those who, like Miller, are willing to accept ethically constitutive accounts that articulate a common national identity but who oppose stories that can easily be used to challenge such identities. Instead, I believe that in our political interactions, we ought to be most receptive to the (many) accounts of peoplehood that, though partly supportive of particular existing political communities, nonetheless define "peoples" in ways that can rarely if ever be equated with the current memberships of any regimes.

Thus, instead of political realms that display a great but generally forced consensus on a shared ethically constitutive story, or ones that seek to confine participation in political debates to their current members or some subset thereof, or ones that strive to purge all ethically constitutive stories, religious, ethnic, cultural, national, and otherwise, from public discourse, I urge a different vision. In it political loyalties inspiring committed political engagement, but also skepticism toward "sovereign" authorities and willingness to accept change, are all fostered by a public life in which a variety of particularistic as well as more universalistic ethically constitutive stories are openly advocated, critiqued, modified, and sometimes profoundly transformed, by leaders, by citizens, and by outsiders as well.

The fears that drive the alternative positions I am challenging are sensible. Liberals like Rawls fear that if religious, ethnic, racial, and other ethically constitutive stories are too prominent in public life, they will prove explosively divisive. "Difference democrats" like Young instead welcome certain public articulations of long-subordinated group identities; but they fear that if common citizenship is based on anything more than democratic procedures, old unjust political and cultural hegemonies will be reproduced. Contemporary republicans like Miller worry in turn that if we do not accept particularistic senses of national identity, citizens will not be motivated to participate politically or to sacrifice for each other. They are uncomfortable with assertions of subgroup identities or transnational identities that challenge national solidarities. The upshot is that all these writers might well be aghast at precisely the spectacle I propose: one in which different groups seek to gain power within existing political communities, and sometimes to forge new communities, in part by advancing conflicting ethically constitutive stories that, once in power, they seek to institutionalize.

Yet in light of the characteristic tendencies of the politics of people-building previously reviewed, this approach seems the only realistic one available. Efforts to confine ethically constitutive stories chiefly to the "richer" life of the subgroups and civil associations within a liberal democratic regime are, in all likelihood, quixotic and ultimately counterproductive. They are quixotic because political actors inevitably interpret the shared procedural principles that are supposed to ground common citizenship from different perspectives, reflecting embrace of different ethically constitutive stories. Furthermore, most political participants know this; so the stories still end up playing powerful roles in political life. Efforts to limit the role of such stories are also counterproductive, because in the end nothing can really prevent aspiring leaders from summoning support by advancing compelling constitutive accounts of shared political identity. Such stories confer enough of a political advantage that at various times, their proponents are bound to gain the upper hand in the competitive politics of people-building that is part of any long-enduring society. Proceduralist positions often simply open the door for the successes of these more full-blooded competitors. Furthermore, by seeking to remove from politics many of the things about which people care most, attempts to relegate constitutive stories to the margins only tend to weaken and falsify political life, making civic activities seem trivial and much public rhetoric disingenuous.

This means that I support a politics in which, for example, the Christian Right can offer a Protestant religious vision of American peoplehood, the Parti Québécois can defend a linguistically based conception of a distinctive Quebec identity, and even neo-Nazis in Germany can offer their racial doctrines of German nationality. To be sure, I would strongly oppose the first and third of these ethically constitutive positions and would seek in some regards to moderate the second. One can favor this sort of more widely and intensely contested politics while still urging sharp criticism of all conceptions of peoplehood that fail to incorporate human rights and democracy as fundamental values, and still advocating the construction and maintenance of political communities through processes that are as broadly democratic as possible. Though I think we must accept that politically potent visions of peoplehood will rely in part on ethically constitutive stories, and that we should neither ban nor discourage articulation in politics of any such stories, however illiberal and undemocratic, this restraint is no bar on sharp denunciation and resistance of their undesirable, sometimes morally reprehensible features. And again, I also am not suggesting that we actively seek to promote forms of politics that are, most of the time, solely or even chiefly about ethically constitutive stories. It is possible and preferable under many circumstances to win allegiance by emphasizing stories of membership that stress economic and political security benefits to constituents and that deliver on those promises.

Yet for all the reasons discussed in Part I, those themes will rarely if ever be able to stand by themselves for long. Not only do economic and political hard times inevitably come to every community; even in good times, many constituents want their primary political membership to possess some larger meaning. The political tasks of maintaining support for larger but still bounded political societies also drive political leaders and constituents to embrace ethically constitutive accounts of those memberships that can respond to claims made by dissidents within their borders and challengers from outside. And vital as they are, doctrines of human rights and democracy are just not able to define the boundaries of particular political communities, which we recurrently have to do. Human rights transcend boundaries; they do not define them. Democratic processes are not enough to do so, because they necessarily presuppose some prior definition of the proper participants in those processes. Such definitions must be provided through means and conceptions of peoplehood beyond those that democratic theories generate.

My alternative approach, calling for embracing ongoing political contestation that includes conflicting ethically constitutive stories, is broadly Madisonian in spirit.[16] I believe we can partly combat the evils of

---

[16] The reference is to James Madison's famed advocacy in *Federalist #10* of a policy of dealing with dangerous factions by multiplying them, not abolishing them (Madison, Hamilton and Jay, 1987, 122–128).

factious particularisms by multiplying and extending them, rather than by futilely seeking to ban them or to consign them to extra-political realms. The reality is, again, that in all extant societies, there are many inherited senses of group identity and interest that are politically woven into many different stories of peoplehood. If we encourage the articulation of all of these stories in political processes, we can reasonably hope that, to a certain degree, conflicting stories will work to check each other's excesses as they vie to win broad support in political contests. We should also especially favor visions of political peoplehood that seek to structure those contests as democratically as possible, though they will often not be very democratic when community boundaries are at stake.

How might such "checking" work politically? Let me briefly suggest an answer by considering issues I discuss more fully in the next chapter. In the US, a story of Americans as a "special people" because they are bearers of traditions of liberty rooted in northern Europe and in Christianity might well have to compete with a story of Americans as "special" because they are bearers of liberty with a shared culture forged in a melting pot of religious and cultural traditions. These two visions of American peoplehood could have different implications for many issues, including boundary questions such as statehood, colonial status, or independence for predominantly Catholic and Hispanic Puerto Rico.

Under reasonably democratic conditions, today the narrower Christian-centered, often Protestant-leaning conception of American nationality almost certainly could not inspire as broad and powerful a coalition in the United States as the more expansive one (though this was not always the case). And at best, in the ensuing political competition, both conceptions might be transformed in ways that would soften any irreconcilable differences. In political competition, even the most ardent essentialist may feel impelled to charm that fabled and widely beloved median voter. If partisans of rival constitutive stories therefore did moderate and modify their appeals, many Americans might then find that they were pondering differing constitutive accounts that nonetheless had common elements, some procedural, some substantive. And they might conclude that they could embrace more than one such account not just with comfort but with enthusiasm. Perhaps, for example, advocates of the most politically popular constitutive narratives would all agree (though I would not) that American nationality is indeed compelling because God favors Americans. They still might accept that there legitimately are very different notions of God and of what divine favor implies in terms of public policies. If so, widespread convictions of the value of civic membership might be sustained regardless of which version of this constitutive story gained political predominance; and some invidious exclusions, such as hostility toward Catholic Latinos and Islamic Arabs, might be further discredited. Yet as that example makes clear, at the same time no such "compromise" or modified constitutive story is ever likely to satisfy fully all members of the governing coalition, much less groups that they have for the time being defeated. Hence that coalition's effort to shape laws and institutions in light of their vision of peoplehood will always be subject to salutary, restraining contestation.

And let me underline: *the approach I am suggesting expects and encourages considerable contestation.* Once ethically constitutive stories are politically advanced as a basis for gaining power and shaping policies, courteous deference to the religious, cultural, ethnic, or other beliefs and preferences of political movements cannot and should not be expected. Forceful arguments denying that certain particularistic conceptions are really intellectually credible enough to justify public measures are to be valued. Such critiques might well lead political aspirants to minimize or alter their more idiosyncratic, undemocratic, and perhaps their more chauvinistic views.

I am in fact enough of an optimistic Enlightenment rationalist to believe that, as I have previously suggested, the sorts of ethically constitutive stories that would become most prevalent over time are secular historical ones (Smith, 1997, 497–498). Purely historical accounts, accounts that present political peoplehood not as the products through time of underlying biological or divine determinants, but rather as the products of contingent historical human actions, can eschew grand, controversial metaphysical and theological claims. Yet they can still claim quite truthfully to be stories of elements that have visibly helped to create the identities of all persons whose life experiences have been deeply shaped by the history in question. Will Kymlicka has complained that such historical conceptions of shared political identity are likely either to be "sanitized" accounts full of "deliberate misrepresentation," or else they will contain truths too bleak to inspire civic pride and loyalty (1995, 189, 238n14). Such misrepresentations will, however, be vulnerable to vigorous challenges in political contests involving those whose interests they neglect or distort, so again I think such contestation should be encouraged. And over time, I believe most people will be more strongly motivated, rather than alienated, if they see their political identities as partly constituted by histories displaying both good and bad elements. Such histories will indicate, quite authentically, that it is now largely up to them to determine in their shared political lives whether and how the best parts of their heritage will be continued and extended, and the worst parts overcome.[17]

---

[17] For related endorsements of historical conceptions of peoplehood, see Hollinger, 1995, and Yack, 1996.

I do not insist, however, that the only acceptable particularistic ethically constitutive stories are secular historical ones, although those are the ones I find most convincing. Even if I had the intellectual resources to demonstrate that only such stories make sense, which I do not, there is no realistic way to keep other kinds of accounts, biological, religious, cultural, linguistic, from playing important roles in political struggles. Contestation must occur among a wide variety of senses of peoplehood. Many liberals will therefore worry all the more that, unless we insist that such conflicts can only end up producing agreement on political procedures, the politics of contested constitutive stories I am envisioning will prove to be a formula for ethnic, religious, and cultural tensions, small- or large-scale civil wars, secessions, or wars of aggression.

I agree that, in regions of the world rent by civil war and massive violations of human rights and democratic values, it often makes sense to give special prominence to accounts of possible forms of peoplehood featuring such commitments. Yet even in such contexts, I cannot imagine that a purely procedural consensus, rather than the temporary triumph of a politically powerful substantive vision of peoplehood, will often be attainable. The strength of the ethically constitutive commitments of the combatants frequently will have to be taken into account and given institutional expression in some form (O'Leary, 2000). And though efforts to reach acceptable accommodations of clashing visions will sometimes fail, and more destructive outcomes will sometimes occur, it is hard to imagine an attainable world in which that will never happen.

I believe, moreover, that if political actors understand that their contests are likely to result in the adoption of some sort of substantive understanding of shared peoplehood that will prevail for a time (though contestation will never end), they will feel that politics matters greatly for their lives, interests, and most basic values. Just as it is true that this sense of having a lot at stake in politics can make compromise difficult, it is also true that it can make failure to achieve successful resolutions of differences unthinkable. And at a minimum, dangers of apathy and disengagement from a politics that seems meaningless should be greatly reduced.

This last claim might be questioned in light of my further recommendation here: that we more fully recognize and encourage a feature of most ethically constitutive stories that many republicans from Rousseau on have sought to alter – again, I believe, quite unrealistically. The feature is this: to a greater or lesser degree, most politically viable constitutive doctrines point to senses of peoplehood that vary from membership in any specific regime, even when they present their forms of "peoplehood" as natural or divinely ordained, and even when they genuinely can justify and inspire allegiance to some particular regimes. This fact of life arises from the reality that no governing officials, institutions, or regime, whether of an existing state, an ethnic association, religion, or any other form of political "people," can credibly claim to have held governing authority over that "people" from time immemorial. All governments and states are commonly known to be human products created within human history, whatever broader mandates they may claim. Hence they all necessarily claim to represent a people that, at least in some important regards, they have not generated and that is usually not simply identical to their current membership. Take, as examples, those officials who have historically presented Israel as the true home of the Jewish people, or those American politicians who have presented the US as carrying the destiny of Anglo-Saxon or English-speaking peoples. The ethically constitutive stories they have invoked could never conceal the reality that they were claiming to speak for a "people" that had not always been represented by their regime and that had always contained members, inside and outside the regime's jurisdiction, who would sharply dispute their vision of common peoplehood.

Nationalist republicans like David Miller are correct to say that this reality is a source of potential political disaffection and unrest, even destruction of "the sense of common nationality" on which, he thinks, "democratic politics depends" (Miller, 1995, 130–154).[18] Those are problems that we must confront. But this republican concern also highlights a valuable consequence of these gaps between the "people" invoked in constitutive stories and the governing officials and current members of actual regimes. Awareness of these gaps can help, morally and politically, to limit the capacities of existing regimes to claim total sovereignty over those they govern. I see the dangers of "strong" peoplehood, of authorities claiming too much power, as very great. I therefore think it is desirable, indeed vital, to embrace the reality that nationalists, republicans, and communitarians sometimes seek to overcome. We should be especially receptive to ethically constitutive stories that acknowledge that no regime is simply natural, even if those stories contend that some "peoples" are; and that all concrete systems of governance and membership are artificial, imperfect vehicles for realizing the aspirations of constituents whose deepest identities are at best only partly expressed through them.

The notions of peoplehood contained in such views may be much more expansive or much less expansive than any concrete regime's

---

[18] That is why, though Miller stresses that nations are not the same as states, and he can accept multinational states, he nonetheless does think it generally desirable for each nation to have its own state, or at least significant powers of political self-determination (1995, 18–19, 81–118).

membership, in terms of time, space, persons, or all three. Some Americans and some Britons might feel, for example, that their political nationality is most valuable because it partly expresses their identities as Protestants, a category that does not include all Americans or Britons and that extends beyond the US and the UK in terms of space, time, and adherents. In contrast, some Canadians might feel themselves most deeply to be culturally British Columbians, a narrower identity that in most respects does not predate Canada and one that certainly does not encompass all people or territories within it, much less many beyond it. But though these memberships are not equivalent to American, British, or Canadian "national identities," they can still be articulated in terms of ethically constitutive stories that strongly affirm the propriety of belonging to the US, the UK, or Canada. They can do so, moreover, in intrinsic rather than strictly instrumental terms. The US or UK might be seen as the right membership for Protestants today in light of the Protestant God's providential plans. Canadian citizenship as well as allegiance to the current British Columbian provincial authorities may seem the best way now available to preserve and advance the British Columbian way of life. But because their embrace of membership in the current regime is only partial, such constitutive conceptions do not inspire unqualified allegiance to any government or polity. They can foster civic loyalties while always also providing bases for resisting totalistic claims of political identity and for suggesting desirable transformations in existing forms of common life, both at the pertinent national levels and at the levels of church or provincial governance.[19]

Particularistic accounts of "peoplehood" that refuse to equate fully their members' shared political identity with allegiance to any particular regime might therefore help us come closer to the best of both worlds. Political leaders can still use them to craft ethically constitutive stories to inspire support for their visions of community in ways that can prompt civic engagement (both in alliance and in opposition to such visions). But when adherents of this sort of ethical/political vision attain power, they do so under auspices that leave their authority open to constructive challenges. They have less warrant for claims of total sovereignty over their political society justified by appeal to the people for whom they speak, because they have acknowledged that their "people" and the members of that political society are not simply the same.

Still, I do not wish to make too much of this argument. It may be rightly said against it that often such beneficial consequences have simply

[19] My thinking here has been influenced by arguments in Bernard Yack's forthcoming book, though he might well have disagreements with my position.

not followed from the fact that actual constitutive stories almost always invoke senses of peoplehood not identical to the membership of any actual regime. The Nazis claimed to speak for the Aryan race, a "people" that encompassed many but not all German citizens and that included many persons dwelling outside Germany's borders. The gaps between "German" and "Aryan" identity certainly did not produce robust political spaces for constructive challenges to Nazi authority. They instead helped justify aggressive military actions both to incorporate German Aryans into the Fatherland and, eventually, to "purify" Germany via the Holocaust.

The problem, however, was that the Nazis sought to crush those who made compelling objections to their vision of peoplehood, not that there were no compelling objections to be made. Hence I still believe that generally, compared to attempting to do without ethically constitutive stories or to reach consensus on one benign constitutive story, it makes sense to pursue the Madisonian course I am advocating. In most contemporary contexts people-building will proceed in healthier ways if we encourage the expression of ethically constitutive stories that can inspire strong senses of membership and political engagement; that can serve as checks on one another; and that can simultaneously foster some sense of distance between persons' deepest political allegiances and the claims of their current governors. I agree, however, that this Madisonian approach is not enough to solve all the problems posed by particularistic constitutive stories. Chauvinistic senses of political peoplehood still need to be combated by persuasive defenses of the rights and interests of those whom they devalue, as well as by force when nothing else can succeed. Analyses of the deployment of force remain beyond my aims here. But to consider how to develop politically persuasive defenses that might either limit the need for force to protect human rights or motivate its constructive use, we must attend further to the role of ethically constitutive stories, this time more universalistic ones.

Universalistic ethically constitutive stories

In the end, all constitutive stories that are highly particularistic, such as stories of racial supremacy, cultural superiority, unique religious purity, "manifest destiny," or simply historical national uniqueness, are all too capable of justifying abusive treatment toward others. The dangers of such doctrines probably cannot be adequately checked unless would-be leaders and constituents connect their particularistic beliefs with some suitable "universalistic," or at least humanity-wide, constitutive story, some account of how and why they share morally important identities and interests with all other human beings. After all, the foregoing analysis has provided many reasons to believe that within any regime, successful partisans will need to offer compelling narratives of common identity, sometimes implicitly, sometimes quite centrally. That is why I suspect that it takes not only favorable material circumstances and reasoned arguments, but also a compelling, more universalistic ethically constitutive story, to counter deplorable particularistic ones peacefully.

Again, it is far from politically impractical to suggest that accounts of particular human communities should be connected to some broader depiction of humanity. The reality is that, because all political communities have to define their relationships to outsiders, virtually all ethically constitutive stories do include accounts of such connections. All too many, however, simply proclaim the rest of humanity to be comparatively inferior and worthless. Historically, such harsh xenophobia has at times been tempered by religious doctrines proclaiming the value of all human beings as children of God, and such moral egalitarianism today also has many secular adherents, most of whom are heirs in one way or another of Kantian idealism. It is likely that religious stories extolling the spiritual worth of all human beings and secular moral doctrines espousing the dignity of all rational beings will remain vital supports for doctrines of human rights, democracy, and humanitarian concern for many years to come. I seek neither to minimize nor to forego their political and moral contributions.

It may, however, be necessary to add to them. Compelling as they can be for believers, religious doctrines generally are persuasive only to those raised in a particular faith; and they have often been sources of bitter political conflicts, perhaps as much as they have fostered moderation and peaceful cooperation. Intoxicating as they can be for initiates, Kantian metaphysical claims are neither broadly understood nor, today, widely defended; and modern neo-Kantians have not provided any very clear ethically constitutive story of human identity in their place, much less a forceful one. I believe, therefore, that today it may well be useful to go beyond the Kantian and religious doctrines of human worth that form the most prevalent types of universalistic stories in modern academic and political discourse. We should seek to elaborate more concrete secular accounts of humanity and of the real and profound dangers and choices that genuinely confront us all, in ways that might prompt us to give greater weight to all our fellow human beings in the conceptions of political values and memberships we adopt.

Contemporary liberal political theorists, in particular, have been reluctant to take this step because it seems to require endorsing speculative and controversial claims about human beings that are not clearly necessary or helpful. But there is, I think, a secular constitutive story about humanity that we may well need to emphasize in the twenty-first century more than we have previously done. A century and a half after Darwin, it now seems clear to all but the most traditionalist fundamentalists that humanity is plausibly understood as a highly evolved and still evolving animate species. Many if not most religious adherents have come to accept this general view, though they may interpret the sources and path of human evolution quite differently than secular rationalists. This view of ourselves as all members of a species striving to survive and thrive in a not entirely hospitable universe certainly can support the idea that we have shared interests with all other human beings stemming from who we truly are in a very primary sense. Even so, widespread beliefs that humanity is in some sense an evolving species do little by themselves to generate any consensus on how we should live, much less one that can temper invidious particularistic claims. Perhaps, as late nineteenth-century scientists thought, humanity has evolved into superior and inferior subgroups – races, sexes, "primitive," and "civilized" peoples.

It is certainly important to oppose such evolutionary doctrines by all intellectually credible means. But many have already been widely discredited; and today it may well prove salutary, even indispensable, to heighten awareness of human identity as shared membership in a species engaged in an ages-long process of adapting to often dangerous and unforgiving natural and man-made environments.[20] When we see ourselves in the light of general evolutionary patterns, we become aware that it is genuinely possible for a species such as ourselves to suffer massive setbacks or even to become extinct if we pursue certain dangerous courses of action. That outcome does not seem to be in any human's interest. And when we reflect on the state of our species today, we see or should see at least five major challenges to our collective survival, much less our collective flourishing, that are in some respects truly unprecedented. These are all challenges of our own making, however, and so they can all be met through suitably cooperative human efforts.

The first is our ongoing vulnerability to the extraordinary weapons of mass destruction that we have been building during the last half century.

---

[20] In so arguing, I am essentially agreeing with David Lorenzo's contentions that we cannot avoid offering some sort of at least tentative "philosophical foundations" for the stories of peoplehood we tell, and that my notions of desirable stories rest on a view of humans as flawed but resourceful beings with some potential to achieve more fruitful relationships with themselves and with the natural world, but no utopias. He terms this a "satirically comedic" view of human nature (Lorenzo, 2002, 366–370, 377).

The tense anticipations of imminent conflagration that characterized the Cold War at its worst are now behind us, but the nuclear arsenals that were so threatening are largely still with us, and indeed the governments and, perhaps, terrorist groups possessed of some nuclear weaponry have continued to proliferate.

The second great threat is some sort of environmental disaster, brought on by the by-products of our efforts to achieve ever-accelerating industrial and post-industrial production and distribution of an incredible range of good and services. Whether it is global warming, the spread of toxic wastes, biospheric disruptions due to new agricultural techniques, or some combination of these and other consequences of human interference with the air, water, climate, and plant and animal species that sustain us, any major environmental disaster can affect all of humanity.

Third, as our economic and technological systems have become ever more interconnected, the danger that major economic or technological failures in one part of the world might trigger global catastrophes may well increase. Such interdependencies can, to be sure, be a source of strength as well as weakness, as American and European responses to the East Asian and Mexican economic crises of the 1990s indicated. Still, if global capitalism were to collapse or a technological disaster comparable to the imagined Y2K doomsday scenario were to occur, the consequences today would be more far-reaching than they would have been for comparable developments in previous centuries.

Fourth, as advances in food production, medical care, and other technologies have contributed to higher infant survival rates and longer lives, the world's population has been rapidly increasing, placing intensifying pressures on our physical and social environments in a great variety of ways. These demographic trends, necessarily involving all of humanity, threaten to exacerbate all the preceding problems, generating political and military conflicts, spawning chronic and acute environmental damages, and straining the capacities of economic systems.

The final major challenge we face as a species is a more novel one, and it is one that may bring consciousness of our shared "species interests" even more to the fore. In the upcoming century, human beings will increasingly be able to affect their own genetic endowment, in ways that might potentially alter the very sort of organic species that we are. Here as with modern weapons, economic processes, and population growth, we face risks that our efforts to improve our condition may go disastrously wrong, potentially endangering the entire human race. Yet the appeal of endowing our children with greater gifts is sufficiently powerful that organized efforts to create such genetic technologies capable of "redesigning humans" are already burgeoning, both among reputable academic researchers and less restrained, but well-endowed, fringe groups.[21]

To be sure, an awareness of these as well as other potential dangers affecting all human beings is not enough by itself to foster moral outlooks that reject narrow and invidious particularistic conceptions of human identity. It is perfectly possible for leaders to feel that to save the species, policies that run roughshod over the claims of their rivals are not simply justified but morally demanded. Indeed, like the writers I have examined here, my own more egalitarian and cosmopolitan moral leanings probably stem originally from religious and Kantian philosophical influences, not from any consciousness of the common "species interests" of human beings. But the ethically constitutive story which contends that we have such interests, and that we can see them as moral interests, seems quite realistic, which is of some advantage in any such account. And under the circumstances just sketched, it is likely that more and more people will become persuaded that today, those shared species interests face more profound challenges than they have in most of human history.

If so, then stressing our shared identity as members of an evolving species may serve as a highly credible ethically constitutive story that can challenge particularistic accounts and foster support for novel political arrangements. Many more people may come to feel that it is no longer safe to conduct their political lives absorbed in their traditional communities, with disregard for outsiders, without active concern about the issues that affect the whole species and without practical collaborative efforts to confront those issues. That consciousness of shared interests has the potential to promote stronger and much more inclusive senses of trust, as people come to realize that the dangers and challenges they face in common matter more than the differences that will doubtless persist. I think this sort of awareness of a shared "species interests" also can support senses of personal and collective worth, though I acknowledge that this is not obviously the case. Many people find the spectacle of the human species struggling for survival amidst rival life forms and an unfeeling material world a bleak and dispiriting one. Many may still feel the need to combine acceptance of an evolutionary constitutive story with religious or philosophical accounts that supply some stronger sense of moral purpose to human and cosmic existence.

---

[21] See e.g. Stock, 2002 (advocacy of genetic enhancement by the director of the UCLA School of Medicine's Program of Medicine, Technology and Society); Talbot, 2001 (discussing more unrestrained efforts to promote genetic experimentation). For scholarly reflections on the implications of genetic enhancement, see Parens, ed., 1998; Buchanan, Brock, Daniels, and Wikler, 2000; Fukuyama (2002).

But if people are so inclined, then nothing I am advocating here stands in the way of such combinations. Many persons, moreover, may well find a sustaining sense of moral worth in a conception of themselves as contributors to a species that has developed unique capacities to deliberate and to act responsibly in regard to questions no other known species can yet conceive: how should we live? What relationships should we have, individually and collectively, to other people, other life forms, and the broader universe? In time, I hope that many more people may come to agree that humanity has shared responsibilities of stewardship for the animate and physical worlds around us as well as ourselves, ultimately seeking to promote the flourishing of all insofar as we are capable and the finitude of existence permits. But even short of such a grand sense of species vocation, the idea that we are part of humanity's endeavor to strive and thrive across ever-greater expanses of space and time may be one that can inspire a deep sense of worth in many if not most human beings.

Hence it does not seem unrealistic to hope that we can encourage increased acceptance of a universalistic sense of human peoplehood that may help rein in popular impulses to get swept up in more parochial tales of their identities and interests. In the years ahead, this ethical sensibility might foster acceptance of various sorts of transnational political arrangements to deal with problems like exploitative and wildly fluctuating international financial and labor markets, destructive environmental and agricultural practices, population control, and the momentous issue of human genetic modifications. These are, after all, problems that appear to need to be dealt with on a near-global scale if they are to be dealt with satisfactorily. Greater acceptance of such arrangements would necessarily entail increased willingness to view existing governments at all levels as at best only "semi-sovereign," authoritative over some issues and not others, in the manner that acceptance of multiple particularistic constitutive stories would also reinforce. In the resulting political climate, it might become easier to construct the sorts of systems of interwoven democratic international, regional, state and local governments that theorists of "cosmopolitan democracy," "liberal multicultural nationalism," and "differentiated democracy" like David Held, Will Kymlicka, Iris Young, William Connolly, and Jürgen Habermas all envision.

Given the persistence of more particularistic interests, identities, and ideals and the likelihood of severe conflicts over how such species-wide interests can be best understood and advanced, I certainly do not anticipate any easy acceptance of a universalistic constitutive story of humanity as an evolving species. Indeed, a world of shifting national boundaries and new transnational communities is one in which the tendencies of the politics of people-building to foster invidious particularistic identities are likely in some respects to become more severe. For example, if regional arrangements like the European Union are to become more than merely economic associations, the analysis here suggests that their partisans will need to generate supportive constitutive stories that valorize European identity while, perhaps, derogating non-European immigrants in order to justify a "fortress Europe." Such tendencies are already visible in European discourse (Farrell, 2002, 208).

And as I have noted, to call even a species-wide perspective "universalistic" is misleading, as champions of animal rights and of the value of preserving all plant species contend. I have personally long been persuaded by Enlightenment-derived moral perspectives that ground moral identity and worth on the possession of basic capacities for reasoning self-governance, not on membership in the human species per se; and I endorse a stewardship ethic toward non-rational beings (Smith, 1985). Hence I would not myself rely exclusively on a species-centered account of human identity, and I do not mean to suggest that we can see any consensus emerging on a species-centered view of human political identity.

Often, moreover, what is advanced under the name of "universalistic" values can be rightly criticized as serving the interests of certain powerful groups far more than others, as feminist and Third World critics of prevailing western versions of "human rights" have long contended. Sometimes, however, such attacks on "universalistic" values are merely useful rhetorical devices for defending invidious local oppressions. I do not suggest that the approach sketched here provides certain answers to all these conflicts. My hope is instead that the variety of "universalistic" and more particularistic stories can be made to work politically to limit the excesses of each, with critics exposing the hidden selfishness and repressiveness of both some "human rights" claims and some claims to have defensible "distinctive" traditional values.

But because my primary concern here is to identify relatively promising ways to combat the worst consequences of the politics of people-building, I admittedly am partisan to more inclusive, egalitarian, species-centered constitutive stories. That partisanship seems prudent because, though the causes of concern for all rational beings and for all life forms are not without adherents, to most people these claims still seem rather abstract and impractical. In contrast, claims for the defensibility of local variations on human rights principles are politically quite potent, and sometimes reasonable; but more often than not they are at least in part excuses for injustices. Hence even while favoring a politics in which all sorts of ethically constitutive stories can be advanced, I think it wise today to stress the case for ones that call attention to the concerns of all humanity. I believe, moreover, that the circumstances I have sketched are already driving more and more people to reconceive their core interests, at least in part, from the standpoint of dangers to the whole of the species, for very good reasons. Hence I believe that the notion of humanity as an evolving species, in its secular scientific formulations and in religious variants, represents an inclusive and politically viable constitutive story on which it is reasonable and desirable to build.

It is, admittedly, a universalistic story that is not as intrinsically supportive of claims for the irreducible worth of all individuals as Kantian morality and many religious systems are. It is, however, hardly illogical to extend a concern for the survival and flourishing of the human species to all its members; and again, a species-centered ethically constitutive story can be combined with other such moral perspectives. It adds to them a focus on concrete and ongoing shared dangers that, if they come to be widely recognized and emphasized, might make it far more common for political actors, leaders and constituents alike, to define their political interests in ways that include such species interests. And if those who spoke for various political "peoples" felt politically impelled to show their supporters and outsiders how their policies, and indeed the very existence of their political communities, contributed to addressing basic species interests threatened by the sorts of problems I have reviewed, the consequences would probably be beneficial. Various forms of militarism, economic exploitation, environmental degradation, and demographic irresponsibility might well be better constrained, though certainly they will not prove easy to eliminate.

For from the perspective of this universalistic ethically constitutive story, governments, states, and other political communities appear as things somewhat akin to what political parties are within existing polities. They are political organizations that simultaneously seek to advance the interests of their members *and* to contribute in some way to the good of a more expansive and inclusive political body. I have previously argued that it is on the whole salutary to see political communities in this way, rather than as things akin to families, clubs, churches, orchestras, neighborhoods, or contractually based businesses (Smith, 1997, 490–496). It is salutary because it highlights the fact that all political communities are ineradicably *partisan* and *political* entities that inherently tend to favor the interests of their own members over outsiders, even though they often profess to be serving everyone. Awareness of this tendency can prompt vigilance in pushing societies to live up to their more universalistic promises. Yet this view of political communities is also salutary because, however much we decry political parties, honest observers know that they remain simply indispensable for the effective conduct of political affairs, even in the United States, where strong identifications with parties have declined. Similarly, however much we may decry the dangers of particularistic political allegiances from cosmopolitan perspectives, it is important to recognize that we simply do not yet have feasible ways of organizing systems of governance except through the division of humanity into many smaller political societies.

This perspective on political societies is salutary, finally, because even though some political parties, like some communities, claim to be the sole, authentic voice for peoples whose existences stretch back to time immemorial, it is in fact always clear that the parties are relatively recent human constructions. It is also clear that they are good for some purposes but not others. Hence it is always imaginable that their members' interests, as well as those of non-members, might be better served if those parties were significantly refashioned or abolished. It also seems proper to most people that individuals should be allowed to change parties or to belong to multiple parties if they are so inclined. Such perspectives on our political communities would again help counter their tendencies to claim total sovereignty and to seek to perpetuate their existence when humanity would be better served through the development of new forms of collective political association and activity. This outlook could also foster greater willingness to countenance fluidity in political memberships for all who desire it, via easy expatriation and naturalization and also acceptance of dual citizenships or even multiple citizenships.

My comparison of political communities to political parties can and has been criticized on many grounds (e.g., Spiro, 1999; Katznelson, 1999). The chief ones are first, that political communities are both of much deeper and enduring importance in people's lives than parties, and far harder to change; so the comparison makes little sense. Second, political parties can be as virulently ethnic or racial or as narrowly religious as chauvinistic political communities, so it does no good to analogize the latter to the former. And finally, many people find political parties unappealing and alienating, so that thinking of political communities as like parties and promoting more fluid memberships among them will only work to undercut further the senses of solidarity and loyalty that generate civic participation and public spiritedness.

I believe these criticisms are insufficiently informed by an understanding of the characteristic tendencies and dangers of the politics of peoplemaking that I am seeking to address. Perhaps the greatest danger of that politics is that it fosters far too demanding doctrines of allegiance to particular regimes and, sometimes, all too unquestioning attachments to them. It is able to do so in part because of the undeniable reality that one's legally recognized political community is in many respects a far more important membership than almost all others, and one that most people cannot easily change. Yet if we are to prompt political leaders and their constituents to accept the more multiple, fluid, and only "semi-sovereign" forms of political community that seem increasingly possible and desirable today, it is important to foster views of membership that combat these powerful tendencies to reify existing regimes. One purpose of advocating a more universalistic perspective is to engender the moderating belief that membership in the human species ultimately matters more than memberships in its political subdivisions, in precisely the way that people often feel their national memberships are more important than their political parties. Such a view reinforces the normative belief that all such "subdivision" memberships ought in principle to be alterable through individual and collective choices, even if many will understandably have no wish to undertake any radical changes.

I also have no illusions about the capacities of parties to champion invidious particularistic ideologies, racial, religious, and otherwise. Still, such parties generally confront the political burdens of either indicating how their vision is good for the whole of their communities, or of justifying their disregard for those who would not benefit from their policies. In contrast, nations and other political societies today can often simply present themselves as embodying the good of the pertinent whole, treating their neglect of their impact on the rest of humanity as unproblematic. If political peoples came to be more widely seen as something like political parties within the human community, these evasions might come less easily.

Finally, even though I regard it as valuable for leaders to promote more flexible forms of political belonging, and for people to have a certain sense of distance between their deepest political identities and their membership in any state, the normative stance urged here also has other political implications. The politics of conflicting stories of peoplehood that I am advocating is more likely to foster intense political engagement within and across existing political communities than apathetic absorption in non-political pursuits. The lack of excitement many Americans feel about their political parties arises, I believe, chiefly from the fact that they have too few parties, not from the inherent character of parties. Quite reasonably, many Americans do not feel that the party with which they are loosely aligned really champions their causes. A world in which people instead believe, with good reason, that they can act individually and collectively to join and shape forms of political community expressive of their deepest values and identities is a world in which political participation is likely to seem vastly more urgent and worthwhile.

The portrait of a competitive politics of particularistic and universalistic ethically constitutive stories that I have sketched does not provide easy guides to a whole variety of issues of political membership that confront us today: how far should we officially recognize racial, ethnic, religious, and gender identities in political institutions? How do we foster effective transnational governing agencies without deepening the "democratic deficit" arising from their inaccessibility? When are consociational arrangements, regional autonomy, even secessions justified? What governmental functions should different levels of government undertake in federated arrangements? Here I have said nothing directly about these and a whole host of other equally important questions. But what I have said is enough, I hope, to suggest some directions for normative reflection that are substantially different than those in which many current writers appear to be heading. These directions are, in fact, different from those that I anticipated I would pursue when I began this work. But they are different because they are based on an understanding of how and why people politically construct distinct communities for themselves, the kind of understanding that, I have suggested, is indispensable for useful normative analyses, yet too often left undone. At a minimum, I think the arguments I have made present some challenges to conventional thinking that may spur some strengthening of the cases typically advanced for the views I have criticized. At best, the directions charted here may prove to be ones which help us to conduct the politics of people-building in our rapidly changing world in ways that prove more constructive than much of what we have done so far.

Readers are more likely to be persuaded that this is the case, however, if they see these arguments worked through more fully in a particular context; and though the analysis here has sought to range far and wide, it originated in a particular context that has concededly shaped my concerns throughout. I conclude, then, by laying out more fully the normative implications of these arguments for the politics of people-making in the United States today; though as they have done throughout the preceding pages, those arguments ultimately lead us beyond American boundaries to the larger world of which that nation, like any nation, is but a part.

4   A pioneering people

Back in the USA

There are many reasons to object to the normative direction mapped out in the previous chapter. A world of moderate political peoples in which multiple, overlapping memberships are common, in which powers are assigned to many governments at many levels, and in which transnational arrangements seek to secure human rights, risks being a world of constantly conflicting authorities, of instability and disorder. It might therefore be one in which few regimes can provide effectively for the needs of their members. And insofar as power is transferred to larger and larger federations and international tribunals, it may also be a world that is in practice strikingly undemocratic, despite widespread professions of democratic commitments and formal opportunities to choose allegiances. Insofar as it actually becomes a stage for multiple, relatively fluid political memberships, moreover, such a world might also be condemned as one in which people do not have the sorts of truly deep and abiding senses of community and belonging that may be desirable for the development of many virtues.

In any case, such a world may simply not be practically attainable. It may appear particularly utopian if its societies feature political contests that involve clashes between competing ethically constitutive accounts of the society's common identity and those of the groups that partly comprise it and surround it. In many contexts, such a politics may seem likely to unleash fierce ethnic, racial, tribal, cultural, ideological, and religious antagonisms that will sooner or later destroy any basis for consensual, cooperative forms of political life. Despite all the problems involved in doing so, it may therefore still seem wisest to continue to place our normative focus on defining the institutional forms that can secure democracy and human rights within regimes in which all more "ethnic" conceptions are understood to be properly subordinated to shared procedural values in the political realm.

I raise these objections not to dismiss them; I am not sure they are wrong. But neither does it seem useful at this point to respond to them either by rehearsing more general philosophic considerations or by further detailing the ideal institutions for a world of moderate political peoples. Whatever one's grand philosophical or institutional blueprints for a well-ordered planet may look like, we are always faced by the question of what sorts of politics have a hope of getting us there from where we are now.

That is a question we can never answer with certainty. Politics is in practice necessarily a matter of uncertain experimentation, even if our experiment is to try to stand pat while many things are changing all around us. The most we can really hope to do is to lay out some next steps that we should take in specific political contexts if we seek to move in a particular direction, and then evaluate how feasible and desirable those concrete measures seem to be. I cannot suggest such steps for each and every current political context and community. But as it happens, no existing political society is likely to play a larger role in shaping world political developments during the foreseeable future than the one to which I primarily belong, the United States of America. In this chapter, then, I consider what it might mean for Americans to draw the sorts of normative lessons just sketched from the account of the politics of people-making provided in Part I – again with a special focus on the role that ethically constitutive stories should play.

This course is open to one immediate objection. By discussing how Americans might best conceive of their national identity and structure their politics, I may appear to be siding with those who insist that nation-states should remain the preeminent form of political community in the modern world. Some critics of my account of a normative vision of American identity in my 1997 book *Civic Ideals*, on which I build here, have seen it as too unthinkingly and profoundly invested in what should be seen as an increasingly retrograde and repressive nationalism (e.g. Spiro, 1999, 599–601; Honig, 2001, 119–120). Other critics have instead accused me of being too negative toward the US and too sympathetic to cosmopolitanism (e.g. Rabkin, 1998, 119–120; Rosen, 1998, 34–36). It is possible that both sets of critics are right; but let me note why both features seem to me all the more normatively appropriate in light of the analysis of people-making provided here.

That account argues that a successful politics of people-making must necessarily begin by drawing on and adapting the existing array of affiliations, interests, and ideologies in particular locales to build support for what is always a partly old, partly new vision of political community. It is not politically realistic to expect to win allegiance for political enterprises that cannot be shown to advance at least some of the deepest concerns that potential constituents harbor. I have also suggested that it is morally appropriate to recognize that the organization of the world into particular political communities has thus far been a necessary precondition for many forms of human development and flourishing; and that people deserve opportunities to participate in deciding to which communities they will assign priority and how the common lives of those communities will be conducted. But I have emphasized that all political communities are nonetheless partisan entities, created to serve the interests of some groups and individuals far more than others, and susceptible to being governed in ways that are harshly unjust to many inside and outside their bounds. It is irresponsible not to be greatly concerned with those propensities, found in greater and less degrees in every form of peoplehood in all times and places. The claims of every particular community must therefore be examined and challenged from many perspectives, especially from the standpoints of more universalistic accounts concerned to promote the flourishing of all humanity.

These general points, juxtaposed with prevailing political circumstances, seem to me to make it particularly imperative to offer constructive conceptions of American peoplehood today. There are indeed many important transformations in the forms of political membership visible around the world today, including the spread of transnational social movements, new systems of partial or full regional confederation, devolution of powers to various political subunits, and new initiatives to create more potent international legal structures, via laws, treaties, and tribunals to enforce them. Yet most analysts recognize that so-called "nation-states" remain very important, if not the most important, structures of political power in today's world; and no one denies that the United States, in particular, is extraordinarily powerful. It is a political community in which hundreds of millions of people are profoundly invested in many ways: through their economic interests; as a vehicle for their personal protection and their source of some share in collective political power; as the prime geographical location for their homes and their kinship and social networks; as an expression of their political ideals; and as a major source of their cultural and psychological identities.

The character of those interests, ideals, and identities varies enormously, of course. But what matters in the first instance is that the American political community is tremendously significant to very large numbers of people who possess the resources and will to maintain and shape its existence. I therefore doubt that any kind of politics of peoplehood, either within or without current US borders, is likely to get far in transforming the world for the better if it simply takes the form of an assault on or dismissal of American national identity. Such assaults are likely either to be ignored by Americans or to be met with hostile responses that may express and reinforce some of the worst aspects of American peoplehood.[1] I also think that many of the reasons that many Americans value their nationality have genuine moral weight. Hence it seems to me both politically unavoidable and morally appropriate to take American national identity as one important starting point for defining a morally defensible politics of peoplehood in today's world, even if, as I shall argue, such a politics must also motivate ongoing projects of reform and transformation if it is to remain defensible.

Let us begin, then, with the United States and its institutions as they are, and first consider what the normative viewpoint elaborated here implies about how the ongoing politics of people-making should be conducted in relation to this society. Despite many limitations, to be discussed in due course, modern American institutions fortunately provide significant opportunities and resources for conducting such politics in morally respectable fashion. The franchise is extended widely, and there are numerous arenas available for democratic political participation. In many instances, non-citizens as well as citizens can be heard and sometimes exercise influence. There are extensive police and military apparatuses that provide a substantial measure of personal security against criminal and political violence, and there are also formal legal institutions and mobilized groups working to check how far collective security for the majority is achieved through abuse of suspect individuals and groups. Personal and institutional legal freedoms of religion and expression are, in comparative perspective, quite expansive. Formal rights of internal movement, expatriation, and emigration are also well established. Prevailing laws promise opportunities for immigration that are fairly broad, seen in either historical or modern comparative perspective. These institutions both express and provide grounds to elaborate political power stories promising considerable personal and collective safety and some opportunities to exercise meaningful choices in regard to whether persons want to remain or become Americans, and in regard to how Americans wish for their political community to be governed. That is to say, in their broad outlines, American institutions give both practical channels and symbolic support to forms of people-building politics that prominently feature stories of democracy and human rights.

[1] As David Hollinger argues (2000, 203), the more chauvinistic strains in American political culture may well "loom all the larger in national politics if more space is left open for the flag-flying far right because the rest of us hide the Stars and Stripes in embarrassment and devote all our political energy to affiliations of more certain virtue but less certain strength."

The legal, political, and social institutions that structure American economic life also provide practical means and symbolic valorization for a wide range of economic pursuits in ways that generate extensive economic opportunities, impressive collective prosperity, and ongoing economic growth, even though these are accompanied by huge domestic and even more gaping international economic inequalities. These circumstances facilitate the elaboration of a range of economic stories featuring the potential of American peoplehood to foster greater and more widespread material prosperity, within and even outside its borders.

There are nonetheless many features of American democratic and economic institutions that can be severely criticized, and in the latter part of this chapter I raise a number of concerns from the standpoint of my own preferred conception of American national identity. But because that conception, like all conceptions of peoplehood, includes an ethically constitutive story as well as ones addressed to economic and political power structures, we must turn first to our core subject here, the sorts of ethically constitutive stories that can and should be told in American processes of people-making. It is on this question, especially, that the normative perspective sketched in the previous chapters has implications that challenge the prescriptions offered by some of the leading voices in contemporary western political theory.

Alternatives for an American public ethos

Notably, John Rawls and many theorists and activists influenced by similar concerns urge political participants in all modern societies, including the United States, to conduct their politics in line with non-mandatory but morally imperative standards of "public reason." Those standards require that whenever political candidates, governing officials, and judges address political issues in any public forum, they must stress reasons for political actions that are acceptable to other reasonable citizens – with those citizens viewed as free and equal persons, and with "reasonable" defined as embracing "a constitutional democratic regime and its companion idea of legitimate law" (Rawls, 1999, 132–133, 136–138).

Such a regime must include rights of free speech, and those rights mean that legally, these public figures can in fact say anything they like. Rawls also accepts that it may be appropriate for them to articulate controversial philosophic and religious grounds for their positions, *along with* arguments that can reasonably be expected to appeal to everyone (1999, 135, 152–54). Yet he still advocates acceptance of a moral "duty of civility" which would exhort political actors, when engaged in public advocacy, to "give up forever the hope of changing the constitution so as to establish" their religion's "hegemony" or to establish measures "to ensure its influence and success. To retain such hopes and aims would be inconsistent with the ideal of equal basic liberties for all free and equal citizens." Rawls maintains that without such an ethos governing political conduct, "without citizens' allegiance to public reason and their honoring the duty of civility, divisions and hostilities are bound in time to assert themselves ... harmony and concord depend on the vitality of the public political culture and on citizens' being devoted to and realizing the ideal of public reason" (1999, 150, 174–175). Throughout his career, Rawls has explained that he is convinced of this sociological proposition especially because of the long history of religious warfare in western societies.

That history is not to be dismissed lightly. But consider what Rawls's view implies in regard to some of the most divisive and repressive political perspectives in US history, all of which remain present in some form today. Despite its ideals and institutions promoting separation of church and state, the US has always had citizens who believed that they were first and foremost a chosen people of the Protestant God, and that American institutions should in various ways express and reinforce this most ultimate comprehensive truth. It has also always had Catholic citizens, many of whom believed, especially prior to Vatican II, that separation of church and state was instrumentally valuable while Catholics were in the minority, but that eventually the US should become an officially Catholic community. Even more notably, the US has always had leaders and movements who argued explicitly that the reality of "white" racial supremacy demanded that whites be privileged in various ways. Those policies, in turn, have in various periods generated powerful African-American political movements advancing ideologies depicting whites as inherently less soulful than blacks, sometimes as ineradicably evil. Proponents of these views have often called for some measure of African-American separation and self-rule, ranging from legally segregated neighborhoods, schools, and businesses, to statehood within a transformed American confederation, to the establishment of an independent African-American nation.[2] Today, there is little doubt that some Americans embrace variants of all these positions, including some Protestant and Catholic extremists, the Ku Klux Klan and some militia organizations, and more radical members of Louis Farrakhan's Nation of Islam.

Such conceptions are rarely advanced by mainstream political figures in public locations, however, and Rawls might argue that this represents a triumph for the sort of ethos he proposes. He does not seek to interfere

---

[2] See generally Bennett, 1990; Anbinder, 1992; Robinson, 2001.

with what is undoubtedly the more open expression of these views in various sectors of the "background culture" of American political society, such as churches, social groups, and private associations. But he does urge all political figures and all citizens to regard public espousal of such views as "unreasonable" and to stigmatize such pronouncements as displays of "incivility." He insists that if these Americans are to be good citizens and generally seen as such, they must give up, publicly at least, any notion of ever seeing the establishment of legislative policies or constitutional changes expressive of their political visions.

Because the alternative perspective I propose calls for robust and explicit contests among all rival political views, including clashing ethically constitutive stories, I certainly do not suggest that Rawlsians should hold back from advancing these contentions, so long as they find them convincing. I also concede that advocacy of the propriety of something like Rawls's ethos has probably played some role in curbing public expression of highly illiberal views. Yet I think that contribution has been and is likely to be less important than the impact of the more Madisonian contestation I have described, which has often occurred in US history, and which I think still needs to occur, probably more extensively than it does now.

Rather than suggesting to political figures that it is "uncivil" to say publicly what they may be saying quite passionately privately or semi-privately, the ethos of honest contestation that I favor would urge them to articulate the visions they favor as fully as possible. Public debate would include elaboration of the ethically constitutive stories they invoke, the manner and degree to which they favor democratic political processes and guarantees of basic rights, and what all this implies for Americans and non-Americans as individuals and group members, and for desirable forms of political peoplehood. Proponents of different viewpoints would then be encouraged to subject these contrasting visions to sharp criticisms, including challenges to any *lack* of forthrightness on these matters. That means, however, that these criticisms would not focus at all on whether these views were sufficiently "civil," or even on whether they were "reasonable" given presumptions of the propriety of liberal rights and democratic governance within the peoples that comprise the world today. They would focus on whether the substantive claims being advanced are intellectually and morally convincing, or whether they rely on factually false premises and propose morally damaging directions.

In other words, I would not say to a fundamentalist Secretary of the Interior that it is inconsistent with political morality to propose conservation policies based on expectations that the second coming of Christ is imminent, as James Watt is alleged to have done. I would argue to him and to my fellow citizens that this expectation is weakly supported even in religious terms, substantively risky, and probably flat wrong. And I submit that through most of US history, our public debates over illiberal religious and racial views, which have now led most public figures to abandon advocacy of extreme positions, have been conducted much more through this kind of robust, substantive critical engagement than through Rawlsian tactics. Instead of political participants publicly saying nothing about their illiberal opponents' views other than that they were "uncivil" and "unreasonably" reliant on arguments that were not "public reasons," it has been more customary for figures like the African-American writer Martin Delany, addressing religious arguments for black subordination in the 1850s, and Massachusetts Senator George Hoar, opposing scientific defenses for racially exclusionary immigration laws in the 1880s, to use every sort of contention that might persuade. They made some arguments that Rawls might feel comfortable with, but they also called attention to the scientific inadequacy and theological weaknesses of the positions they attacked, and they often offered equally contentious alternative interpretations (Smith, 1997, 247–248, 359–360). The account of people-making politics I have provided makes this pattern understandable. It is just not realistic to think that most political figures ever can or ever will avoid invoking more comprehensive accounts, usually including ethically constitutive stories, to bolster their views whenever they think it helpful to do so.

It is true that US history also vividly displays the sorts of dangers of invidious racial and religious ethically constitutive stories, and the clashes between intensely held rival views, that so profoundly alarm Rawls and many others. Changes in more moderate directions have not come without violence and coercion. Yet insofar as the US has moved toward greater acceptance that it is wrong to enshrine one religious viewpoint or doctrine of racial supremacy as nationally authoritative, that progress has been achieved with, not without, deep public engagement with contrasting ethically constitutive visions. To some hard-to-determine degree, those public contests have contributed both to strategic rethinking of what positions can be successfully promoted publicly, and internal reconsideration of what the substantive views of heretofore inegalitarian and illiberal groups actually should be. Americans have not needed to confine official discourses to Rawlsian "public reasons" in order to work toward more inclusive, egalitarian, and pluralistic forms of public life in the past, nor do they need to do so now.

To the contrary, I suspect that many contemporary proponents of extreme religious and racial views may experience strengthening senses of righteous indignation when they are told that their views are too unreasonable even to be debated on the merits in public arenas and that it is "uncivil" for officials to discuss them seriously. And it is likely to be all the more infuriating, and mobilizing, when the champions of "public reason" appear to deny, either hypocritically or foolishly, that their own views also express controversial ethically constitutive accounts of human beings that are far from self-evident truths. Certainly, the most successful leaders of many illiberal American political movements, as well as many liberal ones, have often energetically employed contentions that they and their constituents were being unjustly denied any authentic voice, and that they were being treated with disrespectful condescension, to stir up support for their causes.[3]

I therefore think it is often more practically effective, as well as more morally appropriate, to address the positions advanced by such movements fully and openly, however critically. In many cases, I suspect that leaders and members of such movements may be more likely to accept compromises, and even to reconsider their own demonologies, if their fellow citizens treat them in these antagonistic yet respectful ways. I do not wish to overstate that potential: I do not suppose that any "ethos" for the conduct of public institutions, whether Rawls's, mine, or some other, is likely to play a greatly determinative role in political outcomes. But I think that we can accomplish more to promote concord by urging all parties, groups, and movements to meet opposing views with serious engagement, and by encouraging all participants to articulate their commitments fully and honestly, than we can by encouraging dismissive disregard for all those who fail to offer what academics deem to be appropriate arguments.

Still, the question inevitably arises: what if things go badly? What if, in the course of democratic political struggles among conflicting, openly comprehensive and ethically constitutive positions, an immoderate fundamentalist religious group or a racialist faction gains control of the White House or the Congress, or both, amidst elections splintered among a number of parties? Perhaps, in accordance with my view, they have campaigned openly on platforms promising that they will institutionally favor their religion in public schools, ceremonies, and funding programs, or that they will restore legal racial segregation, with resources disproportionately assigned to their "master" race. Perhaps, in fact, they propose to disfranchise infidels or racial "inferiors." Perhaps they propose to use

[3] James Tully argues persuasively that without "intercultural dialogues" in which different but potentially "complementary stories are exchanged," members of distinct cultural groups may well feel that they are not receiving the recognition and respect that are required to sustain both self-respect and, therefore, mutual respect and willingness to participate cooperatively (Tully, 1995, 183, 189–191). This seems as true for white fundamentalist Christians as it is for members of the native tribes or radical black nationalists.

police and military powers to persecute, imprison, sometimes even execute those who oppose them. What can an advocate of open contestation among conflicting ethically constitutive views say or do when such political forces gain power?

The answer is: much the same sorts of things, with equal or greater conviction, that most Rawlsian liberals or, for that matter, most radical democrats and most conservative American patriots would do. Precisely because my view recognizes all forms of political peoplehood and all accompanying institutions and policies as imperfect human creations, I do not see in it any inner logical compulsion to acquiesce in every way to the results of democratic processes. In regard to any and all governing policies, groups, institutions, and affiliations, it is always a matter of pragmatic judgment as to whether more good can be done in the long run through resistance, acceptance, or compromise. Most of the time, in societies with many valuable institutions and traditions like the United States, the answer to defeat is to seek to win another day through peaceful, lawful democratic processes. At some point, however, strategies must shift.

If, for example, Christian fundamentalists captured the Congress and the Presidency and passed laws requiring that public school curricula acknowledge the God of the Bible to be the one true God, it would certainly be appropriate for all who disagreed, from whatever perspective, to urge the US Supreme Court to overturn that law on the basis of the First Amendment. And if, injecting a modicum of political reality into the discussion, we assume that the fundamentalists could not win a constitutional amendment for their position, so that they instead sought to deny the Court's jurisdiction and to defy its ruling through legislative and executive actions, those measures also should be resisted by the most peaceful yet effective means available. The best means would be to throw the pious rascals out at the next election. That failing, perhaps due to new disfranchising initiatives, forms of peaceful civil disobedience would certainly be appropriate. And if those did not work, then the forms of resistance would have to escalate. If instead it was a white supremacist faction establishing disproportionately funded racially segregated schools, the first resort might be to adjudication of the equal protection clause along with efforts at electoral repudiation, and then similar escalations.

It is hard to imagine in these unlikely cases that any extreme responses would ever really be needed; but admittedly other, more difficult scenarios could arise, "even" in America and certainly in many other societies. Some readers may think that my response amounts to conceding that, if we are to forestall such developments or deal with them successfully, we must first have in place firm agreements, accompanied by enforcing institutions, on liberal democratic constitutional rules of the game, before any ethically constitutive stories are articulated. Stories that fail to endorse those rules should then be understood to be improper, just as Rawls contends.

I believe instead that I am only maintaining that whatever happens, political participants can and should always be expected to continue to struggle to establish their values, taking as much advantage as they can of any and all established traditions and institutions that are conducive to the furthering of those values. I doubt that we can ever hope to escape these sorts of dangerous scenarios by insisting that all political participants are ethically (but not legally) required to commit in advance to support democratic procedures, basic rights, and legitimate law above all else, whatever the costs to their ideological objectives. Questions of proper democratic processes and genuinely fundamental rights are, after all, always subject to contentiously varying interpretations, and it is always possible, I think, to show that those accounts are informed by controversial ethically constitutive views. We can, if we wish, certainly *use* democratic and liberal values to help define and win support for our political objectives, for the institutions we wish to see maintained and established, and for their proper conduct, *as we engage* in ongoing political contests over rival visions, some liberal democratic, some not. But we cannot hope to use those values at some imaginary, unalterable pre-political moment to impose rules that succeed in getting all political groups to abandon their public efforts to work for deeply held beliefs that we regard as unreasonable. Nor can any rules insure that we can defeat any such group simply by pointing out that they are breaking these rules, without having to respond to their substantive appeals. To think that we can do so is, again, to ignore the inescapable realities of the always-continuing, always-competitive politics of people-making.

The impracticality of this course of action becomes even more apparent when we consider a second feature of Rawls's position, one that he shares, as we have seen, with many contemporary theorists. Though he provides much advice about the sorts of controversial and chauvinistic views that should not be offered in the central arenas of public life, and though he urges certain sorts of political and, to a lesser degree, economic institutions, there is very little in Rawls's view to help us determine the substantive accounts of American national identity that political figures should be encouraged to advance. That, of course, is not his aim; nor is it the aim of most liberal or democratic theorists, who are generally more concerned, like Rawls, to highlight forms of political repression that should be resisted.

Yet the arguments of Part I indicate strongly that it is wildly unrealistic to think that political participants in this or any other political community

are likely to win support for their preferred political and economic institutions if they do not also offer some sort of compelling account of the
collective identity of that community. Even if they wish to turn people
away from support for American nationalism, for example, they must still
resist the ethically constitutive stories told on its behalf; and sooner or
later, they will need their own such stories to buttress their rival visions
of appropriate political memberships. If they instead wish for people to
embrace certain conceptions of citizenship and certain types of governing
institutions as defining features in an America capable of inspiring justified allegiance, they will have an even greater need for a story of American
identity that goes beyond abstract defenses of democracy and human
rights. This imperative is so keenly apparent to all who engage in concrete political organizing that every (temporarily) successful American
political party and movement, along with virtually every unsuccessful
one, has offered such accounts, always including potent ethically constitutive elements, usually linked to some sorts of democratic power and
commercial economic stories. There is, then, no realistic escape from the
task of seeking to define a morally defensible conception of American
peoplehood, however provisional and transitional we may think it should
be.[4] There is also no guarantee that we can do so in ways that are proof
against the dangers involved, only reason to hope that some conceptions
may prove more salutary than others.

Historical ethically constitutive stories

Because writers like Rawls, Young, Connolly, Honig, and others eschew
the task of defining any concrete sense of American national identity, we
must look elsewhere to consider what alternatives are available for doing
so. I trust it will be clear that, though I do not think we should treat
any ethically constitutive stories as outside the bounds of permissible
political discourse, I fervently hope that Americans will issue resounding
rejections of extreme religious, racial, and ethnic accounts throughout
their decision-making processes and institutions. As I have contended
in the past (1997, 496–506), I think Americans are best advised instead

---

[4] This, again, is where I part company from William Connolly's proposed "post-national
ethos of engagement," with which I am otherwise in considerable agreement. He hopes
for "a thick public culture of multi-dimensional pluralism well oiled by an ethos of engagement between diverse constituents who reciprocally relinquish the narcissistic demand to
occupy the national center" (2000, 194, 198). Narcissistic such demands may be, but an
ethos that demands that they be abandoned is still likely to be experienced as repressive
and to prove politically unrealistic. I therefore hope only for an ethos that encourages
acceptance of and responsiveness to contestation, and a willingness in most instances to
abide defeats peaceably in the hopes of future victories.

to embrace fundamentally historical accounts of their national identity. And here I wish to stress, more than I have done previously, that to be morally defensible, those stories should be linked to accounts of humanity more broadly in ways that can and do call for ongoing transformations in American peoplehood.

Since most if not all ethically constitutive accounts are structured chronologically, often genealogically, let me emphasize that by "historical" stories, I mean only those positions that present the American political community as something that exists because it has been constructed and maintained through time by the political actions of human beings. The contrast I wish to draw here can be well illustrated by considering one of the most eloquent recent political narratives of American civic identity, President George W. Bush's Inaugural Address, delivered January 20, 2001. There he told his fellow Americans:

> We have a place, all of us, in a long story. A story we continue, but whose end we will not see. It is the story of a new world that became a friend and liberator of the old, a story of a slave-holding society that became a servant of freedom, the story of a power that went into the world to protect but not possess, to defend but not to conquer. It is the American story. A story of flawed and fallible people, united across the generations by grand and enduring ideals. The grandest of these ideals is an unfolding American promise that everyone belongs, that everyone deserves a chance, that no insignificant person was ever born. Americans are called upon to enact this promise in our lives and in our laws; and though our nation has sometimes halted and sometimes delayed, we must follow no other course ... Our democratic faith is more than the creed of our country, it is the inborn hope of our humanity, an ideal we carry but do not own, a trust we bear and pass along; and even after nearly 225 years, we have a long way yet to travel.

In these opening passages in his address, President Bush clearly and movingly defines American peoplehood, and the identity of Americans, in terms of their participation in a shared story stretching beyond them into the past and on into a future that lacks certainty but not direction. His telling of the American story commendably recognizes American shortcomings, while valorizing a democratic faith involving concern and respect for all persons as the "grandest" of American ideals. Accordingly, Bush connects this national story with a more universalistic one, stressing that this ideal is common to and should be realized for all humanity. In all these regards, Bush offers a story of peoplehood that I find admirable, indeed inspiring. It is a civic vision that, I believe, merits the loyalty of Americans even if they are, like me, not partisan supporters of this President.

Yet despite many important points of agreement, Bush's story is still not the one I would prefer, nor is it ultimately a genuinely historical story.

The passage just cited intimates the Protestant notion of a divine vocation or "calling" as our guide to our civic lives, and in the speech's closing passages, the fundamentally religious character of President Bush's view of American identity becomes more explicit:

> After the Declaration of Independence was signed, Virginia statesman John Page wrote to Thomas Jefferson, "We know the race is not to the swift nor the battle to the strong. Do you not think an angel rides in the whirlwind and directs this storm?" Much time has passed since Jefferson arrived for his inauguration. The years and changes accumulate, but the themes of this day he would know, "our nation's grand story of courage and its simple dream of dignity."
>
> We are not this story's author, who fills time and eternity with His purpose. Yet His purpose is achieved in our duty, and our duty is fulfilled in service to one another. Never tiring, never yielding, never finishing, we renew that purpose today; to make our country more just and generous; to affirm the dignity of our lives and every life.
>
> This work continues. This story goes on. And an angel still rides in the whirlwind and directs this storm.[5]

Stirring as they are, these passages come close to the sort of effort to insure the "influence and success" of President Bush's religious views that John Rawls criticizes. Unlike Rawls, I welcome this open expression of the ethically constitutive beliefs that guide this important political actor's sense of American purposes, at least in part. It is not, however, an element of his American story that I can endorse; and it also makes his account at bottom not a genuinely historical one. Though I share many of President Bush's values – more than enough to sustain my qualified but genuine allegiance to the political society he now leads – I do not think it either right or wise to see the United States as an instrument of divine purposes, or its story as authored by God. I do not profess to know the aims of whatever divinities may play a role in human affairs; and I am skeptical of political leaders who suggest that they do, because I believe they claim more knowledge and authority than they legitimately can. I prefer to see the American story as primarily authored by the American people themselves, acting as agents in human history, and to hold them – us – responsible for defining our civic aims and identity.

The case for thus preferring historical ethically constitutive stories rests first on the fact that it is undeniably true that the US, like all other political communities, originated in and has since been sustained through such actions, whatever else one may wish to perceive at work in its history. In the inevitable contestation among different visions of peoplehood, the inclusion of truthful elements is no guarantee of political success; but it

---

[5] Bush's Inaugural Address can be found at http://www.yale.edu/lawweb/Avalon/presiden/inaug/gbush1.htm.

is often advantageous, and it certainly contributes to the intellectual and moral defensibility of the view. Second, such a conception of American national identity ought, at least, to foster fuller acknowledgement of the fact that the United States is an inevitably imperfect and partisan political creation, produced by compromises among coalitions seeking to serve some purposes and some persons and not others. This recognition fosters desirable capacities for critical distance even on the part of those who strongly affirm American national identity. It makes it always appropriate to consider whether the existing form of American peoplehood remains the most suitable instrument for its original purposes; whether those purposes remain desirable and defensible; and whether other purposes and persons ought to be more fully served than they are now.

But third, even though historical accounts certainly cannot naturalize and probably cannot valorize political memberships to anything like the degree that religious and familial accounts often do, they nonetheless can be effective responses to the political and philosophical demands that generate the irreplaceable role of ethically constitutive stories in the politics of people-making. They do present membership in the American political community as participation in a larger entity with an existence and meaning that simultaneously transcend and inform the individual lives of its citizens. Historical stories also have a natural propensity to strengthen senses of civic responsibility and to affirm the propriety of democratic self-governance. For in presenting the political community as something to which citizens have given shape and meaning in the past, these stories make it clear that the decisions of American political leaders and their active constituents today can play a large role in determining their nation's current and future significance – especially if they take their powers and opportunities to do so seriously.

Some writers argue that fundamentally historical stories of peoplehood are undesirable, for if they are to be politically effective at all, they must be sanitized accounts that offer deceptive, self-congratulatory myths about the nation's past leaders and achievements (e.g. Kymlicka, 1995, 189, 238n14; Kiss, 1996, 319). Others equate the notion of a shared historical identity with the conception of a shared cultural identity, so that being American is as much or more a matter of the dominant language, folkways, consumption and work habits, and social practices as it is a sense of participation in and responsibility for the developing life of a historical political people (e.g. Brimelow, 1995, xix; Lind, 1995, 5, 14–15, 285–286).

I have previously argued that the first claim is unconvincing, because people can feel profoundly committed to and inspired to assist even quite flawed memberships if they see those memberships as deeply constitutive of their identities, as in the cases of unhappy families and scandal-plagued churches. And I remain profoundly wary of the second argument, because concerns to preserve common cultural identities so often and so easily serve to justify harsh, needlessly repressive policies of assimilation and exclusion (Smith, 1997, 488, 498–499, 514n31, 642–643nn66–67). The distinction I am making here between "historical political" and "cultural" stories of peoplehood probably warrants some clarification.

Again, I disagree with proponents of civic nationhood, who believe that political communities can be sustained by agreement on shared political principles alone; and I also disagree with those who suggest that those agreements must be supported by a particular culture and history, but that these must be a culture and history that are understood to converge on universal liberal democratic principles. Actual political communities like the United States are better understood as historical political creations that have been produced both by force and, usually, a great range of ideological traditions, and all the traditions that retain support, democratic and undemocratic, secular liberal, militantly religious, and narrowly ethnic, must be recognized as authentic elements of that national identity. We can and should designate some as more preferable and worthy of development, but it is wrong to deny that other elements are constitutive parts of a community like the United States. But just as it is a mistake to pretend that only certain of these traditions are "really" American, it is an even greater mistake to treat putatively "extrapolitical" cultural patterns as definitively American traits that can legitimately be imposed on all in the name of preserving the "national identity." This course really represents a choice in favor of more narrowly ethnic political traditions.

It is true that an awareness of and sense of participation in the historic life of a particular political people in itself represents a kind of political cultural identity that has "something of the flavor of a community of descent," as David Hollinger argues (2000, 217). That is an important reason why historical ethically constitutive stories can be politically potent. But I do not see why these stories need to feature any "extrapolitical" cultural elements, which a number of present and potential Americans may neither share nor value, in order to play this role. Accounts focused on the diverse, conflictual, sometimes great, sometimes vicious, and sometimes mundane experiences and activities of the historical American political community can be felt to be powerfully constitutive, and ethically constitutive, by any and all who believe that this history and these actions have, for better and for worse, deeply shaped who they are and who they wish to be.

Recent developments have strongly affirmed the power of ethically constitutive historical stories of American peoplehood because, in the wake
of the terrible destruction wrought by terrorists on September 11, 2001,
these sorts of accounts have multiplied. It might be assumed that those
on the more liberal end of the contemporary political spectrum are more
open to conceiving of nations as historical political creations, rather than
as expressions of organic cultures, distinctive lineages, or divine will.
Many proponents of historical conceptions of membership can indeed
be found in such ranks (e.g. Hollinger, 1995; Yack, 1996; Rorty, 1998).
In contrast, when President Bush spoke to the nation ten days after the
terrorist attacks, he built upon the themes of his inaugural to suggest
that God would not be "neutral" in the long conflict he foresaw between
the United States and terrorists, and that we could again hope for an
angel to guide the nation in this new storm.[6] As the ensuing "war on
terrorism" has precipitated both the largest reorganization of the nation's
security structure since the onset of the Cold War and, at this writing, a
likely resumption of the "Desert Storm" war on Iraq, President Bush has
continued to define American goals in terms of his profoundly religious
sense of American civic identity, rather than simply advancing a secular,
historical account.

Nonetheless, three recent works published by firmly conservative authors show the broad appeal of conceptions of the USA as a distinctive
historical political community. Though in a fuller elaboration of their
views, some or all of these writers might well place significant stress on
religious, cultural, and natural law themes, in a manner more reminiscent of President Bush, their primary focus in these books, all aimed at
general readers, is on the US as a humanly established, humanly shaped
historical project.

In *What's so Great about America*, the conservative commentator Dinesh
D'Souza discusses the United States primarily as the political creation of
the American founders, carried forward by patriots throughout history.
He maintains that out of all aspects of American life, it is one ideological
thread, the "notion of you as being the architect of your own destiny," that
is above all else "behind the worldwide appeal of America." He sees this
immensely inspiring but potentially anarchic idea as skillfully institutionally enshrined and channeled by the founders in a "new regime" in which
problems of scarcity and diversity are largely "solved" by granting citizens "a wide berth of freedom – economic freedom, political freedom,
and freedom of speech and religion – in order to shape their own lives

---

[6] President Bush's September 21, 2001 address can be found at http://www.cnn.com/2001/
US/09/20/gen.bush.transcript/.

and pursue happiness," even as the system directs "the energies of citizens toward trade and commerce." And he tells the story of American history as one in which this idea and these institutions, properly adhered to and defended, have made America "the greatest, freest, and most decent society in existence," an "oasis of goodness in a desert of cynicism and barbarism" (2002, 84, 94, 195).

Former Secretary of Education William Bennett's *Why We Fight: Moral Clarity and the War on Terrorism* articulates a similar historical conception of American national identity, if in yet more militant language. He defines the United States as "a nation created to realize a specific political vision," and he insists that it is our historical sense of this entity,

our collective memory of that vision – the American idea – that defines us as Americans and ineluctably exerts its pull on our patriotic emotions . . . By studying our history, by learning about its heroes, by examining and understanding its failures as well as its incomparable achievements, we grasp the value of our political tradition and what distinguishes it from others.

And Bennett maintains that a "sober, a sophisticated study of our history" shows

beyond cavil that we have provided more freedom to more people than any nation in the history of mankind; that we have provided a greater degree of equality to more people than any nation in the history of mankind; that we have created more prosperity, and spread it more widely, than any nation in the history of mankind; that we have brought more justice to more people than any nation in the history of mankind; that our open, tolerant, prosperous, peaceable society is the marvel and envy of the ages. (2002, 150–151)

He also believes that the history supportive of such conclusions need not be a sanitizing or mythologizing one. Bennett contends:

a positive assessment of American history is not the same thing as an uncritical assessment. If we were created by a political vision, our story is the story of a struggle to realize that vision. A struggle has its ups and downs, its advances and setbacks; it is subject not only to changing circumstance and to the shifting quality of leadership in any generation but to the vicissitudes of human character and the enduring waywardness of the human heart. We have certainly had our failures, some of them shameful.

But in Bennett's view, Americans have never once "lost sight of our moral ideals, which is why, time and again, we have succeeded in confronting, overcoming, and transcending the stains on our record, the stain of slavery foremost among them" (2002, 151–152).

Finally, the distinguished constitutional scholar Walter Berns argues in *Making Patriots* that American patriotism is "twofold," involving allegiance both to the principles of the Declaration of Independence, which are understood to provide guidance to all humanity, and to the United States as a distinctive country with "particular sentiments, manners, and memories" (2001, 4, 9). Because Berns affirms that American principles are in some sense also principles of natural and divine justice, and because he includes particular culture traits as elements of American patriotism, his account does not present American national identity as a purely historical, political human construction. But like the other two authors, he nonetheless stresses the origin of America in acts of conscious creation by human political actors, and he rests his account of its contemporary significance on an understanding of its historical and present role in the world. Berns's account is also substantively similar to the other two. He argues that whether Americans like it or not:

– and it *is* something of a burden, certainly a responsibility – America is to modern history as Rome was to ancient, and not only because we are the one remaining superpower. Modern politics began three hundred-plus years ago with the discovery or pronouncement of new principles, universal and revolutionary principles, respecting the rights of man. In 1776 we declared our right to form a new nation by appealing to these principles. Because we were the first to do so, it fell to us to be their champions, first by setting an example – this was Lincoln's point – and subsequently by defending them against their latter-day enemies, the Nazis and fascists in World War II and the communists in the cold war. Our lot is to be the one essential country, "the last, best hope of earth," and this ought to be acknowledged, beginning in our schools and universities, for it is only then that we can come to accept the responsibilities attending it. (2001, ix–x)

But if these examples illustrate that Americans across the political spectrum seem eager to embrace fundamentally or strongly historical conceptions of American national identity today, they will also confirm in many minds the limitations and dangers of such conceptions. Despite William Bennett's protestations, which may seem to echo mine, these are stories of America that mythologize and valorize in order to instill far more reverence toward America than critically reflective attachment. They are all far more concerned to persuade Americans of their special greatness and moral superiority than they are to suggest ways Americans might confront and improve upon their failings. All these writers portray America's human founders as almost godlike figures, since their political vision has made America the greatest, most decent, and most widely beneficial society in history, the marvel of the ages. And all maintain that the heroes of succeeding generations of patriots have kept America, as each author asserts following Lincoln, "the last, best hope of earth" (Berns, 2001, x; Bennett, 2002, 14; D'Souza, 2002, 193).

By trumpeting this resonant phrase, the authors link their stories of America's distinctive historical identity with a universalistic story of all humanity: the US is the "essential nation" that shows the world how to live freely and prosperously and that provides the might and fortitude necessary to withstand the enemies of liberty and civilized progress. Humanity is that species that can best develop by following America's example. D'Souza goes so far as to argue that, as "the American founders knew," the American political experiment

produces a new kind of human being. That human being – confident, self-reliant, tolerant, generous, future oriented – is a vast improvement over the wretched, servile, fatalistic, and intolerant human being that traditional societies have always produced, and that Islamic societies produce now . . . Ultimately, America is worthy of our love and sacrifice because, more than any other society, it makes possible the good life, and the life that is good,

not just for Americans but for all human beings (D'Souza, 2002, 192–193).

Despite such glorifying panegyrics, all three writers do see problems in contemporary American life. The evils they highlight, however, are almost exclusively those of multiculturalism and its allegedly attendant cultural relativism. These are bad because they undermine recognition that the US is indeed far superior to all other nations and political communities, past and present (Berns, 2001, 135–144; Bennett, 2002, 44–70; D'Souza, 2002, 37–42, 187–188). All these authors are deeply concerned that in the absence of this recognition, Americans today may lack the patriotism needed to sustain a war against terrorism. That is why they write.

These books are therefore clearly exercises in American peoplebuilding in a time of heightened conflict, and they plainly show that historical, political stories can express claims of intrinsic moral superiority as passionately as any other ethically constitutive accounts. I think, however, this only means that it is realistic to imagine a sustainable politics of robustly contested people-making that chiefly features varying historical stories, not that historical ethically constitutive narratives have to be extravagantly celebratory to work at all. My own preferred story has agreements with all these positions, making it possible to conceive of us all working cooperatively on many matters. But it also has some basic disagreements that could fuel major debates and clashing political projects. The agreements mean that both they and I would probably see it worthwhile to continue the contestation if our opponents temporarily prevailed. The disagreements mean that very different policies would ensue if power should then shift.

Let me review the agreements. It is unquestionably true that the American founders crafted new political institutions that provided for more extensive political freedoms and forms of self-governance than had previously prevailed in most times and places, as well as institutions providing broad if by no means universal rights to participate as juridical equals in market economies and to engage in a wide range of intellectual and spiritual pursuits. It is also true that these institutions were defended through still-novel doctrines of natural rights, and that over time those institutions and those doctrines have helped generate many great benefits for many Americans and many people in other countries. That is why I and most Americans believe that there is much about America that is worth preserving and extending, in some form or another.

As I have previously argued, however, I think it is misleading to suggest that the American founders were essentially agreed on a single "specific political vision." They had serious disputes among themselves on many things, including the ultimate desirability of democracy; on its implications for where governmental powers should be allocated; on the propriety of slavery; on the relationship of doctrines of human rights to the different sexes and "races"; on the proper place of religion in American life; and on questions of how extensively the US should engage the other nations of the world and toward what ends. Due to these disagreements, the system they produced and the policies it pursued were from the start the results of both high and low compromises among distinct but overlapping visions and interests. Their works were, in short, impressive but fallible human creations resulting from the complex interplay of competing conceptions of political peoplehood.

It is therefore unsurprising, but also unavoidably important, that America's subsequent history has indeed included great failings as well as great accomplishments. Those failings include not only slavery but also longer-lasting, elaborate legal structures of racial and gender hierarchy; the forcible displacement even of peaceful, cooperative native tribes; wars of imperial expansion against Mexico and Spain; the recurrent generation of gross economic inequalities, often accompanied by violent repression of would-be reformers; and overt public discrimination against adherents of "extreme" minority religions, among other shortcomings. Major reforms of many of those features of American political experience have certainly been achieved, and in this Americans can and should take pride. But it is misleading to say that Americans never "lost sight of" their moral ideals. Rather, proponents of some American ideals eventually won out over rivals with bona fide claims to be championing different, but equally authentic versions of American ideals.

Or so I have argued, in *Civic Ideals* and other works. As a result, the historical ethically constitutive accounts of these authors seem to me to overstate greatly the visionary character of the framers and to mischaracterize the nature and extent of American political struggles, the sources of their positive achievements, and their damaging consequences. I have instead told what seems to me a more accurate and no less meaningful, but admittedly less glorious and less teleological tale in which progress has come, when it has come, through contingent, ongoing contestation, not through simply following the framers' blueprints. In so doing, however, I have not sought simply to reverse the acclaim offered by authors like these: I have not contended that the US has been on balance much worse than most other societies. I have not done so partly because I do not think that is the case; but even more, the whole question of whether or not the US is much better or worse than all other societies has not seemed especially pertinent. America's historical and contemporary deficiencies seem far too serious to brush aside, whatever the nation's comparative standing. And besides, truly scholarly assessments of the achievements and worth of whole societies seems like a tremendously demanding task, if it can be done at all.

These authors, of course, have not seriously undertaken that task. Their sweeping comparative assertions about American worth are used to structure their universalistic story, their claim that humanity has progressed in the modern world chiefly because of America's distinctive, particular political community. That universalistic story makes attention to America's limitations seem not so much unpatriotic as foolishly short-sighted. To make this remarkable strategy respectable, they all rely heavily on one of the few statements by Lincoln that should be forgiven as a bit of understandable hyperbole, rather than taken as a serious factual claim. To be sure, Lincoln was certainly profoundly serious about the idea that the United States should seek to be a shining example to the world, and he was right to define that goal. But he gave us no warrant to presume that it was or is the "last" political community anywhere that retains any potential to give "hope" to humanity. There were and are other societies with much to contribute; today there are many other democracies that honor human rights. To contend that America is an "oasis" amidst a "desert of cynicism and barbarism" is obviously to stoke unjustified xenophobia toward many other decent societies and peoples, contrary to Lincoln's intent.

It is nonetheless true today that the US has unique political, military, and economic preeminence among the political communities of the world; and as a recent American hero has averred, with this great power does indeed come great responsibility. But if the United States is to be the "best," or even simply better, at benefiting humanity, it will only be because Americans acknowledge and address the limitations in what they have achieved so far. I believe that instead of historical stories that minimize those limitations, Americans need honest accounts that can help us draw from our failures an agenda for what we should do to realize our finest aspirations more fully today.

But before elaborating what might be involved in doing so, let me call attention to another basic contrast between the ethically constitutive story of American historical identity I prefer to tell and those contained in these recent books. All these works are fundamentally backward-looking accounts in which America's founders hit upon all the right basic answers, and the task of Americans since has been simply to preserve the basic institutions and ideals the framers established, operating them under changing conditions but in the original spirit. This deeply conservative view of American life seems to me not only unwarranted; it is paradoxical. It implicitly urges us to ignore one major defining trait of the founding generation, a characteristic at least as central to their story as any other: the creators of America were pioneers.

They were pioneers, of course, in establishing settlements on lands not previously occupied by Europeans. But they were also pioneers in a whole range of other ways. They did not simply establish systems of republican self-governance; they pioneered new ones. They did not simply establish commercial institutions; they pioneered many new legal structures and forms of governmental economic assistance in order to generate a novel, more prosperous, essentially commercial society. They did not simply adopt religious toleration; they pioneered unprecedented forms of separation of church and state. They also pioneered new types of protections for an unprecedented array of individual and community rights, including limits on police tactics and trials by local juries, as well as newly expansive liberties of speech and press. In so doing they gave new concreteness to what were still novel philosophical assertions of universal rights.

As I have stressed, they did not all agree on any of these innovations – but they nonetheless collectively created a pattern of pervasive pioneering, throughout an extraordinary range of human arenas. All these forms of pioneering had both successes and failures, desirable and undesirable consequences – to which Americans have responded by continuing to innovate, again in ways both positive and negative. The pioneers usually displaced the tribes through unjust means and they sometimes verged on committing genocide; and US policy toward aboriginal Americans has been a fluctuating mix of just and repressive measures ever since. Americans were also among the world's pioneers in elaborating legal systems of chattel slavery, and then race-based naturalization and immigration exclusions, and eventually legal racial segregation, even though American abolitionist and civil rights struggles have been sources of inspiration worldwide. The founding Americans' roles as architects of the first successful modern republic also included pioneering ideological and legal efforts to harmonize patriarchy with allegedly egalitarian republican citizenship, mostly at women's expense, again sparking movements for gender equality that have had global impact. The many innovations that contributed to their pioneering creation of a modern commercial economy included numerous institutional and legal devices to secure employer power over sometimes exploited workers, even as many millions oppressed by the poverty under other economic systems have sought to develop their own commercial systems.

Not all American pioneering, then, has been commendable. But it is undeniable that Americans began as, in a staggering variety of ways, a pioneering people, and that they have been so again and again throughout history. They have done so because they have often recognized that they faced both enduring and unprecedented problems; they have had confidence that it was worth trying to find ways to do better; and they have believed that sometimes, at least, they could do so. This, I submit, is the way Americans should still see themselves, today and into the future, until and unless Americans ever decide that the next experiment to undertake is the embrace of forms of political peoplehood considerably different from those they have thought best to try so far. This sense of Americans as a pioneering people seems to me actually to capture much of what was best and boldest about the nation's founding generation, in contrast to approaches that transform all their works into barriers to further innovation. I also suspect that more Americans would like to see themselves as pioneers of progress than as pious preservers of past achievements. But far more importantly, I believe that a willingness to pioneer new policies and political arrangements is likely simply to be necessary if Americans are to respond to challenging new global conditions in ways that are wise and beneficial, for themselves and the broader world.

Pioneering in the twenty-first century

What are the implications of telling the story of American political identity today as the history of a pioneering people, whose pioneering included their own creation as a new type of political people? No concrete conclusions flow from that broad conception alone, other than a general spirit open to what seems like promising and constructive experimentation. Instead, all those who wish to participate in some way in shaping the direction of American life must look at that history for themselves, in light of whatever standards seem to them intellectually and morally compelling, in order to judge which aspects of American pioneering have enduring value, which represent moral or practical failures, which represent initiatives desirable in their day but greatly in need of reconstruction and transformation now. The different verdicts on the lessons of that history that ensue ought, in my view, to become contenders in robust democratic contestation among different senses of American identity and purpose. But I acknowledge that even that preference represents a debatable inference about what American historical experiences, along with more general considerations, indicate to be politically feasible and desirable.

Impressive candidates for such contending American stories can already be found. Of all recent writers on national identity, David Hollinger has produced the most compelling account of how Americans might define and embrace morally defensible senses of solidarity and shared purposes through awareness of their nation as a "finite historical entity with a record of specific tragedies, successes, failures, contradictions, and provincial conceits" (2000, 215).[7] Yet out of his understandable concern to strengthen humane conceptions of American political community, Hollinger is, I think, unduly resistant to ways of continuing the American story that might ultimately transform American nationalism into a much more moderate form of political peoplehood. By examining how my preferred view of Americans as a pioneering people builds on Hollinger's account in some respects and departs from it in others, we can get a more concrete sense both of alternative conceptions that might be pursued in the contemporary American politics of people-making, and of the value of conducting that politics through full critical engagement with differing views.

Hollinger advances a conception of "post-ethnic America" that has the priceless virtue of highlighting not only the nation's historical quest to build new and better forms of democracy, but also an agenda defined by its most important shortcomings in that regard. He argues that the "United States now finds itself in a position to develop and act upon a cultural self-image as *a national solidarity committed – but often failing – to incorporate individuals from a great variety of communities of descent, on equal but not homogeneous terms, into a society with democratic aspirations inherited largely from England*" (2000, 216). Even more fully than Bennett,

---

[7] Though Richard Rorty properly describes American identity as an ongoing political achievement and argues, as I do here, that "Competition for political leadership is in part a competition between differing stories about a nation's self-identity, and between differing symbols of its greatness," he ultimately insists that commitments to democratic processes form the heart of the "true" American story, a view that seems to me both excessively procedural and essentialist (1998, 4).

D'Souza, and Berns, Hollinger sees America's historic establishment of legal systems of chattel slavery and subsequent forms of racial hierarchy and exclusion as the greatest moral stain on the American experiment in self-government, and the source of the deepest pathologies in American life. But he also sees in that terrible historical reality an opportunity for the United States to play an inspiring role in today's world. He argues that the US has the potential to become "a formidable engine of ethno-racial change." If Americans so choose, their "historically particular entity" can be what it "often has been, and can be even more effectively in the future, an instrument for worthy transnational ends." And no end available to the US is more worthy, Hollinger eloquently contends, than "the project of liberating human selves from the color-coded prisons in which they have been locked by 'time's blood-rusted key.'" If Americans not only celebrate the best features of their past but seek ways to overcome the enduring injustices generated by the worst, especially racial divisions and inequities, then the United States "may yet serve humbly to remind a heavily racialized world that even a society with a deeply racist past can incorporate individuals from a great variety of communities of descent on terms of considerable intimacy within a civic solidarity" (2000, 208, 214, 218).

I fully agree with Hollinger that rather than shrugging off America's criminal racial history as an aberration that still leaves us morally superior to all other peoples, the US as a political community and Americans as citizens should see themselves as possessing both distinctive responsibilities and distinctive opportunities to show that the poisonous legacies of racist institutions can be overcome. In so doing, I do not mean to minimize the importance of addressing the broader gaping economic inequalities and the often oppressive conditions of employment in certain sectors that American market systems have generated, along with great wealth, all through US history up to the present. I believe that both democratic values and American traditions of constructive innovation would be well served by pursuing Ian Shapiro's recommendation: insofar as governments do not underwrite "social wage" guarantees against poverty, unemployment, malnutrition, illness and disability, inadequate housing and education, they must more intensively regulate employer–employee relations and corporate conduct, to strengthen the power of labor representatives to win adequate protections for themselves, and, I would add, to protect consumers and to safeguard the environment and other more general public interests (Shapiro, 1999, 184–190). Even so, I think Hollinger is right to say that America's political history makes it also necessary to give special attention to the challenge of alleviating the nation's deeply entrenched racial inequalities.

How to do so remains an enormously difficult question. Though feelings run strong on all sides, no one, left, right, or center, can credibly claim to have all the answers. The familiar, fundamental problem is that it is very hard to combat enduring racial inequities effectively without also reinforcing antagonistic senses of racial identity that are fertile ground for the propagation of invidious racial myths. The analysis of the politics of people-building here only underscores the daunting dangers involved. People genuinely and deeply concerned to further racial and civic progress can all too reasonably disagree about how best to proceed.

My own judgment is that racial disadvantages remain so pervasive in the United States, due in large part to the past policies of American governments and the arrays of racially divided interests, identities, and ways of life that they fostered, that many race-conscious governmental measures are still needed if we are to battle both inherited inequities and ongoing discrimination successfully. I have therefore long favored not only vigorous enforcement of laws banning invidious racial discrimination in financial, real estate, and consumer markets, but also racially targeted affirmative efforts in public and private employment and educational admissions policies. I also think that, when and where a racial or ethnic group can be shown to have been systematically locked out of effective participation in a political system, the adoption of devices to promote their representation, perhaps including the creation of districts with moderately sized "minority majorities," may be advisable. Furthermore, it does not seem to me inappropriate for those who can show that their families suffered from slavery and Jim Crow laws to sue companies that can be shown to have benefited from those governmentally sanctioned systems of oppression. It also might be useful to create a national trust fund as a source of targeted investment to improve housing, schools, and employment opportunities in economically disadvantaged, predominantly non-white communities. As part of a larger agenda noted below, it is also desirable for the United States to seek to form beneficial economic agreements, over trade, aid, consumer and environmental protection, and workers' rights, particularly with any and all communities in Africa and Latin America who can be shown to have been harmed by American policies encouraging slavery and, especially, more recent forms of racially and ethnically structured economic exploitation and military aggression (Klinkner with Smith, 1999, 347–351; Robinson, 2000, 244–246).

Support for these sorts of directions in public policy clearly places me on the side of those who risk perpetuating the evils of racial identity through their strategies to overcome them. Those risks are real, and I cannot show that other strategies for alleviating America's continuing racial and ethnic injustices are clearly worse. The only approach that seems to me plainly morally indefensible is to have no strategy or concern at all. As Philip Klinkner and I have argued, what is essential is for policy-makers and citizens to ask themselves in every pertinent context, "If we go down this road, will we perpetuate or even intensify the racial inequalities government has done so much to create in this country, or will we lessen them?" That recommendation reflects a sense of national purpose embraced not only by Hollinger but also, we have contended, by Lincoln: the conviction that all those who share in the benefits of American peoplehood also must share in addressing the harms inflicted by the public policies that have been the nation's most profound moral failure and the leading source of many of its most severe contemporary problems (Klinkner with Smith, 1999, 347, 350–51).

Perhaps more controversially yet, I do not think our goal in these efforts should be eventually to eliminate all conceptions of racial identity, making the nation truly "color-blind." I therefore do not envision or seek any future politics of people-making in America in which racial stories disappear. Neither, however, do I think the goal should be to achieve complete equality among what would have to be fairly rigidly defined and fixed racial groups. Rather, my hope for the longer-range consequences of an ongoing politics of democratic contestation that generated racial reform measures would be wider and wider acceptances of newer and truer senses of racial and ethnic identity. Political life pursued in accordance with an ethos of honest, critical engagement with rival ethically constitutive stories, including racial stories, might well foster awareness over time that all racial identities are themselves historical political constructions – often established and maintained for purposes of economic and political exploitation, yet also often sustained as suitable bases for solidarity among the oppressed as they struggled for survival and constructive change. The fact that, in the course of these struggles, racial identities became deeply entrenched historical and social realities may well mean that many will continue to see them as defining meaningful memberships even if the nation should some day reach a point where race is no longer systematically associated with unequal sets of disadvantages and opportunities in American life.

If many people did decide to sustain racial conceptions of themselves and their communities under those more halcyon conditions, my hope is that they would do so as voluntarily, culturally defined identities and communities that would represent, at most, moderate to weak forms of political peoplehood. And I would like to see those identities and communities constructed in ways that would make them open to people of any biological origins who shared a sense of the importance of the historical experiences that helped constitute that group's identity. All those who valued and wished to preserve and extend aspects of the historical ways of life of African-Americans, Mexican-Americans, Japanese-Americans, and other groups would have opportunities to participate in doing so. All those who wished to distance themselves from those particular member-ships would also have some real option to do, whatever their ancestry, since racial identities would no longer be so fraught with implications for social status.

But again, I am not suggesting that only these sorts of historical, volun-taristic conceptions of racial and ethnic identity can properly be advanced or recognized in American political processes. I wish only to clarify what my endorsement of race-conscious measures is aimed at achieving. I also think that it is as likely that a democratic politics in which racial and eth-nic constitutive stories are openly advanced and critiqued will eventually foster these kinds of racial and ethnic conceptions, as it is to believe that they will necessarily reinvigorate older notions of unalterable, hierarchi-cal, "natural" racial identities.

Hence I do not imagine or seek to contribute to an America that is quite so "post-ethnic" as Hollinger may favor (though it is clearly older, more inflexible forms of racial and ethnic identity that most concern him). Our views also diverge in another, perhaps more fundamental way. Though I firmly agree with Hollinger about the centrality of goals of racial reform to all morally defensible conceptions of American political identity today, he appears more committed to maintaining US nationality as a rather strong form of political peoplehood than, I think, contemporary condi-tions warrant. The role he imagines for the US is as an exemplary but otherwise typical nation-state within what we have come to assume to be a world of nation-states. The US is to remain a "national solidarity" that seeks to "incorporate" persons from a variety of descent communities within it, without effacing all differences but still with a goal of establish-ing the primacy of a shared, democratic, national cultural and political identity. There are many good reasons for this emphasis. With David Miller, Hollinger believes that a "stronger national solidarity enhances the possibility of social and economic justice within the United States" (2000, 201). People are more likely to be willing to provide support and to correct injustices when the persons affected are those with whom they share a strong sense of community. Hollinger is also vividly aware that in the American political context, an emphasis on national identity, pow-ers, and responsibilities has often been necessary to counteract the use of claims of state's rights to shelter local systems of racial, gender, and class subjugation.

That concern has also led me previously to stress the importance of compelling senses of American national community. And even though there are sensible arguments that democratic self-governance can better be achieved in smaller political units, so that devolution of powers, at least in regard to issues amenable to local policy-making, is desirable, I continue to fear that many calls for decentralization in the US today reflect not so much commitments to democracy as opposition to desirable but disruptive national reform initiatives (Klinkner with Smith, 1999, 328–329). It is also true that there simply are not immediately available transnational or international forms of political community that can hope to be as effective in meeting a wide variety of human needs as the United States is, despite its limitations. I therefore agree with Hollinger, against many more cosmopolitan writers, that it remains desirable today to strengthen appropriate senses of American national identity in relation to some rival contenders for political allegiances (cf. e.g. Bosniak, 1998, 2000).

But not all such rivals. In a number of regards, I believe that fidelity to what is most morally compelling in many of America's past political innovations now points in favor of further changes. Some of these would simply strengthen desirable features and ameliorate ills in the nation's domestic institutions and policies. Others, however, would transform the United States more deeply, making the world's only superpower a leader in helping to construct a world, and to reconstruct itself, in accordance with the vision of a globe comprised of a great multiplicity of moderate, cooperative forms of semi-sovereign political peoplehood.

Let us begin with the most centrally political of American's pioneering initiatives: the establishment of a federal republic, made up of state republics, all organized as various institutional expressions of bedrock commitments to popular self-governance. That system in itself represents an embrace of the legitimacy of dividing sovereignty among different levels of political community; and again, though I favor a nationally centered view of American federalism, I recognize that there are benefits to maintaining state and local governments with some genuinely meaningful authority. They can help to expand opportunities for democratic participation, increase the role of local knowledge in confronting distinctive problems, and check excesses of the national regime.

Yet there is clearly much that could and should be done to make the American federal republic a fuller realization of democratic aspirations, more than I can possibly discuss here. Many of the topics are highly complex, such as efforts to control the influence of money in politics via campaign financing laws without limiting the participation of various advocacy groups, and attempts to promote a greater multiplicity of political viewpoints in the media without fostering greater political fragmentation. But let us take a more straightforward example. The 2000 presidential election shocked some observers by revealing that the Constitution still assigns the authority to choose the members of the electoral college to the state legislatures, not to voters directly. Whatever one's concerns about the evils of majority tyranny and the dangers of unbridled direct participatory democracy, there is no even mildly persuasive reason for reserving this power to state legislators. The situation should be remedied by constitutional amendment (Caraley, 2001, 1–3). Doing so, however, would and should raise questions about the validity of state laws disfranchising felons, which American governments do to a greater extent than virtually any other, as well as about the prevailing denial of the right to vote for President to US citizens residing in Puerto Rico (Keyssar, 2002). Those questions might prove sufficiently controversial to block even this obvious reform. It may take heightened public acceptance of conception of the US as an innovative, pioneering democratic people to create a climate in which the case for such a relatively minor but virtually indisputable reform becomes inarguable.

There is reason to think, moreover, that if we do strongly affirm the democratic aspirations in American traditions but acknowledge the past and present failings of American institutions of self-governance, a political consensus in favor of constructive changes can be built. In a number of ways the 2000 elections results showed that the widely varying local systems of voter registration and balloting in the US are so unreliable that literally millions of votes are not counted properly in every national election, with poor and racial and ethnic minorities disproportionately disfranchised (Ansolabehere, 2001; Klinkner, 2001). Many Americans were ashamed to discover that despite their rightful pride in the US as a pioneer of modern democratic republicanism, in fact it lags behind many less wealthy and technologically advanced political communities in the efficiency of its basic electoral institutions. As a result, after a number of missteps, a bipartisan congressional coalition approved the creation of a federal Election Assistance Commission to test both existing and proposed voting equipment and to provide funds for state and local reforms, including anti-fraud measures in voter registration but also systems permitting the casting of provisional ballots in cases of doubt, enhancing access for the disabled, and making counting procedures more uniform (Pear, 2002, A13). It remains true that officeholders elected under any arrangements are unlikely candidates to change them, and the efficacy of these measures remains to be seen. Still, they underscore the reality that pioneering reforms are possible if Americans face up to our obvious political shortcomings and do not just complacently tell ourselves that the framers got almost everything right and that we have the greatest system in the world.

There are, however, much more sweeping changes implied by accepting a sense of Americans as a people concerned to enhance meaningfully democratic self-governance that will be far more difficult to achieve. Currently the US Supreme Court treats electoral laws designed to protect the two-party system against third-party competitors as positive contributions to the public interest, even as it opposes electoral structures drawn to amplify the political voices of racial and ethnic minorities.[8] If Americans valued robust competition among honest, conflicting political views, they would instead be more receptive to voting systems that gave groups that shared a political outlook, whether for ideological, economic, ethnic, or other reasons, real chances to win a proportionate share of political power. These are the sorts of democratic innovations that a nation that prided itself on pioneering effective forms of representation should wish to explore. Yet many instead argued that mere academic advocacy of such ideas made Lani Guinier unfit for high office (Guinier, 1994).

More fundamentally still, a historical sense of America's distinctive achievements and misdeeds would make it imperative to consider adaptations and extensions of American federalism more radical than any undertaken so far, as one possible route to terminating the still-continuing American imperial system in all its parts. These include the continuing exercise of ultimate US sovereignty not only over Puerto Rico but also over the partly self-governing native tribes; Guam; the Virgin Islands; and a variety of other American possessions and protectorates. These communities, added to the United States only as a result of coercive military actions, all possess varying forms of "home rule" – but, according to prevailing legal doctrines, they all do so only at the sufferance and discretion of the US government, in which they have no real representation (Aleinikoff, 2002, 183–186).

A people committed to pioneering new and more effective systems of popular self-governance, in the name of human rights, cannot be an imperial people. The federal government should instead permit those communities to define decision-making processes through which they decide on their preferred relationship with the United States. Answers might include statehood or some variant, still involving federal voting rights and representation, in the case of Puerto Rico or some of the larger tribes. They might include a greater measure of autonomous self-governing power and a looser confederation with the US. There are countless possible variations. The US should then either constitutionalize the preferred arrangements, making them less vulnerable to congressional abrogation; or,

---

[8] Cf. e.g. *Gaffney v. Cummings* (412 US 735, 1973) (upholding districts drawn to favor the two major parties) with *Shaw v. Reno* (509 US 630, 1993) (striking down districts drawn to favor racial minorities).

if the terms seem unacceptable, it should actively assist the communities
involved in achieving a viable form of independence, insofar as possible.[9]
One option, discussed by Will Kymlicka in relationship to indigenous
tribes, would constitute a still greater transformation in American peoplehood. Some tribes wish to remain affiliated with the United States
and are generally satisfied with the scope of autonomous legislative and
executive powers they possess. They object, however, to the manner in
which US federal courts have final say in all conflicts between tribal laws,
local and state laws, and US laws and treaties. Some might prefer resort to an international tribunal mandated to enforce the rule of law and
human rights and void of any interest in which of these levels of government prevailed (Kymlicka, 2001, 83–87). But of course, acceptance of
the authority of such tribunals would amount to transferal by the US government of some of its "sovereign" power to a new governmental level,
and the establishment of a less strong, more moderate form of American
political peoplehood.

As I have noted at several points, that sort of choice is being raised in a
great, indeed somewhat bewildering variety of contexts today. Regional
and indeed global trade associations like NAFTA and the World Trade
Organization exercise a certain measure of regulatory authority bestowed
by treaties, and many advocate adapting these organizations or creating
new ones to address problems of environmental degradation, immigration flows, fair wages, workers' rights, women's rights, and consumer
protection, among other topics. To do so fully and effectively, these organizations may well need to incorporate not only national governments
and corporations, but representatives of transnational labor unions, environmental groups, women's groups, and consumer and public health advocacy organizations, among others, into their regular decision-making

---

[9] Aleinikoff, 2002, also argues forcefully for transforming territorial as well as tribal statuses
via "negotiated, bilateral compacts that provide space for political and cultural diversity
sought by the people of the subnational polities" (186); though I would stress more the
duty of the US to accept whatever status is preferred by those it has colonized, unless the
arrangements are so unacceptable as to make assisted separation preferable. Aleinikoff
also contends, much as I do here, that acceptance of these arrangements can and should
flow from embrace of a new, "future oriented," and optimistic "American narrative"
of "decentered citizenship" that he identifies with Randolph Bourne's "transnational
Americanism" (Aleinikoff, 2000, 193–196). Because of its more explicit embrace of multiple memberships, the view I develop here is also closer to Bourne's than the earlier
version in *Civic Ideals* (see e.g. Smith, 1997, 638n3). I still stress more than Bourne a
politics in which not only contrasting subnational and transnational identities but also
competing views of national identities are articulated and contested.

Tully, 1995, also provides important reflections on the form and prospects of constitutional arrangements that would grant more autonomy and recognition to aboriginal peoples, among others; though he, too, gives less attention to the topic of common
identities.

processes, instead of confining them to the role of outside advisory or pressure groups. Otherwise, these regional or international regulatory bodies may work against rather than for efforts to develop better ways to promote democratic self-governance and material well-being for as many as possible.

Along with the growth of these sorts of treaty-based administrative bodies, in recent decades support has also grown for the protection of human rights via the creation of international legal tribunals of various sorts, with the International Criminal Court having been finally established, however precariously, while this book has been written. Although this "judicialization" of political problems provokes many legitimate worries from a democratic standpoint, it seems clear that these institutions have growing potential to check some prevalent forms of abusive political conduct. In a related development, numerous members of the international political community also are increasingly urging that states should no longer use military force unilaterally, except in cases of immediate self-defense. Many insist that to prevent wars of aggression, modern political communities should accept that only multilateral military actions, under the auspices of the UN or perhaps a regional defense organization such as NATO, are legitimate. As one recent advocate of democratic republicanism, Philip Pettit, has argued, although particular republican states remain valuable for many purposes, many analysts and activists are coming to believe that "there is nothing sacred from the republican point of view about the state or about the state's sovereignty. Given the existence of multinational bodies of various kinds, there are some domestic issues on which it may be better from the point of view of promoting freedom . . . to give over control to those bodies and thereby to restrict the local state" (1997, 152, 183).

As the world's preeminent military and economic power, the stance the US takes toward these appeals is obviously crucially important for shaping global developments. But though American groups and some American governmental leaders have been actively involved in all these endeavors, overall the US stance toward the development of more meaningfully empowered international institutions has been at most ambivalent, and more often, and increasingly, adversarial. The US has shaped international institutions to represent the interests of powerful states and major corporations more than those of workers, small farmers, weaker political societies, or environmental and human rights groups. Indeed, it has a long history of reluctance to ratify international human rights agreements; it has opposed the Kyoto treaty seeking to regulate environmental damages; and it has repeatedly sought to exempt its military personnel from the jurisdiction of the new International Criminal Court, among other examples (e.g. Sewall and Kaysen, eds., 2000, 1–26). Under President George W. Bush, it has also begun to emphasize for the first time that national foreign policy alternatives include unilateral, preemptive wars. The US remains committed to consulting the United Nations Security Council in regard to its military interventions in foreign countries, but it rejects the notion that the UN or any other international body can really bind America's sovereign prerogatives.

Indeed, since an influential Wall Street Journal essay by Irving Kristol in 1997 argued that "One of the days, the American people are going to awaken to the fact that we have become an imperial nation," many more American policy advocates have come to argue openly that at this point in world history, the US is indeed the "new Rome," as Walter Berns suggests. Kristol argued that America's imperial role has emerged "because the world wanted it to happen, needed it to happen," and that it "lacks the brute coercion that characterized European imperialism." But, he worried, "it also lacks the authentic missionary spirit of that older imperialism, which aimed to establish the rule of law while spreading Christianity ... It is an imperium with a minimum of moral substance."[10] As the speeches of President Bush and the writings of commentators like D'Souza, Bennett, Berns, and many others indicate, many now see the September 11 attacks as indicating what America's moral mission should be: to rid the world and the American homeland of terrorist threats, especially those driven by an Islamic extremism that despises much of what most Americans see as civilization. In November of 2002, Fouad Ajami, Professor of Middle Eastern Studies at Johns Hopkins University, wrote that the events of the preceding year had "revealed hatreds of America and malignancies beyond our wildest imagination." He concluded: "Where Britain once filled the void left by the shattered Ottoman Empire in the aftermath of the First World War, now the failures – and the dangers – of the successor Arab states are drawing America to its own imperial mission" (Ajami, 2002, 28). From such perspectives, calls for the US to reject all forms of imperialism and to seek to pioneer a more genuinely multilateral world can seem not only wildly unrealistic but morally irresponsible.

Without espousing an explicitly imperial conception of American peoplehood, the Bush administration has responded by committing itself to maintaining unrivalled US military supremacy, conducting unilateral, first-strike warfare when the US deems it necessary, and establishing a Department of Homeland Security with powers that abolish the longstanding "wall" between domestic criminal justice measures and

---

[10] The full text is at http://www.aei.org/oti/oti7998.htm.

international espionage.[11] These policies are by no means simply unreflective expressions of US chauvinism. Terrorists threats are transparently real and overwhelmingly serious today. And again, the position of the US in the world today is undeniably exceptional. Because its wealth and power influence the rest of the globe more than those of any other nation, in practice, international treaties and institutions may well be used to challenge American economic, diplomatic, and military practices more than those of any other signatory to such arrangements. Sometimes those challenges will express envy, resentment, and greed, rather than collective policy wisdom or cosmopolitan senses of justice. And precisely because the consequences of its policies are so broad ranging, the United States cannot shirk responsibility for being a leading contributor to global economic, political, and security developments. It is understandable that many American leaders feel that if their discretion is constrained by the preferences of other less influential and, perhaps, less conscientious participants in the international community, the US may not be able to act effectively on behalf of any conception of legitimate interests, not just for its own.

Yet though caution may often be prudent, it is fundamentally unwise, as well as contrary to the pioneering spirit that is a valuable part of the distinctive American historical identity, to respond to the trends moving toward a more complex world of interlocked, moderate, semi-sovereign political peoples simply with recalcitrant resistance. Instead, as it has at its best moments in the past, the United States should seek to play a leading role in helping to construct that world in desirable ways. Precisely because today we increasingly face problems that can have tremendous impact on the whole of humanity, traditional commitments to responsive self-governance and human rights do point to the establishment of effective cooperative arrangements among representatives of all those concerned. And to be effective, institutions must be acknowledged to wield legitimate if limited powers. To take the most novel yet all too rapidly emerging example, whatever regulations about human genetic experimentation may seem desirable, they cannot protect the species if they apply only within a few geographical locations.[12]

It is true that achieving responsible, democratic, rights-respecting transnational and international institutions is an enormously complex

---

[11] These commitments are expressed in Secs. III and V of the Bush administration's September 17, 2002 National Security Strategy document, obtainable at http://www.whitehouse.gov/nsc/nssall.html.

[12] At this writing, wire services have reported that an Italian physician, Severino Antinori, has announced, but not yet proven, that he has successfully cloned a human being. His past expressions of intent to do so helped prompt the UN to begin drafting an international treaty to ban such experiments. See e.g. http://www.thestate.com/mld/thestate/3008410.htm.

challenge. Even conceiving of plausible answers, given the scale and diversity of the populations involved, much less gaining political support for
them, is tremendously difficult. But that is why these challenges cannot
possibly be met well unless the world's most powerful nation takes a lead
role, a pioneering role, in helping to craft suitable initiatives – including
the voluntary relinquishing of aspects of its sovereignty, at appropriate
points, so that those initiatives can succeed.

Where would that success lead? It is plainly impossible to say with
any certainty. I anticipate that it would lead to a world where "plural
citizenships," meaningful, participatory membership in multiple forms
of political peoplehood, would become more prevalent.[13] In that world
many more memberships would come to be conceived, ideally through
democratic contests, compromises, and political constructions, as
"moderate" political peoples, and by the same token as forms of what the
philosopher Samuel Scheffler has termed "moderate" cosmopolitanism.
They would be seen as particular associations that do legitimately embody special claims on our loyalties, because they represent special joint
endeavors of all those involved; but ones that do not claim full sovereignty
over their members, and that recognize an obligation to work cooperatively with other associations for more general human benefit. Though
persons might well preserve genuine allegiances to particular national and
cultural traditions, they would be more concerned with "how the integrity
of a tradition can be maintained, and what would count as maintaining
it, given the inevitability of cultural change," rather than with preserving cultural "purity." And though people would also seek to promote
new, freer, and more just political arrangements, they would be aware
of the need to do so in ways that are respectful of "special loyalties and
attachments" and that "incorporate the sort of stable infrastructure of responsibility that more traditional ways of life have always made available
to their adherents," insofar as possible (Scheffler, 2001, 129–130).

These are clearly difficult goals to keep in balance. As I said at the
outset of this chapter, I cannot guarantee that a political world that predominantly seeks to do so is possible or desirable. But neither can critics
claim with any certainty that it is not. The reality is that powerful historical trends; pressing contemporary needs; and many compelling enduring
values point toward the wisdom of seeking its creation. I therefore believe
that this is the sort of world that a proudly pioneering people, committed
not only to its own welfare but also to broader values of democracy, human rights, and human progress, ought to try to help humanity to achieve
today.

[13] For a nuanced assessment of the costs and benefits of plural citizenship by a scholar
deeply appreciative of the positive features of American nationality, yet still receptive to
its modification in this regard, see Schuck, 1998.

This, then, is the ethically constitutive historical story of America that I would like to see become part of a vigorous, engaged modern politics of people-making, in the US and beyond. What kind of story, in the end, is it? Readers of my earlier work have attributed to me a preference for stories of peoplehood that fall in the genre of Harlequin romances or satirical comedies. That is to say, they read me as advocating "happy-ending love" stories involving flawed but ultimately successful participants seeking a more perfect American union (Honig, 2001, 109, 119; Lorenzo, 2002, 368–369).

Though there is some basis for those readings, I hope it is clear at this point, if it has not been so evident previously, that I do not advocate *perpetual* union with any specific form of political community, that I see limitations and dangers in them all, and that I am far from certain that those dangers can be overcome. Still, it is true that I think this analysis of the realities of political people-making leaves room for hope that human beings, including Americans, can construct their political communities and identities in ways that are more morally defensible and humanly desirable than they have in the past. Although doing so is a tremendously difficult endeavor with no assurances of success, it is an endeavor that I wholeheartedly support.

If we wish to assign a genre to this sort of narrative of peoplehood, I think it best to depart a bit from the categories, derived from Northrop Frye and Hayden White, that my critics employ. I would classify the sorts of stories I favor as, first and foremost, political adventure stories – ones that present some exciting possibilities but also some terrible ones. The more important "generic" question, however, may seem to be whether we should perceive these sorts of stories as comic or tragic – can we expect them to end happily or sadly?

That is a question I cannot answer. For if my analysis is at all correct, then the future chapters of all stories of peoplehood are always contingent things that human beings create collectively, through both conflictual and cooperative processes, with some elements that are patterned and predictable, but others that may be novel and unanticipated. The most that we can say is that, if we are wise enough to curb our own tendencies to conduct our political processes in catastrophic ways, then for as far as we can foresee, the writing, telling, and living of these stories, which do so much to give shape and meaning to who we are and how we fare, will never come to an end.

References

Ackerman, B. A. 1980. *Social Justice in the Liberal State*. New Haven: Yale University Press.

Ajami, F. 2002. "Hail the American Imperium." *U.S. News and World Report* 133: 28.

Aleinikoff, T. A. 2002. *Semblances of Sovereignty: The Constitution, the State, and American Citizenship*. Cambridge: Harvard University Press.

Allen, C. T. 1990. "Northeast Asia Centered around Korea: Ch'oe Namsn's View of History." *Journal of Asian Studies* 49: 787–806.

Anbinder, T. 1992. *Nativism and Slavery: The Northern Know Nothings and the Politics of the 1850s*. New York: Oxford University Press.

Anderson, B. 1983. *Imagined Communities: Reflections on the Origin and Spread of Nationalism*. New York: Verso.

1991. *Imagined Communities*. Rev. edn. New York: Verso.

Annan, K. A. 2000. *We the Peoples: The Role of the United Nations in the 21st Century*. New York: United Nations Department of Information.

Ansolabehere, S. 2001. "The Search for New Voting Technology." Available online at http://bostonreview.mit.edu/BR26.5/ansolabehere.html.

Arendt, H. 1958. *The Human Condition*. Chicago: University of Chicago Press.

Aristotle. 1968. *The Politics of Aristotle*. Ed. E. Barker. New York: Oxford University Press.

Armstrong, J. A. 1982. *Nations before Nationalism*. Chapel Hill: University of North Carolina Press.

Asher, R. E. 1993. *National Myths in Renaissance France: Francus, Samothes, and the Druids*. Edinburgh: Edinburgh University Press.

Baker, D. 1998. "Christianity 'Koreanized.' " In H. I. Pai and T. R. Tangherlini, eds., *Nationalism and the Construction of Korean Identity*. Berkeley: Institute of East Asian Studies, University of California, Berkeley.

Balibar, Etienne and Immanuel Wallerstein. 1991. *Race, Nation, Class: Ambiguous Identities*. New York: Verso.

Barber, B. 1984. *Strong Democracy: Participatory Politics for a New Age*. Berkeley: University of California Press.

1995. *Jihad v. McWorld*. New York: New York Times Books.

Barry, B. 2001. *Culture and Equality: An Egalitarian Critique of Multiculturalism*. Cambridge: Polity Press.

Becker, M. 1995. "Indigenismo and Indian Movements in Twentieth-Century Ecuador." Paper delivered at the 1995 Meeting of the Latin American

Studies Association, the Sheraton Washington, Sept. 28–30. Online at http://lanic.utexas.edu/project/lasa95/becker.html.

Bederman, G. 1995. *Manliness and Civilization: A Cultural History of Gender and Race in the United States, 1880–1917*. Chicago: University of Chicago Press.

Begaye, K. A. 1999. "State of the Nation Address and Second Quarterly Report: The First 100 Days." Presented to the Navajo Nation Council, April, 1999, available at http://www.navajo.org/presrpt.html.

Bennett, D. H. 1990. *The Party of Fear: From Nativist Movements to the New Right in American History*. New York: Vintage Books.

Bennett, W. J. 2002. *Why we Fight: Moral Clarity and the War on Terrorism*. New York: Doubleday.

Berkowitz, P. 2002. "John Rawls and the Liberal Faith." *Wilson Quarterly*. Spring: 60–69.

Berns, W. 2001. *Making Patriots*. Chicago: University of Chicago Press.

Bhabha, H. K., ed. 1990. *Nation and Narration*. New York: Routledge.

Blake, R. and W. R. Louis, eds. 1996. *Churchill*. Oxford: Clarendon Press.

Bloch, Marc. 1970. *French Rural History: An Essay on its Basic Characteristics*. Transl. Janet Sondheimer. Berkeley: University of California Press.

Bosniak, L. 1998. "A National Solidarity? A Response to David Hollinger." In N. Pickus, ed., *Immigration and Citizenship in the Twenty-First Century*. New York: Rowman & Littlefield Publishers.

2002. "Citizenship Denationalized." *Indiana Journal of Global Legal Studies* 7: 447–509.

Breuilly, John. 1982. *Nationalism and the State*. Manchester: Manchester University Press.

Brownlee, J. S. 1997. *Japanese Historians and the National Myths, 1600–1945: The Age of the Gods and Emperor Jinmu*. Vancouver: UBC Press.

Brubaker, W. Rogers. 1992. *Citizenship and Nationhood in France and Germany*. Cambridge: Harvard University Press.

1996. *Nationalism reframed: Nationhood and the national question in the New Europe*. Cambridge: Cambridge University Press.

Brudny, Y. 2002. "National Identity and Democracy in Postcommunist Russia." Unpublished MS. On file with author.

Buchanan, A., D. W. Brock, N. Daniels, and D. Wikler. 2000. *From Chance to Choice: Genetics and Justice*. New York: Cambridge University Press.

Burke, E. 1968. *Reflections on the Revolution in France*. Harmondsworth: Penguin.

Burnham, P. 1996. *The Politics of Cultural Difference in Northern Cameroon*. Washington, DC: Smithsonian Institution Press.

Burtt, S. 1992. *Virtue Transformed: Political Argument in England, 1688–1740*. New York: Cambridge University Press.

Buruma, I. 2001. " 'The Emperor's Secrets,' Review of *Hirohito and the Making of Modern Japan* by Herbert P. Bix." *New York Review of Books*, March 29: 24–28.

de la Cadena, M. 2001. "Reconstructing Race: Racism, Culture, and Mestizaje in Latin America." *NACLA Report on the Americas* 34: 18–23.

Cairns, A. C., J. C. Courtney, P. MacKinnon, H. J. Michelmann, and D. E. Smith, eds. 1999. *Citizenship, Diversity, and Pluralism: Canadian and Comparative Perspectives*. Montreal: McGill-Queen's University Press.

Canovan, M. 1996. *Nationhood and Political Theory*. Brookfield, VT: Edward Elgar Pub.
  2000. "Patriotism Is not Enough." *British Journal of Political Science* 30: 413–432.
Caraley, D. J. 2001. "Editor's Opinion: Why Americans Deserve a Constitutional Right to Vote for Presidential Electors." *Political Science Quarterly* 116: 1–3.
Carens, J. H. 2000. *Culture, Citizenship, and Community: A Contextual Exploration of Justice as Evenhandedness*. New York: Oxford University Press.
Castoriadis, C. 1987. *The Imaginary Institution of Society*. Transl. K. Blamey. Cambridge: MIT Press.
Caulfield, S. 2000. *In Defense of Honor: Sexual Morality, Modernity, and Nation in Early-Twentieth Century Brazil*. Durham: Duke University Press.
Chambers, S. C. 1999. *From Subjects to Citizens: Honor, Gender, and Politics in Arequipa, Peru 1780–1854*. University Park, PA: Pennsylvania State University Press.
Chow, K. 2001. "Narrating Nation, Race, and National Culture: Imagining the Hanzu Identity in Modern China." In K. Chow, K. M. Doak, and P. Fu, eds., *Constructing Nationhood in Modern East Asia*. Ann Arbor: University of Michigan Press.
Colley, L. 1992. *Britons: Forging the Nation, 1707–1837*. New Haven: Yale University Press.
Connolly, W. E. 1991. *Identity/Difference: Democratic Negotiations of Political Paradox*. Ithaca: Cornell University Press.
  1995. *The Ethos of Pluralization*. Minneapolis: University of Minnesota Press.
  1999. *Why I Am not a Secularist*. Minneapolis: University of Minnesota Press.
  2000. "The Liberal Image of the Nation." In D. Ivison, P. Patton, and W. Sanders, eds., *Political Theory and the Rights of Indigenous Peoples*. Cambridge: Cambridge University Press.
Connor, W. 1994. *Ethnonationalism: The Quest for Understanding*. Princeton: Princeton University Press.
Conyers, J. 1999. "An Afrocentric Study of the Philosophy of Edward Wilmot Blyden." Doctoral dissertation, Temple University. Ann Arbor: UMI Dissertation Services.
Cott, N. F. 2000. *Public Vows: A History of Marriage and the Nation*. Cambridge: Harvard University Press.
Cunningham N. E. 2000. *Jefferson v. Hamilton: Confrontations that Shaped a Nation*. Boston: Bedford/St. Martin's.
Dagger, R. 1997. *Civic Virtues: Rights, Citizenship, and Republican Liberalism*. New York: Oxford University Press.
Dahl, Robert A. 1989. *Democracy and its Critics*. New Haven: Yale University Press.
  1992. "The Problem of Civic Competence." *Journal of Democracy* 3: 47–51.
  1998. *On Democracy*. New Haven: Yale University Press.
Degras, J., ed. 1960. *The Communist International, 1919–1943: Documents*. London: Oxford University Press.
Diagram Group. 2000. *Encyclopedia of African Peoples*. New York: Facts on File.
Dikötter, F., ed., 1997. *The Construction of Racial Identities in China and Japan: Historical and Contemporary Perspectives*. London: Hurst & Co.

Doak, K. 2001. "Narrating China, Ordering East Asia: The Discourse on Nation and Ethnicity in Imperial Japan." In K. Chow, K. M. Doak, and P. Fu, eds., *Constructing Nationhood in Modern East Asia.* Ann Arbor: University of Michigan Press.

Dower, J. W. 1993. *Japan in War and Peace.* New York: New Press.

Driedger, L. 1988. *Mennonite Identity in Conflict.* Lewiston, NY: The Edwin Mellen Press.

D'Souza, D. 2002. *What's so Great about America.* Washington, DC: Regnery Publishing, Inc.

Du Bois, W. E. B. 1992 (orig. 1935). *Black Reconstruction in America.* New York: Atheneum.

Dunn, J. 1984. "The Concept of 'Trust' in the Politics of John Locke." In R. Rorty, J. B. Schneewind, and Q. Skinner, eds., *Philosophy in History: Essays on the Historiography of Philosophy.* Cambridge: Cambridge University Press.

Ettinger, S. 1976. "The Modern Period." In H. H. Ben-Sasson, ed., *A History of the Jewish People.* Cambridge, MA: Harvard University Press.

Falk, R. 1996. "Revisioning Cosmopolitanism." In M. C. Nussbaum, *For Love of Country: Debating the Limits of Patriotism,* ed. J. Cohen. Boston: Beacon Press.

Falola, T. 2001. *Nationalism and African Intellectuals.* Rochester: University of Rochester Press.

Farr, J. 1988. "The History of Political Science." *American Journal of Political Science* 32: 1175–1195.

Farrell, M. 2002. "Conclusion: Possible European Futures." In M. Farrell, S. Fella, and M. Newman, eds., *European Integration in the Twenty-First Century: Unity in Diversity?* London: Sage Publications.

Favell, A. 1998. *Philosophies of Integration: Immigration and the Idea of Citizenship in France and Britain.* London: Macmillan.

Fearon, J. D. and Laitin, D. D. 1996. "Explaining Interethnic Cooperation." *American Political Science Review* 90: 715–735.

Feldblum, M. 1999. *Reconstructing Citizenship: The Politics of Nationality Reform and Immigration in Contemporary France.* Albany: State University of New York Press.

Finkelstein, I. and N. Silberman. 2001. *The Bible Unearthed: Archaeology's New Vision of Ancient Israel and the Origins of its Sacred Texts.* New York: Free Press.

Fitzmaurice, J. 1996. *The Politics of Belgium: A Unique Federalism.* Boulder, CO: Westview Press.

Foucault, M. 1979. *Discipline and Punish: The Birth of the Prison.* Trans. Alan Sheridan, 1977; orig. edn. 1975. New York: Vintage Books.

Frederickson, G. M. 1971. *The Black Image in the White Mind: The Debate on Afro-American Character and Destiny, 1817–1914.* New York: Harper & Row.

Fukuyama, F. 2002. *Our Posthuman Future: Consequences of the Biotechnology Revolution.* New York: Farrar, Straus and Giroux.

Gellner, E. 1965. *Thought and Change.* Chicago: University of Chicago Press. 1983. *Nations and Nationalism.* Oxford: Basil Blackwell.

Gerstle, G. 2001. *American Crucible: Race and Nation in the Twentieth Century.* Princeton: Princeton University Press.

Giddens, A. 1985. *The Nation-State and Violence*. Cambridge: Polity Press.

Gilbert, P. 2000. *Peoples, Cultures, and Nations in Political Philosophy*. Washington: Georgetown University Press.

Gramsci, A. 1971. *Selections from the Prison Notebooks*. Ed. and transl. Q. Hoare and G. N. Smith. New York: International Publishers.

Gray, J. 1992. "Against the New Liberalism: Rawls, Dworkin, and the Emptying of Political Life." *Times Literary Supplement* July 3: 13–15.

——— 1995. *Enlightenment's Wake: Politics and Culture at the Close of the Modern Age*. New York: Routledge.

Greenfeld, L. 1992. *Nationalism: Five Roads to Modernity*. Cambridge: Harvard University Press.

Guinier, L. 1994. *The Tyranny of the Majority: Fundamental Fairness in Representative Democracy*. New York: Free Press, 1994.

Gunnell, J. G. 1993. *The Descent of Political Theory*. Chicago: University of Chicago Press.

Guy, D. J. 1992. " 'White Slavery,' Citizenship and Nationality in Argentina." In A. Parker, M. Russo, D. Sommer, and P. Yaeger, eds., *Nationalisms and Sexualities*. New York: Routledge.

Habermas, J. 1995. "Multiculturalism and the Liberal State." *Stanford Law Review* 47: 849–853.

——— 1996. *Between Facts and Norms: Contributions to a Discourse Theory of Law and Democracy*. Transl. W. Rehg. Cambridge: MIT Press.

——— 1998. *The Inclusion of the Other: Studies in Political Theory*. Ed. C. Cronin and P. de Greiff. Cambridge: MIT Press.

Hanchard, M. G. 1994. *Orpheus and Power: The Movimento Negro of Rio de Janeiro and São Paulo, Brazil, 1845–1988*. Princeton: Princeton University Press.

Held, D. 1995. *Democracy and the Global Order: From the Modern State to Cosmopolitan Governance*. Stanford: Stanford University Press.

Helg, A. 1990. "Race in Argentina and Cuba, 1880–1930: Theory, Policies, and Popular Reaction." In R. Graham, ed., *The Idea of Race in Latin America, 1870–1940*. Austin: University of Texas Press.

Hirschman, A. O. 1977. *The Passions and the Interests: Political Arguments for Capitalism before its Triumph*. Princeton: Princeton University Press.

Hobbes, T. 1968 (repr. 1651). *Leviathan*. Ed. C. B. Macpherson. Harmondsworth: Penguin.

Hobsbawm, E. J. 1990. *Nations and Nationalism since 1870: Programme, Myth, Reality*. Cambridge: Cambridge University Press.

Hofstadter, R. and Hofstadter, B. K., eds., 1981. *Great Issues in American History: From Reconstruction to the Present Day, 1864–1981*. New York: Vintage Books.

Hollinger, D. A. 1995. *Post-Ethnic America: Beyond Multiculturalism*. New York: Basic Books.

——— 2000. (Rev. ed.) *Post-Ethnic America: Beyond Multiculturalism*. New York: Basic Books.

Honig, B. 2001. *Democracy and the Foreigner*. Princeton: Princeton University Press.

Hooghe, L. 1991. "A Leap in the Dark: Nationalist Conflict and Federal Reform in Belgium." Western Societies Program, Occasional Paper Number 27, Cornell University, Ithaca, NY.

Horowitz, D. L. 1985. *Ethnic Groups in Conflict*. Berkeley: University of California Press.

Hutchings, K. and R. Dannreuther, eds. 1999. *Cosmopolitan Citizenship*. New York: St. Martin's Press.

Ignatieff, M. 1994. *Blood and Belonging: Journeys into the New Nationalism*. New York: Farrar, Straus and Giroux.

   1999. "Benign Nationalism? The Possibilities of the Civic Ideal." In E. Mortimer with R. Fine, eds., *People, Nation and State: The Meaning of Ethnicity and Nationalism*. New York: I. B. Tauris.

Ivison, D., P. Patton, and W. Sanders, eds. 2000. *Political Theory and the Rights of Indigenous Peoples*. New York: Cambridge University Press.

Jackson, J. T. R. 2000. *And we Are Doing it: Building an Ecovillage Future*. San Francisco, CA, Robert T. Reed Publishers.

Jacobson, D. 1996. *Rights across Borders: Immigration and the Decline of Citizenship*. Baltimore: Johns Hopkins University Press.

Jager, S. M. 1996. "Women, Resistance and the Divided Nation: The Romantic Rhetoric of Korean Unification." *Journal of Asian Studies* 55: 3–21.

Jones, J. B. and D. Balsom, eds. 2000. *The Road to the National Assembly for Wales*. Cardiff: University of Wales Press.

Jung, C. 2000. *Then I Was Black: South African Political Identities in Transition*. New Haven: Yale University Press.

Kant, I. 1965. *The Metaphysical Elements of Justice*. Transl. J. Ladd. Indianapolis: Bobbs-Merrill.

Katznelson, Ira. 1999. "Review: Civic Ideals." *Political Theory* 27: 565–570.

Kedourie, E. 1961. *Nationalism*. Rev. edn. New York: Praeger.

Kerber, L. 1980. *Women of the Republic*. Chapel Hill: University of North Carolina Press.

Keyssar, A. 2002. "Shoring up the Right to Vote: A Modest Proposal." Paper presented at the Academy of Political Science September 27th Symposium on "Electing the President," Barnard College, New York.

King, D. S. 2000. *Making Americans: Immigration, Race, and the Origin of the Diverse Democracy*. Cambridge: Harvard University Press.

Kirk, D. 2002. "Korean Lawmakers Reject President's Choice for Prime Minister." *New York Times*, August 1, 2002: A5.

Kiss, E. 1996. "Five Theses on Nationalism." In I. Shapiro and R. Hardin, eds., *Nomos XXXVIII: Political Order*. New York: New York University Press.

Klinkner, P. 2001. "Whose Votes Don't Count? An Analysis of Spoiled Ballots in the 2000 Florida Election." Available online at http://www.usccr.gov/pubs/vote2000/report/appendix/app11.htm.

Klinkner, P. with R. M. Smith. 1999. *The Unsteady March: The Rise and Decline of Racial Equality in America*. Chicago: University of Chicago Press.

Knight, A. 1990. "Race, Revolution, and *Indigenismo*: Mexico, 1910–1940." In R. Graham, ed., *The Idea of Race in Latin America, 1870–1940*. Austin: University of Texas Press.

Kohn, H. 1944. *The Idea of Nationalism, a Study in its Origins and Background.* New York: Macmillan.

1955. *Nationalism, its Meaning and History.* Princeton, NJ: Van Nostrand.

1957. *American Nationalism.* New York: Macmillan.

Kuper, Andrew. 2000. "Rawlsian Global Justice: Beyond *The Law of Peoples* to a Cosmopolitan Law of Persons." *Political Theory* 28: 640–674.

Kymlicka, W. 1989. *Liberalism, Community, and Culture.* New York: Oxford University Press.

1995. *Multicultural Citizenship: A Liberal Theory of Minority Rights.* New York: Oxford University Press.

1998. *Finding our Way: Rethinking Ethnocultural Relations in Canada.* New York: Oxford University Press.

2001. *Politics in the Vernacular: Nationalism, Multiculturalism and Citizenship.* New York: Oxford University Press.

Laitin, D. 1998. *Identity in Formation: The Russian-Speaking Populations in the Near Abroad.* Ithaca: Cornell University Press.

Levi, M. and Brathwaite, V., eds. 1998. *Trust and Governance.* New York: Russell Sage.

Lieberman, R. C. 1998. *Shifting the Color Line: Race and the American Welfare State.* Cambridge: Harvard University Press.

Lind, M. 1995. *The Next American Nation: The New Nationalism and the Fourth American Revolution.* New York: Free Press.

Lindblom, C. E. 1977. *Politics and Markets: The World's Political-Economic Systems.* New York: Basic Books.

Linklatter, A. 1999. "Cosmopolitan Citizenship." In K. Hutchings and R. Dannreuther, eds., *Cosmopolitan Citizenship.* New York: St. Martin's Press.

Locke, J. 1965. *Two Treatises of Government.* Ed. P. Laslett. New York: New American Library.

Long, V. P., ed. 1999. *Israel's Past in Present Research: Essays on Ancient Israelite Historiography.* Winona Lake, IN: Eisenbrauns.

Lorenzo, D. J. 2002. "Attaining Rogers Smith's Civic Ideals." *Political Theory* 30: 357–383.

McCormick, J. P. 2001. "Machiavellian Democracy: Controlling Elites with Ferocious Populism." *American Political Science Review* 95: 297–313.

MacDougall, H. A. 1982. *Racial Myth in English History: Trojans, Teutons, and Anglo-Saxons,* Hanover, NH: University Press of New England.

Machiavelli, N. 1950. *The Prince and the Discourses.* Ed. M. Lerner. New York: The Modern Library.

MacMaster, R. K. 1985. *Land, Piety, Peoplehood: The Establishment of Mennonite Communities in America, 1683–1790.* Scottsdale, PA: Herald Press.

Madison, J., A. Hamilton, and J. Jay. 1987. *The Federalist Papers.* Ed. I. Kramnick. New York: Viking Penguin.

Malkki, L. H. 1995. *Purity and Exile: Violence, Memory, and National Cosmology among Hutu Refugees in Tanzania.* Chicago: University of Chicago Press.

Mallon, F. E. 1995. *Peasant and Nation: The Making of Postcolonial Mexico and Peru.* Berkeley: University of California Press.

Mamdani, M. 1996. *Citizen and Subject: Contemporary Africa and the Legacy of Late Colonialism*. Princeton: Princeton University Press.

Mansbridge, J. J. 1986. *Why we Lost the ERA*. Chicago: University of Chicago Press.

Markell, Patchen. 2000. "Making Affect Safe for Democracy? 'Constitutional Patriotism.'" *Political Theory* 28: 38–63.

Marquez, B. 2001. "Choosing Issues, Choosing Sides: Constructing Identities in Mexican-American Social Movement Organizations." *Ethnic and Racial Studies* 24: 218–235.

Marx, A. 1998. *Making Race and Nation: A Comparison of South Africa, the United States, and Brazil*. New York: Cambridge University Press.

Mendel, A. P., ed. 1961. *Essential Works of Marxism*. New York: Bantam Books.

Mettler, S. 1998. *Dividing Citizens: Gender and Federalism in New Deal Public Policy*. Ithaca : Cornell University Press, 1998.

Miller, D. 1995. *On Nationality*. Oxford: Clarendon Press.

1999. "Bounded Citizenship." In K. Hutchings and R. Dannreuther, eds., *Cosmopolitan Citizenship*. New York: St. Martin's Press.

Moghadam, V. M., ed. 1994. *Gender and National Identity: Women and Politics in Muslim Societies*. New Jersey: Zed Books Ltd.

Montesquieu, C. d. 1949. *The Spirit of the Laws*. New York: Hafner Publishing Co.

Morton, D. 1993. "Divided Loyalties? Divided Country?" In W. Kaplan, ed., *Belonging: The Meaning and Future of Canadian Citizenship*. Montreal: McGill-Queen's University Press.

Mosse, G. L. 1985. *Nationalism and Sexuality: Respectability and Abnormal Sexuality in Modern Europe*. New York: Howard Fertig.

Motyl, A. J. 2002. "Imagined Communities, Rational Choosers, Invented Ethnies." *Comparative Politics* 34: 233–250.

Mouffe, C. 2000. *The Democratic Paradox*. New York: Verso.

Nicolet, C. 1982. *L'idée républicaine en France (1789–1924): essai d'histoire critique*. Paris: Gallimard.

Nobles, M. 2000. *Shades of Citizenship: Race and the Census in Modern Politics*. Stanford: Stanford University Press.

Nussbaum, Martha C. 1996. "Patriotism and Cosmopolitanism" and "Reply." In M. C. Nussbaum, *For Love of Country: Debating the Limits of Patriotism*, ed. Joshua Cohen. Boston: Beacon Press.

Ober, J. 1989. *Mass and Elite in Democratic Athens: Rhetoric, Ideology, and the Power of the People*. Princeton: Princeton University Press.

O'Leary, B. 1998. "Ernest Gellner's Diagnoses of Nationalism: A Critical Overview or, What Is Living and What Is Dead in Ernest Gellner's Philosophy of Nationalism?" In J. A. Hall, ed., *The State of the Nation: Ernest Gellner and the Theory of Nationalism*. Cambridge: Cambridge University Press.

2000. "An Iron Law of Federations? A (Neo-Diceyian) Theory of the Necessity of a Federal Staatsvolk, and of Consociational Rescue." *Nations and Nationalism* 7: 273–96.

Omi, M. and H. Winant. 1994. *Racial Formation in the United States: From the 1960s to the 1990s*, 2nd edn. New York: Routledge.

Ong, A. 1999. *Flexible Citizenship: The Cultural Logics of Transnationality*. Durham: Duke University Press.

Oommen, T. K. 1997. *Citizenship, Nationality and Ethnicity: Reconciling Competing Identities*. Cambridge: Polity Press.

Paine, T. 1967 (orig. 1776). "Common Sense." In *Tracts of the American Revolution, 1763–1776*, ed. Merrill Jensen. New York: Bobbs-Merrill.

Palais, J. B. 1995. "A Search for Korean Uniqueness." *Harvard Journal of Asiatic Studies* 55: 409–425.

Parens, E., ed. 1998. *Enhancing Human Traits: Ethical and Social Implications*. Washington, DC: Georgetown University Press.

Pateman, C. 1988. *The Sexual Contract*. Stanford: Stanford University Press.

Pear, R. 2002. "House and Senate Negotiators Agree on an Election Bill." *New York Times* Oct. 5: A13.

Peters, S. F. F. 2000. *Judging Jehovah's Witnesses: Religious Persecution and the Dawn of the Rights Revolution*. Lawrence, KS: University of Kansas Press.

Pettit, P. 1997. *Republicanism: A Theory of Freedom and Government*. Oxford: Clarendon Press.

Pilkington, C. 2001. *Britain in the European Union Today*, 2nd edn. Manchester: Manchester University Press.

Pitkin, H. 1984. *Fortune Is a Woman: Gender and Politics in the Thought of Niccolò Machiavelli*. Berkeley: University of California Press.

Pitts, J. 2000. "Empire and Democracy: Tocqueville and the Algerian Question." *Journal of Political Philosophy* 8: 295–318.

Plamenatz, J. 1976. "Two Types of Nationalism." In E. Kamenka, ed., *Nationalism*. New York: St. Martin's Press.

Pocock, J. G. A. 1967. *The Ancient Constitution and the Feudal Law: A Study of English Historical Thought in the Seventeenth Century*. New York: W. W. Norton.

1975. *The Machiavellian Moment: Florentine Political Thought and the Atlantic Republican Tradition*. Princeton: Princeton University Press.

Purnell, J. 2002. "Citizens and Sons of the *Pueblo*: National and Local Identities in the Making of the Mexican Nation." *Ethnic and Racial Studies* 25: 213–237.

Putnam, R. D. 1995. "Bowling Alone." *Journal of Democracy* 6: 64–79.

2000. *Bowling Alone: The Collapse and Revival of American Community*. New York: Simon & Schuster.

Rabkin, J. 1998. "Elective Citizenship?" *The Public Interest* #131: 117–121.

Radcliffe, S. and S. Westwood. 1996. *Remaking the Nation: Place, Identity and Politics in Latin America*. New York: Routledge.

Ramos, E. R. 2001. *The Legal Construction of Identity: The Judicial and Social Legacy of American Colonialism in Puerto Rico*. Washington, DC: American Psychological Association.

Ranger, T. 1999. "The Nature of Ethnicity: Lessons from Africa." In E. Mortimer with R. Fine, eds., *People, Nation and State: The Meaning of Ethnicity and Nationalism*. London: I. B. Tauris.

Rawls, J. 1971. *A Theory of Justice*. Cambridge: Cambridge University Press.

1993a. *Political Liberalism*. New York: Columbia University Press.

1993b. "The Law of Peoples." In S. Shute and S. Hurley, eds., *On Human Rights*. New York: Basic Books.

1993c. "The Law of Peoples." *Critical Inquiry* 20: 36–68.

1999. *The Law of Peoples with "The Idea of Public Reason Revisited."* Cambridge: Harvard University Press.

Read, J. H. 2000. *Power versus Liberty: Madison, Hamilton, Wilson, and Jefferson*. Charlottesville: University Press of Virginia.

Reed, A. 2000. *Class Notes: Posing as Politics and Other Thoughts on the American Scene*. New York: The New Press.

Robinson, D. E. 2001. *Black Nationalism in American Politics and Thought*. New York: Cambridge University Press.

Robinson, R. 2000. *The Debt: What America Owes to Black America*. New York: Penguin Putnam Inc.

Rogin, M. P. 1975. *Fathers and Children: Andrew Jackson and the Subjugation of the American Indian*. New York: Vintage Books.

Rorty, R. 1998. *Achieving our Country: Leftist Thought in Twentieth-Century America*. Cambridge: Harvard University Press.

Rosen, J. 1998. "America in Thick and Thin: Exclusion, Discrimination, and the Making of Americans." *The New Republic*. January 5 and 12: 29–36.

Rousseau, J. J. 1973. *The Social Contract and the Discourses*. Transl. G. D. H. Cole. New York: Dutton.

Rubenstein, M. 2000. "Citizenship Law: Citizenship and the Centenary – Inclusion and Exclusion in Twentieth Century Australia." *Melbourne University Law Review* 24: 576–611.

Rushton, J. P. 1995. *Race, Evolution, and Behavior: A Life History Perspective*. New Brunswick, NJ: Transaction Publishers.

Safford, F. 1991. "Race, Integration, and Progress: Elite Attitudes and the Indian in Colombia, 1750–1870." *Hispanic American Historical Review* 71: 1–33.

Sandel, M. J. 1996. *Democracy's Discontent: America in Search of a Public Philosophy*. Cambridge: Harvard University Press.

San Juan, Jr., E. 1999. "From the Immigrant Paradigm to Transformative Critique: Asians in the Late Capitalist United States." In P. Wong, ed., *Race, Ethnicity and Nationality in the United States: Toward the Twenty-First Century*. Boulder, CO: Westview Press, 1999.

Scheffler, S. 2001. *Boundaries and Allegiances: Problems of Justice and Responsibility in Liberal Theory*. New York: Oxford University Press.

Scheindlin, R. P. 1998. *A Short History of the Jewish People: From Legendary Times to Modern Statehood*. New York: Macmillan Publishing.

Schnapper, D. 1998. *Community of Citizens: On the Modern Idea of Nationality*. Transl. Séverine Rosée. New Brunswick, NJ: Transaction Publishers. Orig. 1994. *La communauté des citoyens: sur l'idée moderne de nation*. Paris: Gallimard.

Schuck, P. H. 1998. *Citizens, Strangers, and In-Betweens: Essays on Immigration and Citizenship*. Boulder, CO: Westview Press.

Schuck, P. H. and R. M. Smith. 1985. *Citizenship without Consent: The Illegal Alien in the American Polity*. New Haven: Yale University Press.

Scott, J. C. 1985. *Weapons of the Weak: Everyday Forms of Peasant Resistance*. New Haven: Yale University Press.

1990. *Domination and the Arts of Resistance: Hidden Transcripts*. New Haven: Yale University Press.

1998. *Seeing like a State*. New Haven: Yale University Press.

Seidelman, R. and E. J. Harpham. 1985. *Disenchanted Realists: Political Science and the American Crisis, 1884–1984*. Albany: State University of New York Press.

Sewall, S. B. and C. Kaysen, eds. 2000. *The United States and the International Criminal Court: National Security and International Law*. New York: Rowman & Littlefield Publishers.

Shapiro, I. 1996. *Democracy's Place*. Ithaca: Cornell University Press.

1999. *Democratic Justice*. New Haven: Yale University Press.

Silverman, M. 1992. *Deconstructing the Nation: Immigration, Racism and Citizenship in Modern France*. New York: Routledge.

Singer, B. 1995. "Cultural versus Contractual Nations: Rethinking their Opposition." *History and Theory* 25: 309–337.

Skidmore, T. E. 1990. "Racial Ideas and Social Policy in Brazil, 1970–1940." In R. Graham, ed., *The Idea of Race in Latin America, 1870–1940*. Austin: University of Texas Press.

Skowronek, S. 1993. *The Politics Presidents Make: Leadership from John Adams to Bill Clinton*. Cambridge: Belknap Press.

Smith, A. 1776. *An Inquiry into the Nature and Causes of the Wealth of Nations*. Edinburgh: W. Creech.

Smith, A. D. 1983. *Theories of Nationalism*, 2nd edn. New York: Holmes & Meier.

1987. *The Ethnic Origins of Nations*. New York: Basil Blackwell.

1991. *National Identity*. London: Penguin Books.

1995. *Nations and Nationalism in a Global Era*. Cambridge: Polity Press.

1999. *Myths and Memories of the Nation*. Oxford: Oxford University Press.

Smith, R. M. 1985. *Liberalism and American Constitutional Law*. Cambridge: Harvard University Press.

1992. "If Politics Matters: Implications for a New Institutionalism." *Studies in American Political Development* 6: 1–36.

1994. "Unfinished Liberalism." *Social Research* 61: 631–670.

1997. *Civic Ideals: Conflicting Visions of Citizenship in U.S. History*. New Haven: Yale University Press.

1999. "Liberalism and Racism: The Problem of Analyzing Traditions." In D. F. Ericson and L. B. Green, eds., *The Liberal Tradition in American Politics: Consensus, Polarity, or Multiple Traditions?* New York: Routledge Publishing Co.

2001. "Citizenship and the Politics of People-Building." *Journal of Citizenship Studies* 5: 73–96.

Spinner, J. 1994. *The Boundaries of Citizenship: Race, Ethnicity, and Nationality in the Liberal State*. Baltimore: Johns Hopkins University Press.

Spiro, Peter J. 1999. "The Citizenship Dilemma." *Stanford Law Review* 51: 597–639.

Stephanson, Anders. 1995. *Manifest Destiny: American Expansionism and the Empire of Right.* New York: Hill and Wang.

Stock, G. 2002. *Redesigning Humans: Our Inevitable Genetic Future.* Boston: Houghton Mifflin.

Strikwerda, C. 1997. *A House Divided: Catholics, Socialists, and Flemish Nationalists in Nineteenth-Century Belgium.* New York: Rowman & Littlefield Publishers.

Tadmor, H. 1976. "The Period of the First Temple, the Babylonian Exile and the Restoration." In H. H. Ben-Sasson, ed., *A History of the Jewish People.* Cambridge: Harvard University Press.

Talbot, M. 2001. "A Desire to Duplicate." *New York Times Magazine* Feb. 4: 40–45, 67–69.

Tamir, Y. 1993. *Liberal Nationalism.* Princeton: Princeton University Press.

Taylor, C. 1989. "Cross-Purposes: The Liberal–Communitarian Debate." In N. L. Rosenblum, ed., *Liberalism and the Moral Life.* Cambridge: Harvard University Press.

1999. "Democratic Exclusion (and its Remedies?). In A. C. Cairns, J. C. Courtney, P. MacKinnon, H. J. Michelmann, and D. E. Smith, eds., *Citizenship, Diversity, and Pluralism: Canadian and Comparative Perspectives.* Montreal: McGill-Queen's University Press.

Thompson, N. 1996. *Herodotus and the Origins of the Political Community: Arion's Leap.* New Haven: Yale University Press.

Thucydides. 1954. *History of the Peloponnesian War.* Transl. R. Warner. London: Penguin Books.

Tichenor, D. J. 2002. *Dividing Lines: The Politics of Immigration Control in America.* Princeton: Princeton University Press.

Tocqueville, A. de. 1969. *Democracy in America.* Ed. J. P. Mayer. Garden City, NY: Anchor Books.

Tully, J. 1995. *Strange Multiplicity: Constitutionalism in an Age of Diversity.* New York: Cambridge University Press.

Turner, B.S. 1986. *Citizenship and Capitalism: The Debate over Reformism.* Boston: Allen & Unwin.

1990. "Outline of a Theory of Citizenship." *Sociology* 24: 189–217.

Twinam, A. 1980. "From Jew to Basque: Ethnic Myths and Antioqueno Entrepreneurship." *Journal of Interamerican Studies and World Affairs* 22: 81–107.

Vail, L. ed. 1989. *The Creation of Tribalism in South Africa.* Berkeley: University of California Press.

Vaillant, J. G. 1990. *Black, French, and African: A Life of Léopold Sédar Senghor.* Cambridge: Harvard University Press.

Van den Berghe, P. L. 1981. *The Ethnic Phenomenon.* New York: Elsevier.

van Gunsteren, H. 1998. *A Theory of Citizenship: Organizing Plurality in Contemporary Democracies.* Boulder, CO: Westview Press.

Vasconcelos, J. 1926. "The Latin American Basis of Mexican Civilization." In J. Vasconcelos and M. Gamio, *Aspects of Mexican Civilization.* Chicago: University of Chicago Press.

Velasco, J. d. 1994. *Historia del reino de Quito en la América meridional.* Quito: Casa de la Cultura Ecuatoriana.

Ver Steeg, C. L. and R. Hofstadter, eds. 1969. *Great Issues in American History: From Settlement to Revolution, 1584–1776*. New York: Vintage.

Wade, P. 1993. *Blackness and Race Mixture: The Dynamics of Racial Identity in Colombia*. Baltimore: Johns Hopkins University Press.

2001. "Racial Identity and Nationalism: A Theoretical View from Latin America." *Ethnic and Racial Studies* 24: 845–865.

Wald, P. 1995. *Constituting Americans: Cultural Anxiety and Narrative Form*. Durham: Duke University Press.

Walzer, M. 1983. *Spheres of Justice: A Defense of Pluralism and Equality*. New York: Basic Books.

1992. *What it Means to Be an American*. New York: Marsilio.

Weil, P. 2002. *Qu'est-ce qu'un Français? Histoire de la nationalité française depuis la Révolution*. Paris: Bernard Grasset.

Wendt, A. 1999. *Social Theory of International Politics*. Cambridge: Cambridge University Press.

Williams, P. M. and M. Harrison. 1973. *Politics and Society in de Gaulle's Republic*. New York: Anchor Books.

Wills, G. 1978. *Inventing America: Jefferson's Declaration of Independence*. New York: Random House.

Xenos, N. 1996. "Civic Nationalism: Oxymoron?" *Critical Review* 10: 213–231.

Yack, B. 1996. "The Myth of the Civic Nation." *Critical Review* 10: 193–211.

2001. "Popular Sovereignty and Nationalism." *Political Theory* 29: 517–536.

Yew, L. K. 1993. "The Loyalty of Overseas Chinese Belongs Overseas." *International Herald Tribune* Nov. 23. Online at http://ptg.djnr.com/ccroot/asp/publib.

Young, I. M. 2000. *Inclusion and Democracy*. New York: Oxford University Press.

Index

aboriginal peoples *see* native tribes in the
US, governance
accountability *see* public reason
Ackerman, B. A. 89, 146
AFL-CIO 21, 26–27
Africa
"African" personality 99, 115
identity in 112–115
"negritude" 114–115
race as basis for people-making 112–115
African Union, liberalism and 78
Ajami, F. 209
Akayev, A. *see* Kyrgyz Republic; Manas
story
Aleinikoff, T. A. 206, 207
Algeria, imperialism as buttress for
republicanism 80
allegiance 19–24, 31–32
Calvin's Case (1608) 84
political nature of people-making
process and 172–173
right to change 136–137
Allen, C. T. 106
Amish 31
Anbinder, T. 180
Anderson, B. 20, 22, 33, 57, 106
Annan, K. A. 13
Ansolbehere, S. 205
Antioquia 21, 26
race as basis for people-making 26
Arendt, H. 86
Argentina, "whitening policies" 108
Aristotle 75, 81
armed conflict, as pressure on
story-making 44
Armstrong, J. A. 12, 88
Asher, R. E. 103
asymmetry of people-making process 32,
39, 42, 52, 53, 63–64
ethically constitutive stories and 69
Athens, marriage laws and the formation
of peoples 80–81

Australia, nationality/immigration laws
49–50
Awolowo, O. 113, 120

Baker, D. 7
Bale, J. 116
Balibar, E. and I. Wallerstein 37, 41, 57
Barber, B. 57, 75
Barry, B. 11
Bederman, G. 81
Begaye, K. A. 25
Belgium 21
Accord de la St Michel 25
Bennett, D. H. 180
Bennett, W. J. 192, 193, 209
Berns, W. 209
Beveridge, A. 117, 125
Bhabha, H. K. 45
bin Laden, Osama 22
Blair, A. 55
Blake, R. and W. R. Louis 80
Bloch, M. 33–34, 67
Blyden, E. W. 99, 114–115
Bosniak, L. 31
Bourne, R. 207
Brazil, "whitening policies" 110
Breuilly, J. 2, 14, 52
Brimelow 189
Britain
chosen people
see also Brutus/Arthur legend; Wales
Brooklyn 21, 28
Brownlee, J. S. 112
Brubaker, W. R. 14, 51, 57, 75, 86,
96
Brudny, Y. 83, 96
Brutus/Arthur legend 84, 103–104
Buchanan, A., D. W. Brock, N. Daniels,
and D. Wikler 168
Burke, E. 83
Burnham, P. 113
Burtt, S. 54